JAN WURM

GLASS STRUCTURES

DESIGN AND CONSTRUCTION OF SELF-SUPPORTING SKINS

Birkhäuser
Basel · Boston · Berlin

Jan Wurm works for Arup Materials and Arup Facade Engineering in
London as an architect, designer, and project manager.

www.arup.com

PVB film for laminated safety glass
www.trosifol.com

DORMA

www.dorma-glas.de

DELO

SAINT-GOBAIN
GLASS

SCHOTT

Translation from German into English: Raymond Peat, Aberdeenshire, UK,
and Elizabeth Schwaiger, Picton /Canada

Library of Congress Control Number: 2007924610

Bibliographic information published by the German National Library
The German National Library lists this publication in the Deutsche Nationalbibliografie;
detailed bibliographic data are available on the Internet at http://dnb.d-nb.de.

This book is also available in a German language edition (ISBN 978-3-7643-7607-9).

© 2007 Birkhäuser Verlag AG
Basel · Boston · Berlin
P.O. Box 133, CH-4010 Basel, Switzerland
Part of Springer Science+Business Media

Printed on acid-free paper produced from chlorine-free pulp. TCF ∞

Layout concept and cover design: Muriel Comby, Basel
Typesetting: Continue AG, Basel
Cover photograph: Arup

Printed in Germany

ISBN: 978-3-7643-7608-6

9 8 7 6 5 4 3 2 1

www.birkhauser.ch

FOREWORD

The use of glass as a structural component first came to prominence in the early 1990s, when the developments in engineering practice were documented by key publications: in addition to Rice and Dutton, whose book *Le Verre structurel* (Paris, 1990) set out the first engineering explanation of bolted structural glass as practiced by Rice Francis Ritchie, the glass industry began to demystify the role of glass in building through the publication of *Glass in Building* by David Button and Brian Pye (Oxford/Boston, 1993). Michael Wigginton's *Glass in Architecture* (London, 1996), finally, offered a comprehensive overview of the technology and significance of glass in contemporary architecture.

These seminal works were followed by numerous studies and publications containing detailed analyses of construction in the expanding field of structural glass construction. At the same time, a small but growing band of architects and engineers energetically developed new techniques, based on the accumulated experience, in response to the demands of their diverse projects.

When Jan Wurm joined our glass team in London he was about to present his PhD thesis, and his research struck me as clarifying a train of development beginning long before the recent period of activity and indicating numerous exciting potential routes following the present change in the direction of glass architecture. He had designed and built with his students numerous prototypes at a range of scales up to full size, exploring the process and results of using glass in many intriguing ways, freed from the obligation to succeed in meeting a client's brief. The designs were not randomly or perversely generated to challenge conventional wisdom but followed from a logical analysis of the geometry of self-supporting skins and an appreciation of the need for stability, robustness and practicality of construction.

This book presents the research projects and a selection of work in practice, and summarises the key findings of Jan's research: that glass manufacture and processing methods produce material with a set of mechanical properties and a set of physical properties within a range of forms and sizes; the combination of designed glass elements in chosen geometry delivers structural properties; and in combination the structural and physical properties can efficiently enclose unique spaces in beneficial ways.

In addition to a thorough catalogue of the current processes and the resulting properties and sizes, he systematically classifies spanning glazed enclosures and presents a geometrical typology which extends from the defining works of the early masters through contemporary projects to illustrate the potential for rational use of the inherent and modified properties of glass in the future.

Graham Dodd, Arup, London, May 2007

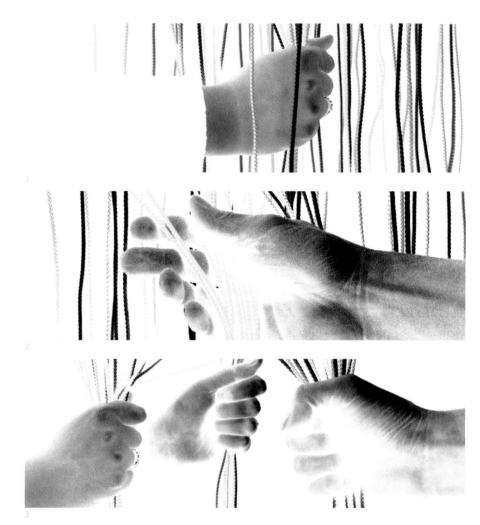

1 3 Visualisation of changes in the professional profile
      of architects and engineers: the strings symbolise
      the decision-making processes associated with
      building and the colours indicate allocations to
      functional, structural and aesthetic questions.
   1 Today, the growing complexity and technological focus
      in building puts the sole decision-making competency
      of the planner/designer as a generalist into question.
   2 The inclusion of experts makes it possible to bundle
      decision-making within limited competencies.
      Integrated planning requires intense communication
      and coordination among the experts, to solve
      the building task as a synthesis of functional,
      structural and aesthetic challenges.
   3 The development of new "creative" approaches
      to solutions requires that "specialised generalists"
      provide the overarching thematic coordination of
      decision-making processes. One possibility is to
      explore the functional, structural and aesthetic
      questions of the different building materials from the
      erspective of a "grammar of building materials".

PREFACE AND ACKNOWLEDGMENTS

"What the structural engineer sees as a load-bearing truss is seen as a sculpture by the architect – naturally, it is both."

– Ove Arup

Based on its geometry, its mechanical, building physical and visual qualities, every material is uniquely suited as a load-bearing component, as a building skin or design element. Within this *Grammar of Materials,* as Anette Gigon called it, no other material opens up as comprehensive a range of possibilities to the designer as flat glass, which increasingly dominates our built environment. [1]

The traditional genesis of material and architectural form, the link between constructional, functional and aesthetic aspects is today rendered more difficult in glass construction as a result of the technological complexity and the necessary specialisation of structural engi-

neers, specialist glass designers, fire engineers, etc. In contrast to steel-, timber- and concrete construction, no specific structural forms have therefore emerged for load-bearing glass structures. [2]

This book aims to close this gap in building research by developing a methodology of design and construction for flat glass, centred on the compression-resistant flat load-bearing element – universal building skin material and a surface that is luminous in a multitude of ways – as an elemental building block for load-bearing structures across wide spans. The technical recommendations contained in the book reflect the current state of technology; it is important to stress, however, that expert planners and designers in charge of a specific project must check and, if necessary, adapt them to the established and current laws, guidelines and standards in each country. Neither the author nor the publisher can be held in any way accountable for the design, planning or execution of faulty glass structures.

I thank everyone who has guided, accompanied and supported

4 Colleagues and students who participated in
the design, planning and realisation of the Tetra
Glass Arch after its completion in 2000

4

me through the various stages of this book. Thanks are due first and foremost to Prof. Dr. Eng. Wilfried Führer for his intensive and unfailingly positive support during my scientific training and to my guide in this field, Prof. Dr. Eng. Ulrich Knaack. I would like to thank my former colleagues Dr. Eng. Rolf Gerhardt, Dr. Eng. Katharina Leitner, Dr. Eng. Helmut Hachul, Cert. Eng. Thorsten Weimar and Cert. Eng. Jochen Dahlhausen for technical suggestions and practical assistance. I am equally grateful to Prof. Alan Brookes and Prof. Dr. Mick Eekhout for the valuable experiences during my research residency at the TU Delft in 2002 and to Prof. Dr. Phil. Andreas Beyer, Prof. Dr. rer. nat. Reinhard Conradt and Prof. Eng. Jochen Neukäter for their helpful comments.

I gratefully acknowledge the firms and my direct contacts, whose extensive sponsorships made the realisation of my research projects and the printing of this book possible. Thanks to my colleagues Graham Dodd and Bruno Miglio at Arup for providing me with the opportunity to review and revise the manuscript.

I would also like to express my gratitude to Ulrike Ruh and Odine Osswald from the publishing house for their substantial support and help in the making of this book.

Special thanks are due to my colleagues and friends at the university – Philipp Berninger, Britta Harnacke, Ron Heiringhoff, Maren Krämer, Alex Kruse, Stefan Steffesmies, Julia Wehrs and especially Ralf Herkrath – who contributed greatly to the successful completion of this work. For their personal support, as well as corrections to the content and language of this work, I extend my heartfelt thanks to my parents Charlotte and Johann Peter, and also to Anke Naujokat, Andres Tönnesmann and especially Silke Flaßnöcker and my silk baldachin. Thanks are due to all students who participated in the projects with tremendous dedication.

Jan Wurm, im März 2007

1

INTRODUCTION

1 Glass lenses in the dome vaulted steam room of the
   Al Bascha hammam, 18th century, Akko, Israel

2 Palm house in Kew Gardens, London, 1845–1848,
   Arch.: D. Burton, Eng.: R. Turner

Flat glass has been used to enclose space for nearly two millennia and is one of the oldest manmade building materials. At the same time continual improvements to the manufacturing and refining processes make glass one of the most modern building materials today, one that shapes the appearance of contemporary architecture unlike any other. Almost any task associated with a modern building skin could be fulfilled with the help of this material. This made it possible to overcome the contradiction between the fundamental need for shelter from the elements and the simultaneous desire for openness to light, paving the way for building structures that "provide shelter without entombing [the dweller]". [1/1]

The roots of modern glass construction reach back to early 19th-century greenhouses in England. Horticulturists and landscape gardeners such as Claudius Loudon (1783–1843) and Joseph Paxton (1803–1865) pioneered a new development. While responding to the desire for cultivating exotic plants under controlled climatic conditions,

they also discovered that the greenhouse proved ideal for experimenting with the new building materials of glass and iron. To best use the incident sunlight, they reduced the ratio of cast and wrought iron to glass panes and developed freestanding enclosures with domed and folded glazed roofs. The stability of these delicate structures was largely achieved by the bracing provided through small glass shingles embedded in putty. As a result of avoiding flexural tensile stress in glass, more by intuition than design, the outcome was folded plate and shell structures in which the iron skeleton formed a structural and functional unity with the glass skin. The successful synthesis of material, form, construction and purpose in these buildings where glass was employed for the first time as a load-bearing structural element created an aesthetic that has lost none of its fascination to this day. [1/2]

The significance of these 19th-century greenhouses as forerunners in the evolution of glass construction should not be underestimated. Experience in working with the new building materials was an

3   Halle au Blé (now: Bourse du Commerce) Paris, 1806–1811, the world's first iron grid shell structure, Arch.: F. J. Bélanger, Eng.: F. Brunet

4   Palm house at Bicton Gardens, Arch.: D. & E. Bailey after plans by C. Loudon, circa 1843

5   Large greenhouse at Chatsworth with ridge-and-furrow glazing, 1840 (demolished in 1920), Arch.: J. Paxton

essential prerequisite for the subsequent construction of large railway terminals and atria. These glass and iron constructions were nothing short of pure feats of engineering. As the understanding of the structural characteristics deepened, the evolution of the form adhered increasingly to the emerging rules of skeleton construction. Although the separation of the skin from the load-bearing structure that was now taking place was accompanied by progress in glass technology, which subsequently led to larger sheet sizes and improved quality, by the mid-19th century glass had become a mere covering and had almost lost its constructional significance. Engineers shifted their focus to reducing the load-bearing framework that supported the glass panes.

At the beginning of the 20th century a young generation of architects recognised the visual potential of the new construction method. The openness and abundance of light in glazed halls, the aesthetics of transparent and orthogonally divided planes became the credo of a "modern" style that sought to abolish the boundary between inside and outside and abandoned traditional ideas on spatial organisation. Larger and larger window panes and glazed surfaces were more than merely a purposeful desire to improve natural daylight conditions in interior spaces: they represented a deliberate emphasis on the abstract and aesthetic qualities of the transparent material itself. Le Corbusier's call for a "struggle between the need for light and the limitations imposed by building materials and construction methods" anticipated the continual efforts of architects and engineers throughout the 20th century to reduce the facade structure to an absolute minimum. Towards the end of the 20th century the gain in transparency achieved through the "invisible" material glass became increasingly dogmatic in character as a symbol of "openness", "democracy" and "modernity", replacing the original pragmatism which had been associated with the term.

As the ratio of glazed to non-glazed surface increased, culminating in the fully glazed skin, so did the conflict between the desired trans-

6 Glass and transparency, Reichstag dome, Berlin, 1998,
   Arch.: Foster and Partners,
   Eng.: Leonhardt, Andrä und Partner

7 Courtyard roof Sony Plaza Berlin, 1998,
   Arch.: H. Jahn, Eng.: Arup
   The fabrics beneath the glass structure provide
   protection from weather, glare and noise.

parency and the physical requirements. Large glazed surfaces create additional heat losses in winter; conversely, they also generate energy gains in summer, at times even to the point of overheating. Even with the use of contemporary, highly selective coatings the energy that is transmitted into the interior in summer is often so great that the unwanted phenomenon of a "glass sauna" can only be avoided with the help of elaborate climate controls. Retrofitting and upgrading the building systems in an effort to control the internal climate is hardly a good argument for the usefulness of such glasshouses.

Today, glass has regained its significance as a building material thanks to the search for enhanced transparency. The initiative for the long-neglected research into the structural properties of glass was set in motion by steel construction institutes and companies, who also assumed responsibility for designing and executing early experimental projects. In contemporary buildings, glass is integrated into delicate load-bearing steel structures in the form of wind fins, beams, columns or props, chiefly with the goal of achieving the greatest possible dematerialisation of the skin. In this manner, constructional principles from skeleton construction are adopted for load-bearing glass structures, even though the properties of the materials differ in a fundamental manner. The "mastery" of the brittle material glass made possible by technological progress is most evident in the wide product palette for bolted point fixings for glass building components. [1/3] Glass construction is still dominated by the tectonics of steel construction to such a degree that it has yet to develop its own formal language.

The dynamic evolution of transparent skins and structures – culminating in the light-flooded spaces that dominate our public environments, the airport and railway termini, the sports and leisure arenas, the exhibition halls, shopping centres and atria in modern city centres – seems to have reached a plateau, begging the question of what the future significance of structural glass architecture might be. [1/4]

8 Canopy structure composed of printed polycarbonate multi-skin sheets, Ricola warehouse, Mulhouse, 1993, Arch.: Herzog & de Meuron

9 Glass and translucency, Schubert Club Band Shell, Saint Paul (USA), 2002, Arch.: James Carpenter Design Associates (JCDA)

10 Dichroic coated glass panes form a three-dimensional structural system, glass sculpture "Refractive Tensegrity Rings", Munich airport, 1992, Arch.: James Carpenter Design Associates (JCDA)

It is notable that the "materiality" of the material is increasingly pushed to the foreground as a new quality. Contemporary architects gain an understanding of the material based on qualities that were already expressed in the early 20th century in the projects of the German group *The Glass Chain* and in Mies van der Rohe's early expressionist works. Architects such as Herzog & de Meuron or Bernard Tschumi understand the transparency of glass as a changeable state and emphasise the variety and sensuality of the material through deliberate mirror effects, colouring and diffused scattering of light: "One moment it is transparent; then it is reflective only to turn semi-transparent in the next minute". [1/5] Interpreting glass as a tangible, optically ephemeral boundary between interior and exterior inspires a new attitude towards its transparency in relationship to the physical aspects of the building skin and towards employing it as a visible "filter". The tremendous potential of structural glass to not only promote transparency but to utilise the liveliness of reflecting surfaces and the presence of a col-ourful absorbent building fabric is highlighted in the work of New York architect and designer James Carpenter ____Figs 9, 10. [1/6]

In modern glass architecture we see a growing convergence of two trends: the aforementioned aesthetics of the materiality itself and a new focus on mechanical forms, in which glass is understood as a planar structural element and no longer as a substitute for linear steel beams and columns. Load-bearing skin structures are the embodiment of unity between the building skin and the load-bearing structure. Although these structures had already been employed in 19th-century English greenhouses, it is only recently that their unique fitness for modern glass construction has been rediscovered. One of their characteristics is greater tolerance for the brittleness of glass because they allow for a far more even distribution of the flow of force than is generally achieved in skeleton structures. Curt Siegel describes load-bearing skin structures as *structural forms* that emerge as a synthesis of the possibilities inherent in the building material, the struc-

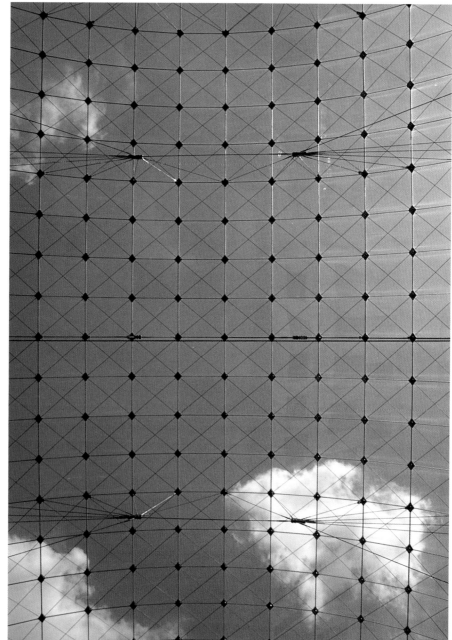

11 Glass as a load-bearing, protective and pictorial element:
    prototype for a space framework composed of glass,
    Tetra glass arch, 2000; design: Wilfried Führer and Jan
    Wurm, Lehrstuhl für Tragkonstruktionen, RWTH Aachen

12 Concept for a station roof; design: Christof Schlaich
    and James Wong, Lehrstuhl für Tragkonstruktionen,
    RWTH Aachen

13 Concepts for structural forms in glass construction:
    glass panels replace linear structural elements.
    Glass barrel shell with a 14 m span, Maximilianmuseum
    Augsburg, 2000; design and coordination: Ludwig und
    Weiler Ingenieure

tural and functional parameters and performance criteria of the building task, and the visual intent of the designer. [1/7, 1/8] To paraphrase
Vitruvius, structural forms are the result of a creative process on the
part of the architect/engineer which unifies the fundamental characteristics of utility (*utilitas*), firmness (*firmitas*) and beauty (*ve-
nustas*).[1/9]

The aim of this work, therefore, is to reveal new approaches to structural forms for contemporary glass construction of building skins and
load-bearing roof structures with wide spans. At the same time, the
tremendous advances in working with glass as a material are linked to
the construction principles and design possibilities that are suitable for
structural skins. Given the often contradictory demands arising from
the functional, structural, technical and visual perspectives in engineering and designing, the geometries of the skin and the load-bearing structure have to be reconsidered for each new building task. Such

a synthesis can only be successfully achieved through a direct explo-
ration of the concrete brief in combination with an intense collaboration between architect, engineer and specialist designers. [1/10] Thus
far structural forms for glass construction have only been sketched out
and any attempt at formulating a specific formal vocabulary for glass
structures must spring from an experimental approach. In addition to
current projects by renowned architects and engineers, this work also
presents case studies and prototypes, which the author developed in
collaboration with students – an endeavour in which he was supported
by the industry. The projects share the goal of strengthening the necessary integrated design approach to glass structures through experimental construction, planning and design. In addition to documenting the
appropriate use of the building material, the systems presented in this
volume also demonstrate how load-bearing components can be employed to environmental climate control. In other words, the concept of
this book is to create a formal vocabulary and to recognise the aes-

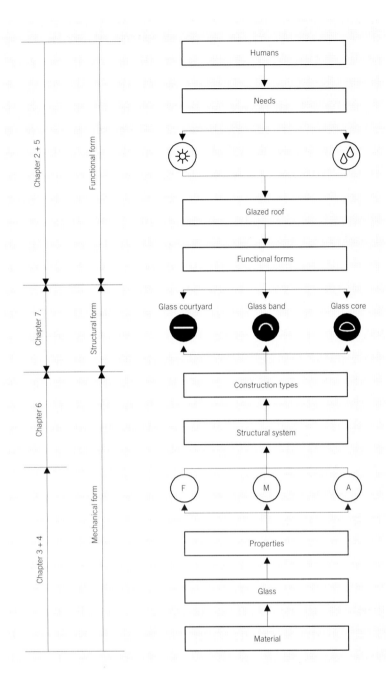

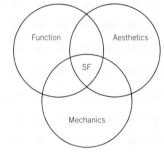

14 Overview

15 Design workshop during the seminar entitled
    "Glasbau – Konzept und Konstruktion"

16 The structural form (SF) as a synthesis of
    mechanical, functional and aesthetic qualities

thetic quality rooted in the poetry of these load-bearing, enclosing and luminous surfaces.

To this end, Chapter 2 is devoted to an overview of the interactions between form, function and construction in roof structures. The technical foundations are systematically explored in the chapters that follow: the properties of the material including working and refining methods are explained in Chapter 3; the principles of material-appropriate jointing techniques and construction in the context of using flat glass as a spatial and structural element are introduced in Chapter 4; Chapters 5 and 6 outline the conclusions drawn from the material properties for the functional technical requirements of glass skins and for the construction principles for glass skin structures; the projects featured in Chapter 7, both realised glass buildings and experimental projects, illustrate the wide range of possible structural forms; in conclusion, Chapter 8 offers an outlook of future developments and perspectives ____ Fig. 14.

11 Domed vault with ceiling frescoes in
Florence cathedral, 1434–1461

12 Ceiling fresco by Correggio in Parma
cathedral, 1526–1530

13 The Pantheon in Rome, AD 118–128

(1434–1461). [2.1/6] With the advent of the domed centralised build-ing, the central skylight became first the characteristic of sacred pub-lic buildings and later of profane public structures.

The celestial symbolism was often emphasised by painting the vault cells, for example with stars on a sky-blue background, as in the early Christian baptistery San Giovanni in Fonte in Naples (approx. AD 400). During the Late Gothic, the vaulted surfaces were decorated with painted foliage. At the same time, the structural system was plas-tically enhanced, so that ribs and transverse arches were rendered as branches and vines: the ceiling now took on the appearance of an ar-bour – a direct illustration of the Garden of Eden. [2.1/7] Painting the vaulted ceilings served to enhance the dematerialisation of the ceiling construction, becoming an integral element of the architecture. In the Baroque and Mannerist periods, the symbolic meaning of ceiling fres-coes began to give way increasingly to a depiction of the real world. Thus the blue sky painted in the background was both a reference to the heavens above and a realistic illustration of the physical sky behind (or above) the construction and, by this means, a deliberate expansion of the interior space. [2.1/8] In other words, painted ceilings that creat-ed the illusion of a dissolved or immaterial structure constituted the final stage in the evolution towards the fully-dissolved glazed roofs of the 19th century.

THE MODERN ERA

THE GREENHOUSE

With the advances in technology brought about by the industrial revo-lution, the dream of a dematerialised roof constructed of iron and glass could finally be realised. English greenhouses featured the first glazed roofs in the history of architecture. Greenhouses became an oasis, a place promising to be the "embodiment of the dream of a happy unity of nature and man". [2.1/9] The abundance of tropical plants, exotic scents and sounds created a dream world that gave city dwellers an

14 Large greenhouse in the Botanical Gardens at
    Dahlem, 1905–1907, Arch.: Alfred Koerner

15 Interior of the People's Palace, Muswell Hill,
    London, 1859 (project)

16 "Coloured glass destroys hatred". Glass pavilion by
    Bruno Taut, Werkbund exhibition in Cologne, 1914

escape from life in the metropolis. The climate control systems, necessary for the survival of the plants, were carefully hidden from the eye of the visitor in order to preserve the illusion of a Garden of Eden in the rough climate of northern Europe. [2.1/10]

Public winter gardens and botanical buildings incorporating concert halls, restaurants and libraries elevated the individual pursuit of leisure into a bourgeois movement of recreating nature. A contemporary report describes the winter garden in Regent's Park as follows: "A veritable fairy tale land has been planted into the heart of London, a most agreeable garden that transforms all our wishes into reality." [2.1/11]

___THE "GLASS CRYSTAL"

At the beginning of the 20th century the Expressionist artists' group The Glass Chain, the most prominent members of which were Bruno Taut (1880–1938) and Paul Scheerbart (1863–1915), embraced utopian social visions associated with the use of glass as a building material. Taut designed crystalline urban domes such as the "Haus des Himmels": "The ceiling is constructed of prisms composed of colourful glass joined by electrolytic fusion; the walls are constructed of cast prisms." [2.1/12]

Scheerbart writes: "The face of the earth would be much altered if brick architecture were ousted everywhere by glass architecture. It would be as if the earth were adorned with diamond and enamel jewellery. Here on earth, we would have [environments] more precious than the gardens in the Arabian Nights. We should then have a paradise on earth." [2.1/13]

___THE CLIMATE SKIN

During the 19th century there was a universal need for living independently of weather conditions coupled with protection from the dirt and polluted atmosphere in large cities, which was architecturally ex-

17 Project for a geodesic dome over Manhattan,
    circa 1960, Arch.: Buckminster Fuller

18 Project for a pneumatically supported climate
    skin in the arctic, 1970, Arch.: Frei Otto in
    collaboration with Kenzo Tange and Ove Arup

19 USA pavilion by Buckminster Fuller at Expo '67
    in Montreal

20 The large biospheres of the "Eden Project"
    in Cornwall, 2001, Arch.: Nicolas Grimshaw,
    Eng.: Arup and Anthony Hunt Associates

pressed in the idea of covering urban space in glass on a large scale. The desire for hygiene and cleanliness was combined with physical and metaphysical aspects. As early as 1808 Charles Marie Fourier (1772–1837) sought to counter the "ravages of civilisation" with his idea of the *phalanstères*, describing the ideal of a city completely covered in a glass dome that was also intended to serve as a catalyst for a new societal order. [2.1/14]

In 1822 J. C. Loudon developed the visionary idea of placing entire cities in "northern regions" under glass roofs for the purpose of improving living conditions. "The most economic method of creating an agreeable climate will be to cover entire cities with monumental glass roofs." [2.1/15]

Nearly 150 years later this vision was resurrected in Buckminster Fuller's (1895–1983) concept for a geodesic dome over Manhattan with a diameter of three kilometres and in Frei Otto's project for a climate skin in the arctic with a diameter of two kilometres. [2.1/16]

With a diameter of roughly 75 metres, Fuller's dome for EXPO '67 in Montreal represents a realisation of this vision on a smaller scale. Fuller writes: "From the inside there will be uninterrupted visual contact with the exterior world. The sun and moon will shine in the landscape, and the sky will be completely visible, but the unpleasant effects of climate, heat, dust, bugs, glare etc. will be modulated by the skin to provide a Garden of Eden interior." [2.1/17]

Today tremendous progress in building systems and glass refining processes have made it possible to regulate the flow of energy between interior and exterior in just such a manner. Glass building skins that are dynamic and self-adaptive – characterised by a harmonised energy balance sheet that is independent of non-regenerative energy resources thanks to utilising solar energy and the ability to adapt to the needs of occupants and the changing climate conditions of the environment – are associated with a yearning for a future where humankind will once again be able to live in harmony with nature.

21   The foliage canopy made of glass: Art Academy on
     Berliner Platz, Berlin, 2002, Arch.: Behnisch Architekten

22   "Tropical Island" in Berlin Brand, 2004

23   Staged nature, photo montage by Taiteilija Ilkka Halso,
     Orimattila

Thus many contemporary projects display the yearning for paradise
that has been associated with the glasshouse since the 19th century
as a synthesis between humans and nature. Lounging beneath the
colourful glazed roof of the thermal baths at Bad Colberg or taking a
break in the atrium of Berlin's Academy of Art is designed to induce in
the visitor a feeling of "dwelling beneath a canopy of leaves". [**2.1/18,
2.1/19**]

Modern examples of *leisure paradise* environments such as the
"Tropical Island" near Berlin, which accommodates a tropical rainfor-
est with lagoons, auditoria and bars, aim to present visitors with quasi-
pristine nature in an over-the-top fun and entertainment package – a
combination that is "purchased" at the cost of an excessive invest-
ment into building services and energy supply for air conditioning and
control technology.

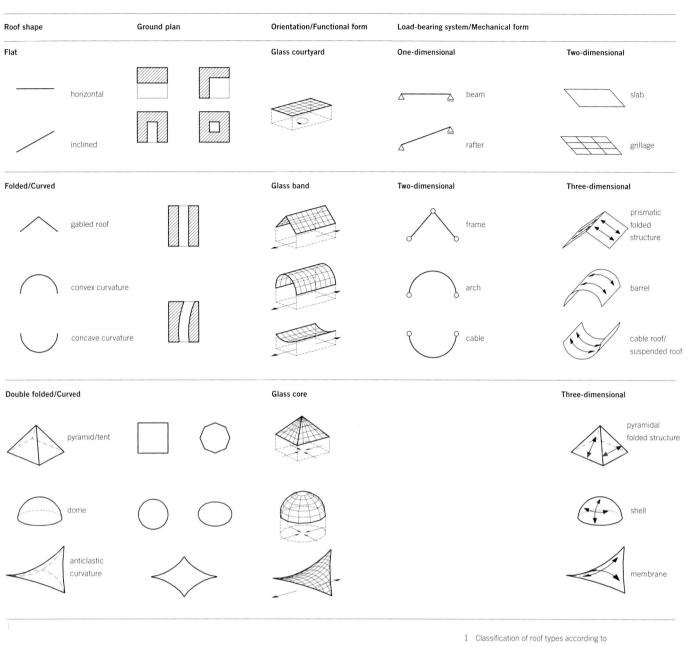

Roof shape		Ground plan		Orientation/Functional form	Load-bearing system/Mechanical form	
Flat				**Glass courtyard**	**One-dimensional**	**Two-dimensional**
	horizontal				beam	slab
	inclined				rafter	grillage
Folded/Curved				**Glass band**	**Two-dimensional**	**Three-dimensional**
	gabled roof				frame	prismatic folded structure
	convex curvature				arch	barrel
	concave curvature				cable	cable roof/ suspended roof
Double folded/Curved				**Glass core**		**Three-dimensional**
	pyramid/tent					pyramidal folded structure
	dome					shell
	anticlastic curvature					membrane

1 Classification of roof types according to
shape and orientation into glass courtyard,
glass band and glass core

__2.2

THE GLASS ROOF: FORM, FUNCTION AND CONSTRUCTION

___THE FUNCTIONAL AND MECHANICAL FORM

The 19th century witnessed the advent of dematerialised structural systems composed of linear compression-resistant and tensile materials such as wood or steel. For the first time, these structures were partially or entirely clad in glass. In central and northern Europe, the separation of structure and skin that emerged during the industrial revolution was born out of the necessity to protect large spaces in railway terminals, factory and assembly halls or arcades against the elements, while at the same time supplying them with natural daylight. The evolution of the glass roof is thus closely linked to that of *low-rise construction*. The interaction between functional and mechanical aspects in defining a form is particularly evident in these large-span roof structures.

After plan and cross-section, the *functional form* of the skin is usually developed on the basis of the intended use and the functional requirements of the building task. Structural systems can only fulfil their function by transferring all dead and imposed loads acting on them to the subsoil. All load-bearing elements necessary for this load transfer to occur must be combined into a complete structure capable of carrying loads – the *mechanical form*. The properties and the availability of building materials are important aspects in the constructional and technical design of roof structures. [2.2/1]

In this work, glass roofs are differentiated according to functional and mechanical form based on the typology of skylight designs estab-

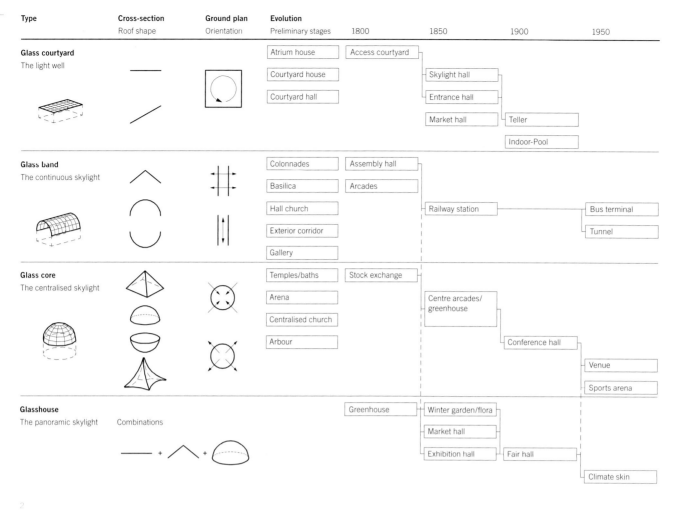

Type	Cross-section Roof shape	Ground plan Orientation	Evolution Preliminary stages	1800	1850	1900	1950
Glass courtyard The light well			Atrium house	Access courtyard			
			Courtyard house		Skylight hall		
			Courtyard hall		Entrance hall		
					Market hall	Teller	
						Indoor-Pool	
Glass band The continuous skylight			Colonnades	Assembly hall			
			Basilica	Arcades			
			Hall church		Railway station		Bus terminal
			Exterior corridor				Tunnel
			Gallery				
Glass core The centralised skylight			Temples/baths	Stock exchange			
			Arena		Centre arcades/ greenhouse		
			Centralised church			Conference hall	
			Arbour				Venue
							Sports arena
Glasshouse The panoramic skylight Combinations				Greenhouse	Winter garden/flora		
					Market hall		
					Exhibition hall	Fair hall	
							Climate skin

2 Diagram representing the evolution of different glass roof types

lished by J. F. Geist. The basic types of *"glass courtyard"*, *"glass band"* and *"glass core"* are summarised in ___Fig. 1. The glass courtyard is defined by a planar (two-dimensional) roof, the glass band by a single folded or curved roof and the glass core by a double-folded or curved roof. Typologically, the *glasshouse* is characterised by a glass skin on all sides, the sculptural quality of which liberates it from unequivocal typological references. [2.2/2]

The flow of force in the structural system and the stresses exerted on the load-bearing elements are dependent on the geometry of cross-section and plan, and it is for this reason that the form and dimension of structural systems are interdependent. For large spans, a flat roof will quickly prove to be uneconomical, whereas a double-folded or curved roof can be realised with relatively little material expenditure. In this sense, glass courtyard, glass band and glass core also differ in terms of the spatial expanse and dimension of the area they cover.

___HISTORIC EVOLUTION

The historic evolution of the glass roof and its typical appearance in the glass courtyard, glass band, glass core and glasshouse is illustrated in the diagram ___Fig. 2. The overview presents the trends and evolutionary lines of cross-section (roof shape) and plan (orientation) from the first glass roof constructions circa 1800 to the present day. Solid construction typologies which are characterised by a similar spatial configuration are given as examples in the column headed "preliminary stages".

The overview provides a sketch of the evolution from the start of the industrial revolution around 1800 to today in 50-year increments. Circa 1850, the need for large skylights gave rise to plans designed for new building tasks such as museums, market halls, stock exchange buildings and libraries. Large halls were needed for the manufacture, distribution and presentation of trade goods and as convening places for a new urban public interested in recreation and the pursuit of cul-

A　　B

C　　D

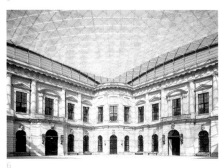

3　Plan types for the glass courtyard
  A　The annexed glass courtyard
  B　The corner glass courtyard
  C　The inserted glass courtyard
  D　The interior glass courtyard (atrium)

4　Teller hall of main post office in St. Petersburg

5　Semi-public circulation space Familistère de Guise,
  circa 1860

6　Interior of glass courtyard as constructional completion,
  the Schlüterhof at the Deutsches Historisches Museum
  in Berlin, 2003, Arch.: I. M. Pei

7　The annexed glass courtyard, shed roof Museum
  Meteorit, Essen, 1998, Arch.: Propeller Z

8　The annexed glass courtyard, expansion
  Museum Rietberg, Zurich, 2007,
  Arch.: ARGE Grazioli Krischanitz GmbH

tural education. Towards the end of the 19th century, new social structures translated into an increase of administrative bodies and the emergence of the modern service-oriented society. Large entertainment and sports arenas are the architectural expression of the leisure society as we know it today.

THE FLAT OR INCLINED ROOF – THE GLASS COURTYARD

A planar roof area is horizontal or pitched, the roof profile is one-dimensional.

The top-lit courtyard screened off from the external surroundings is one of the oldest forms of spatial organisation. It serves to provide light and access to adjacent spaces and is defined by a tranquil, introverted ambience that is an invitation to linger. The interior square atrium terminating in a horizontal glass ceiling, in which none of the lateral enclosing elements are dominant, constitutes the purest form of a glass courtyard. Originally an open light well in Roman homes, the atrium is today often annexed to existing light wells and used as a lobby, exhibition space or cafeteria. With the growing dematerialisation of the wall, glass courtyards emerge in less introverted forms in which one or several directions are singled out. The opening can be additionally emphasised through a rectangular plan or the incline of the roof area. In the case of an "inserted glass courtyard", only three sides are enclosed by solid building components, and the orientation towards the open, often fully-glazed front assumes a prime importance for the organisation of the floor plan. A "corner glass courtyard" has two adjacent open sides, reinforcing the diagonal flow in the interior space. The "glass courtyard annex", finally, is open on three sides. The tranquil character of the glass courtyard can be preserved even in the case of shed and saddle-roof constructions with the help of interior dust or luminous ceilings suspended from the primary structure. A double-skin construction of this kind marks the skylight hall as a variation on the classic glass courtyard. [2.2/3]

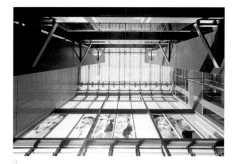

9 The inserted glass courtyard (view towards
  ceiling), Sparkasse Düsseldorf, 2001,
  Arch.: Ingenhoven Overdiek and Partners

10 The corner glass courtyard, Art Museum in Tel
  Aviv, 1998, Arch.: D. Eytan, Eng.: M. Eekhout

11–15 Glass band with convex curvature
  11 Verdeau arcades, Paris, 1847

12 GUM arcades in Moscow, 1893
  Eng.: V. G. Suchov

13 Central fair hall Leipzig, 1996
  Arch.: von Marg und Partner, Eng.: V. G. Suchov

Structural systems for planar roofs include beam and slab systems. The bending resistance necessary for load transfer requires an increase in material and this affects the cross-sectional dimensions of the structural elements. The roof area for longitudinal plans is realised by installing a series of individual cross beams. If the distance between these is large enough to warrant secondary beams, the result is a multilayered, hierarchic system. Slabs, on the other hand, can transfer loads across two or several axes and are suitable for spanning areas that are nearly square in plan. Beams can be dissolved into systems subjected only to normal forces with more slender cross-section when they are executed in the form of trusses. Two-way span truss grillages or space frame slabs allow for greater span widths.

___THE FOLDED OR CURVED ROOF – THE GLASS BAND

The roof types under discussion in this section are two-dimensional in profile: folded in the case of gabled roofs or prismatic folded-plate structures and curved in the case of arched or suspended (cable) roofs. In arched roofs the curvature is convex; in cable roofs it is concave.

The term glass band is used to denote a continuous, elongated skylight that is bounded on its longitudinal sides by predominantly solid building structures. In contrast to the glass courtyard, the glass band is a space designed for traffic – pedestrian or vehicular. The glass band is predominantly employed for "transit-related" building tasks such as arcades and railway terminals. The inserted atrium, bounded by a U-shaped solid structure, is a variant combining both the glass courtyard and the glass band.

The enclosure that is folded or curved in the cross direction supports the dynamics of the space designed for traffic. Gabled and barrel roof result in a strong longitudinal orientation and a "channelling" of the plan. Thus the arcades and railway terminals of the 19th century were initially characterised by symmetrical saddleback roofs and later on by barrel roofs.

14, 15 Platform on Lehrter railway station, Berlin, 2002
     Arch.: von Gerkan Marg und Partner,
     Eng.: Schlaich Bergermann und Partner

16, 17 The folded glass band
  16 Central hall: Züblin house Stuttgart, 1985
     Arch.: Gottfried Böhm, Eng.: Jörg Schlaich
  17 Platform hall Gare d'Austerlitz in Paris, 1862

18, 19 The concave glass band
  18 Cable roof: Central railway station Ulm, 1993,
     Eng.: Schlaich Bergermann und Partner
  19 Cable roof: Station forecourt Heilbronn, 2001,
     Eng.: Schlaich Bergermann und Partner

It wasn't until the 20th century that the enclosure with a convex curvature – the suspended or cable roof – emerged as a building type. The cross-sectional form opening onto the longitudinal sides promotes movement across the transverse axis and marks an entrance or threshold area.

Frames and arches are among the two-dimensional structural systems. The form of the structural system adapts to the natural flow of force in the centre line of pressure or axis line. As a result of the arch effect, there are hardly any bending stresses on curved structural systems and the required material expenditure is reduced. The ratio of bending and compression stresses is dependent on the geometry and the load profile. Every deviation in the load profile leads to a different line of pressure: the greater the deviation between axis line and system geometry, the greater is the bending stress. [2.2/4]

When arches are sequenced in a row, the result is a barrel-shaped, three-dimensional skin geometry with a single axis load path. If the arches are connected in a shear-, compression- and tension-resistant manner in the longitudinal and transverse direction, loads can also be carried across two axes on the curved surface; the resulting form is a barrel vaulted shell. The barrel vaulted shell is a skin structure which loads are transferred across the longitudinal and transverse axes of the barrel given the appropriate support conditions. The longitudinal stress distribution is similar to that of a beam, e.g. the compression zone is located at the apex and the tension zone is located at the lower edges. Since they do not feature a secondary structural system curvature, barrel shells are relatively flexible and must be stabilised in the transverse plane, for example with stiffening arches. If the stabilising measures create a continuous secondary plane, the result is a two-layered system with greater rigidity. [2.2/5]

____THE DOUBLE-FOLDED OR CURVED ROOF – THE GLASS CORE
Pyramidal folded plate structures, domes, shells or tents are charac-

20–22 The glass core: Synclastic dome structures
  20 Halle au Blé (Today: Bourse de Commerce)
      in Paris, 1809–1811, Arch.: F. J. Bélanger

21 Reichstag dome Berlin, 1998,
    Arch.: Foster and Partners

22 Greenhouse at the National Botanical Garden
    of Wales, 1999, Arch.: Foster and Partners

23 Pyramidal folded roof: Bewag Glaspyramide
    Berlin, 1999, Arch.: A. Liepe, H. Siegelmann

24 Anticlastic lattice grid structural system: Schubert
    Club Band Shell Minnesota, 2002, Arch.: JCDA

terised by a fold or curvature in the longitudinal and transverse direction; they are three-dimensional, spatial structures. In domed roofs with a synclastic curvature, the curvature is the same in both cross-sectional axes. In anticlastic membrane and tent roofs, the curvatures are transverse to each other and lie in opposite directions.

The glass core is the centralised skylight in an ideal, circular plan. The lateral enclosures are usually homogeneous. The gathering gesture defines this type as an assembly space. Given their imposing character, centralised pyramidal or domed roofs also exude a unique pretension to power. An anticlastic curvature reverses the spatial form of the dome and results in an extroverted, opening gesture.

The domed shell, which has considerable more rigidity in comparison with the barrel shell owing to the double curvature, is suitable for the large span widths of concert halls and arenas. Load transfer occurs along the meridian and the circumference; all structural elements must be connected to transfer shear, compression and tension forces. When loads are distributed evenly, domes are not subject to moments but to membrane stress, in other words, the area is only subject to normal or axial forces. If the dome geometry corresponds to the supporting plane, the three-dimensional analogy to the line of pressure, the system will be subject purely to compression stress in the direction of the meridian. It is only when the dome geometry deviates from the supporting plane, as is the case in a spherical shell, that ring forces are activated. In a spherical shell the transition from ring compression to ring tension forces in the supporting plane, the "zero ring force line", lies at a polar angle of approximately 52° from the rotational axis. The ideal of the membrane stress is upset by large point or single loads; in extreme cases this can lead to local failure and collapse of the dome surface. The dome shear created by the meridian forces must be absorbed in the supporting plane by a suitable substructure to avoid problems in the load transfer. [2.2/6]

27 Greenhouse in Dahlem, mixed construction,
    1908, Arch.: A. Koerner

26–28 The glasshouse as a mixed type
    26 Convergence of glass band and glass core,
        Wilhelmina Botanical Gardens Stuttgart, 1844,
        Arch.: K.-L. von Zanth

28 Bad Neustadt spa clinic: Membrane as
    a "freely-formed" cable net, 1999,
    Arch.: Lamm, Weber, Donath und Partner
    Eng.: W. Sobek Ingenieure

25 Soccer stadium: Amsterdam ArenA, 1996
    Arch.: R. Schuurman

____THE GLASSHOUSE

According to J. F. Geist, the glasshouse corresponds to the "all-en-compassing skylight". In contrast to other types, the glazing extends across the lateral enclosures down to the floor and forms a weather skin on all sides. Depending on the internal plan, the geometry of the glasshouse can be interpreted as a space defining variation on the glass courtyard, the glass band or the glass core. Typologically, the cubic glass fabric therefore corresponds to the glass courtyard, the glass tube to the glass band and the enclosing dome to the glass core.

Generally speaking, aspects of differing basic types often converge in glasshouses; what emerges are mixed types that do not make an unequivocal statement on functional or mechanical form. Thus the greenhouse, the glasshouse par excellence, has been realised in a multitude of geometric formulations depending on floor-plan layout and the plant species it shelters.

When building in the existing fabric, glasshouse designs may respond primarily to constraints imposed by the urban context rather than to the parameters related to the internal organisation ____Fig. 28.

3

FLAT GLASS
AS A
CONSTRUCTION
MATERIAL

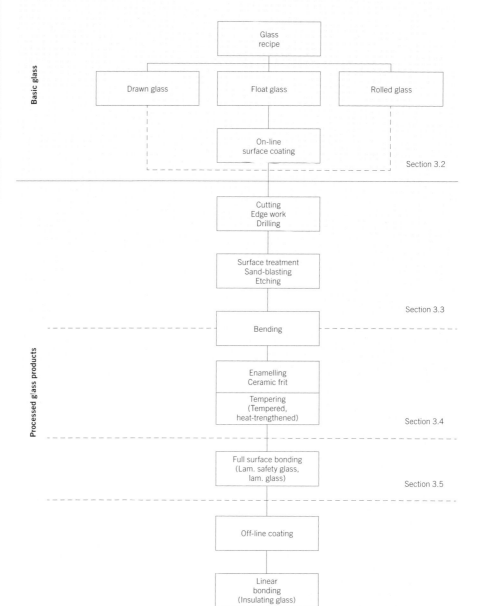

Basic glass

| Glass recipe |

Drawn glass — Float glass — Rolled glass

On-line surface coating

Section 3.2

Processed glass products

Cutting
Edge work
Drilling

Surface treatment
Sand-blasting
Etching

Section 3.3

Bending

Enamelling
Ceramic frit

Tempering
(Tempered,
heat-trengthened)

Section 3.4

Full surface bonding
(Lam. safety glass,
lam. glass)

Section 3.5

Off-line coating

Linear
bonding
(Insulating glass)

Section 3.6

1   Natural glass (obsidian)

2   Various glass types: Small samples of processed
    glass products

3   Overview of the manufacturing and processing stages
    of flat glass in the context of Sections 3.2 to 3.6

3

3.1
PROPERTIES OF GLASS

Glass is a product of fusion. In nature it occurs as solidified volcanic lava and was used by humans in the manufacture of jewellery and other objects at least as long as 5000 years ago. Glass in a hot, viscous state can be formed by mechanical processes into planar, linear or compact semi-finished products. All the products manufactured from glass and used in the construction industry – these include profiled glass and glass blocks but mostly flat glass – are classed as construction materials. Over 70 percent of all flat glass is used in new buildings or in the renovation of building skins. [3.1/1]

The complex and extensive performance criteria which nowadays cover building physics, construction and form, have led to a broad and diverse range of products. The making and forming of the basic glass – normally float glass – is followed by two or more processing stages which optimise the material for specific technical functions such as solar control, structural or safety needs such as the residual strength or purely aesthetic aspects such as colour effect. In glass products used for extensive glass skins, these aspects normally merge with one another to create an overall requirement profile. In these cases the glass is designed to meet all the project-specific requirements relating to structure, building physics and appearance. While basic glass products are now standardised to a very high degree, the end product is often a customized product with special finishing qualities. [3.1/2]

Fig. 3 shows the various manufacturing and processing stages in diagrammatic form. Most basic glass today is manufactured by the float glass process and only about 10 percent of the glass used in

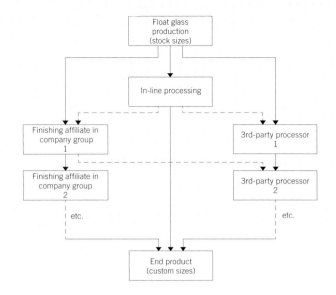

4

Abbr.	Meaning		Glass type	Thickness [mm]	max. size [m x m]
SPG	Annealed glass, non-tempered glass (mainly annealed float glass)		Float glass/ annealed glass	3–19	3.21 x 6.00 (Jumbo size)
TVG	Partially tempered glass (also: heat-strengthened glass)		Tempered Manufacturer A	6–19 4–15	2.70 x 6.00 1.67 x 7.00
ESG	Tempered safety glass (also: fully-tempered glass or toughened glass)		Tempered Manufacturer B	8–19 6–19	2.80 x 6.00 2.50 x 5.00
VG	Laminated glass		Heat-strengthened Manufacturer A	4–12	2.70 x 6.00 1.67 x 7.00
VSG	Laminated safety glass (laminated glass with safety properties)		Heat-strengthened Manufacturer B	6–12	2.80 x 6.00 2.50 x 5.00
MIG	Multipane insulating glass		Laminated Manufacturer A	4–80	2.40 x 3.80 2.00 x 4.00
Low-E	Insulating glass with low emission factor		Laminated Manufacturer B	8–100	2.30 x 5.40 2.40 x 5.00
			Insulating Manufacturer A	up to 45	2.70 x 5.00

5

6

4   The logistics of flat glass processing: Processing takes place either immediately after manufacture in the manufacturer's processing affiliate or by independent or subcontractor laminators

5   Key to common German abbreviations for flat glass products

6   Overview of typical production sizes of processed flat glass products: The dimensions depend primarily on the type of product but also vary from manufacturer to manufacturer.

3.1

construction is drawn or rolled. The group of basic glass types is extended by float glass that is coated in an on-line process directly after forming. Processing lines are often linked directly to production facilities; where this is not the case the basic glass is taken to local or regional finishing or processing works. ___Fig. 4.

The first stage of the further processing chain involves the basic glass, available in the form of *jumbo sheets* initially after manufacture and after cutting as customer-specific *final cut sizes*. Thermal processing may follow further mechanical processing stages such as drilling, grinding and polishing of the edges, surface grinding or sand-blasting. Among these are *bending* of the glass panes and enamelling the glass surface with ceramic frits. *Tempering* or *heat-strengthening* of glass is done by artificially inducing stresses into the glass by forced convective cooling of the pane. These stresses improve the load resistance, but also affect the fracture behaviour in specific ways.

Physical and chemical processes can be used to place *thin film*

coatings (also known as functional coatings) on to the surface of the glass, primarily to change optical properties such as the amount of transmitted light and energy. At the end of the processing chain generally two or more panes are layered and bonded to form *laminated safety glass. Monolithic or laminated panes of glass* are often fabricated into *insulating glass units* by means of a spacer bar along the edges of the panes ___Fig. 5.

The sequence and number of steps involved in the process depends on the degree of required processing and the logistical constraints. Each processing stage has its own specialist equipment such as bending and tempering furnaces or coating plants, all of which have their own limits on maximum size, weight and thickness of the glass elements. These constraints must be taken into account in the design of glass constructions and are described in detail in the following sections ___Fig. 6.

The timing and geographical location of the processing stages are

	Steel S 235	Softwood S 10	Concrete C20/25	Glass Soda-lime glass
Refractive index η	–	–	–	1.5
Density ρ [kN/m³]	78.5	6	22	25
Modulus of elasticity E [kN/cm²]	21 000	1 100	2 900	7 000 (like aluminium)
Tensile strength $f_{t,k}$ [kN/cm²]	24 (yield strength)	1.4	0.22	4.5
Elongation at break ε in %	25	0.7	–	0.006–0.17
Compressive strength $f_{c,k}$ [kN/cm²]	23.5	II 1.7–2.6 $\perp$ 0.4 –0.6	2	approx. 50
Limiting tensile stress σ_{Rd}	21.8	0.9	(~0.1)	1.2/1.8
Safety factor y	$y_M = 1.1$	$y_M = 1.3$	1.8	2.5
Breaking length σ/ρ [m]	2 800	1 500	(45)	480/720
Thermal conductivity [W/m x K]	75	II 0.5 $\perp$ 0.2	1.6	1
Thermal shock resistance ΔT [1/K]	–	–	–	40
Coefficient of thermal expansion α_T [1/K]	12 x 10⁻⁶	II 5 x 10⁻⁶ $\perp$ 35 x 10⁻⁶	10 x 10⁻⁶	9 x 10⁻⁶ 60 K ≈ 0.5 mm/m

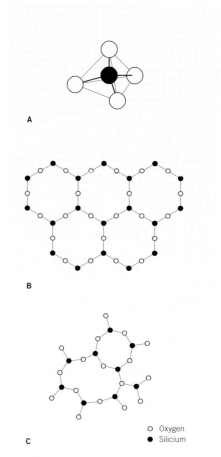

○ Oxygen
● Silicium

7

8

7 Various mechanical and thermal properties of soda-lime glass compared with those of another brittle material (concrete) and two tough materials (wood and steel)

8 Simplified view of the molecular structure of glass
   A Structure of a SiO_4 tetrahedron
   B Representation of a regular crystalline SiO_2 matrix
   C Representation of an irregular crystalline SiO_2 matrix

crucial to the manufacturing costs of a product. Costs rise with the degree of processing works and the dimensions of the finished product, the effort and complexity of transport and the associated risk of breakage. Higher prices also apply if there are limited procurement routes. There may be only a few specialist companies, either inland or abroad, capable of carrying out certain special processes.

This chapter describes the use of flat glass as a building skin and construction material. The building physical, mechanical and optical characteristics of glass are introduced, related to manufacturing and processing methods and interactions discussed to allow a deeper understanding of the often complex conditions of use. Following an introduction of the basic properties of the material, the chapter then discusses the processing stages shown in the previous diagram.

FLAT GLASS AS A LOAD-BEARING MATERIAL

Glass used in construction is composed of almost 75 percent silicon dioxide (silica), which is present in large quantities in the Earth's crust in the form of pure quartz sand, and is therefore generally referred to as *silicate glass*. This *glass former* is combined with sodium oxide (soda), which acts as a *flux* to lower the transformation temperature to approximately 550 °C and simplifies the manufacturing process. Calcium oxide (lime) is added as a *stabiliser* to increase chemical resistance. Further additives in the order of less than one percent can be added to influence the optical properties of the glass. When the molten mass cools, the glass gradually passes from being a liquid to a solid without – as is normally the case with molten products – forming a regular symmetrical or periodic crystal lattice. Glass is often called a *supercooled liquid* because of this non-crystalline (amorphous) molecular structure. Glass is *isotropic*, i.e. its properties do not depend on direction or orientation. [3.1/3]

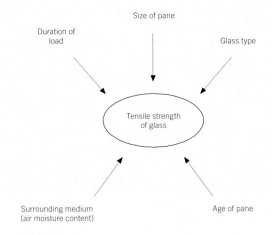

9

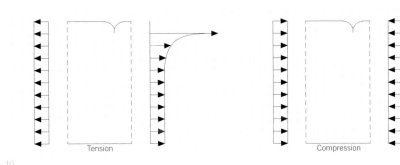

Tension   Compression

10

Fracture strengths [kN/cm²]	Compression (theoretical)	Tension (theoretical)	Bending tensile stress (newly manuf. glass)	Bending tensile stress (aged glass)
Plane dims. 20 cm x 20 cm	70–90	600	4–17	3.8–7
Plane dims. 1 m x 1 m	70–90	600	2–7.5	1.8–5.5

11

9   Factors influencing the tensile (bending) strength of glass: The strength of glass is not a constant value!

10   Stress distribution over the cross section of surface-damaged glass: Stress peaks occur as a result of the notch effect. Under compressive stress the notches are compressed, resulting in no stress peaks.

11   Comparison of strengths of panes of various sizes and ages

_____THE TENSILE AND COMPRESSIVE STRENGTH OF GLASS –
A BRITTLE CONSTRUCTION MATERIAL

An astonishingly high theoretical tensile strength can be calculated based on the bond between the chemical components of glass. This bond largely comes from the high binding energy of the SiO_4 tetrahedron, the basic building block of the irregular molecular structure of glass _____Fig. 11. This is given as up to 800 kN/cm² in the literature – which is about thirty times the yield strength of steel. However the tensile strength achievable in practice is only about one hundredth of this value. This is principally due to glass being a brittle material with a strength that depends on the degree of damage to the glass surface _____Fig. 14. Therefore glass is not a completely compact solid but has a microstructure with many microscopic irregularities and defects. In addition macroscopic damage, such as scratches and notches caused by abrasion, wind and other mechanical effects, accumulates on the edges and the surface of the glass during use. Deflections as a result

of load transfer create fine microcracks on the surface similar to those in concrete. Tensile stresses at these notch sites lead to stress concentrations in the crack root and to propagation of the crack. When the stress peaks exceed a critical value the glass "breaks": the crack propagates at high speed from one edge to the other across the whole area of the pane. The broken glass can be provided with some *residual load-bearing capacity* if required by layering two or more individual panes to form laminated glass. [**3.1/4, 3.1/5**]

The tensile or bending strength of glass therefore reflects the surface quality and is not a constant value _____Fig. 12. It relates directly to the size and age of the pane: the larger and older the pane, the greater the probability of a critical defect _____Fig. 14. The strength of glass depends on the duration of loading and the surrounding medium; humidity promotes subcritical crack propagation.

As a result of its brittle behaviour, the *compressive strength* of glass is about ten times higher than its tensile strength in bending. As

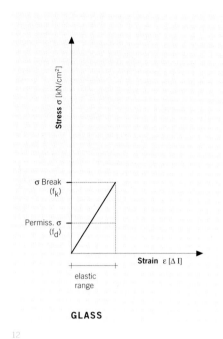

GLASS

12

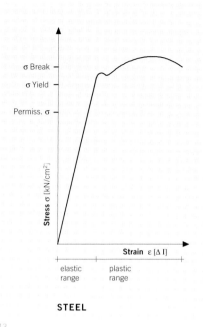

STEEL

13

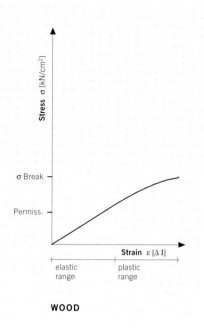

WOOD

14

12–14 Qualitative comparison of the stress-strain
graphs of glass, steel and wood

12 Linear-elastic deformation behaviour of glass:
Glass breaks without warning after its fracture
stress is exceeded.

13 Up to its yield point, steel behaves almost
completely linear-elastically, after this point
steel "yields", i.e. it deforms plastically.

14 Wood has an elastic and a plastic range. Tearing and
splitting of fibres warns of complete failure in wood.

the notch sites are surcharged in compression in the plane of the pane, the defects in the glass surface do not reduce its strength ____Fig. 13. As compressive stresses are always accompanied by tensile shear stresses, the actual compressive strength of about 50 kN/cm² is well below the theoretical value of up to 90 kN/cm². Compressive strength under permanent load is given as about 17 kN/cm² in the literature. [**3.1/6**]

____DEFORMATION BEHAVIOUR UNDER LOADING AND TEMPERATURE EFFECTS

The *modulus of elasticity* of glass is 7000 kN/cm², only about a third of that of steel but five times greater than hardwood. The material deforms linear-elastically under increasing load at right angles to the plane of the pane until it exceeds its load-bearing capacity, when it suddenly fractures without warning on the face under tensile stress. The *strain* e is proportional to *stress* s up to fracture. In this respect

glass is considerably different to other ductile and therefore "good-natured" construction materials such as wood or in particular steel, which are able to deform plastically to a certain extent in order to reduce stress peaks ____Figs. 15–17. The designer must prevent direct contact between glass and glass or between glass and metal in order to avoid stress concentrations. As glass does not strain plastically, it cannot dissipate imposed stresses, such as arise from temperature shock.

The coefficient of thermal expansion α_T expresses the relative longitudinal expansion of a component per degree of temperature rise. The value for the most commonly used glass in buildings, soda-lime glass, is 9×10^{-6} 1/K, i.e. about three-quarters that of structural steelwork. The different amounts by which the various materials expand and contract must be taken into account in all connections and in composite construction. Titanium, with the same coefficient of thermal expansion as glass, is particularly useful in structural glass, despite its high costs. The α_T of special metal alloys can also be adjusted to match glass.

15   Flat glass and the diverse appearance forms of light:
     Church windows with a dichroitic coating, Sweeny
     Chapel Indianapolis, 1987, Arch.: JCDA Inc.

15

The maximum temperature differential that a component can tolerate within its surface without fracturing, often called *thermal shock resistance*, is low for building glass. For untempered soda-lime glass the value is only about 40 Kelvin. The thermal shock resistance of borosilicate glass is more than twice this value due to its lower coefficient of thermal expansion. Tempering or heat-strengthening glass increases its thermal shock resistance.

The brittleness, high compressive strength and elastic deformation behaviour of the material are of prime importance in the design of glass structures. The main physical properties are summarised in ___Fig. 10 and compared with those of other materials.

FLAT GLASS AS A BUILDING SKIN MATERIAL

As an amorphous material, glass has no phase boundaries at which the light rays are scattered and hence glass appears transparent. Its high transparency and good chemical resistance to most corrosive media such as acids and salts means that glass is an excellent material for building skins. Only silica-dissolving hydrofluoric acid attacks the surface of glass. Aqueous alkaline solutions, which may for example arise from leachates out of adjacent concrete or limestone building components or from continuous standing water from condensation on the glass surface, may lead to the glass surface becoming opaque in the long term.

In addition to the optical properties of glass, its thermal and acoustic properties are addressed in the following sections to the extent that they are important to the role of glass as an enclosing element.

___TRANSMISSION, REFLECTION AND ABSORPTION

Glass is not completely transparent – part of the light falling on the glass surface is reflected and a further part is absorbed by the colour of the glass. The diversity and changing interaction of these optical

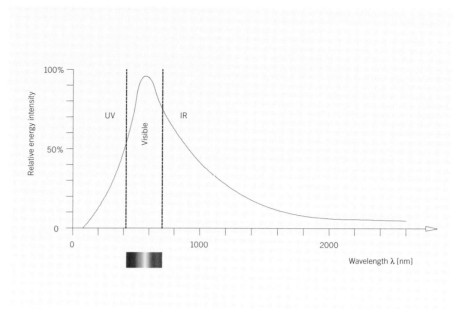

16

18

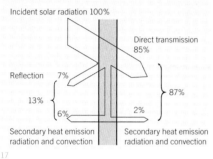

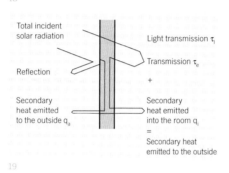

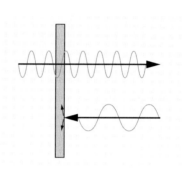

17

19

20

16   Coloured glass Artista, Landeszentralbank
     Sachsen und Thüringen in Meiningen, Arch.:
     H. Kollhoff, Artistic glasswork: H. Federle

18   Schematic representation of the solar spectrum,
     which covers an approximate wavelength
     range of 280 nm (UV) to 3500 nm (IR).

17, 19   The proportions of transmitted, reflected and
         absorbed light add up to 100% of the incident
         light.The g-value is the sum of the directly
         transmitted light and the secondary thermal
         energy qi emitted by the glazing unit into the room
         through radiation, conduction and convection.

20   Greenhouse effect: Short wavelength visible
     light enters the room through the glazing, where
     it is absorbed. The resulting long wavelength
     IR radiation is absorbed by the glass.

phenomena lies at the heart of the unique fascination of glass as a building material ____Fig. 18.

Whilst the *transmittance* (or transmission factor) indicates the proportion of the incident light that passes through a pane without appreciable scattering, *absorption* describes the property of a material to change the light penetrating it into other forms of energy – in most cases into heat. The proportion of absorbed light depends on the thickness of the pane. A detrimental effect on transparency usually considered very distracting is the *reflection* of the incident light off the glass pane. The reflectance between air and glass for a perpendicular incidence of light is 4 percent on the front and back surfaces, 8 percent in total. By applying thin dielectric coatings, reflection can be almost completely eliminated for particular wavelengths of light by using destructive interference. Insulating or solar control glass can be specifically designed to provide glass with particular reflection behaviour with respect to light in UV or IR wavelengths. There is a simple rela-

tionship between the factors of transmittance τ, reflectance r and absorptance a, which illustrates the conservation of light energy:
$\tau+\rho+\alpha=1$.

Glass is a very good transmitter of radiation in the visible light range, which has the highest intensity and occupies over 50 percent of the total radiation in the solar spectrum ____Fig. 19. Ultraviolet (UV) light below 320 nanometres and long wavelength infrared (IR) light above 3000 nanometres are almost completely absorbed. The *greenhouse effect*, which also has important implications for glazed room-defining elements, is based on the phenomenon of different transmission factors for different wavelengths: the visible short wavelength light admitted by the glass is transformed inside the building into long wavelength heat radiation, which is then absorbed by the glass and re-emitted into the building by radiation or convection. The glazing acts as a heat trap ____Fig. 23. [**3.1/7, 3.1/8**]

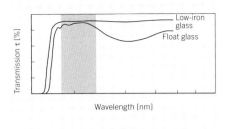

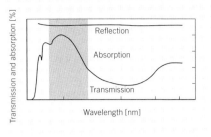

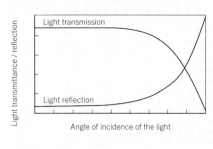

21

23

24

	Visible light [%]			Total radiation [%]		
Thickness [mm]	Transmittance [τ_v]	Reflection [ρ_v]	Absorption [α_v]	Transmittance [τ_e]	Reflection [ρ_e]	Absorption [α_e]
2	91	8	1	87	8	5
3	91	8	1	84	7	9
4	90	8	2	82	7	11
5	90	8	2	80	7	13
6	89	8	3	78	7	15
8	89	8	3	74	7	19
10	88	8	4	71	7	22
12	86	8	6	66	6	28
15	83	8	9	62	6	32

22

25

21   Spectral transmission of low-iron and float glass

22   Overview of the optical parameters relating to visible light (index v) and the whole range of radiation (index e) for float glass of various thicknesses

23   Spectral transmission of green glass, which is suitable for solar control glass because of its high absorption of light in the IR range.

24   Light transmission and reflection graph for various angles of incidence

25   Total reflection at a flat observation angle, Finnish Pavilion, Expo 2000, Hanover

The radiation balance for a particular part of the solar spectrum is therefore as dependent on the composition, thickness and surface qualities of the glass as it is on the prevalent angle of incidence of radiation. These characteristic values are generally referenced either to the range of visible light (τ_v ρ_v and α_v with the index v for *visible*) or to the whole range of radiation (τ_e, ρ_e, α_e with the index e for *energy*) ____Fig. 24. In addition the *total solar energy transmittance g* is important to glazing. This is composed of the directly transmitted proportion of the solar radiation spectrum and the secondary heat transmitted by the glazing as a result of thermal radiation and convection. The ratio of τ to g is known as the *selectivity index S*, where a value of S = 2 represents the physical limit equal to approximately half of the total energy of the solar spectrum. Thus with selective glazing that admits only the visible proportion of light, half the total solar radiation will still enter the building. In other words: in order to counteract overheating, also the gain of visible light must be reduced. [**3.1/9**]

____SOLAR RADIATION BALANCE IN RELATION TO GLASS THICKNESS, COMPOSITION, ANGLE OF INCIDENCE AND SURFACE QUALITY

A 4 millimetres thick soda-lime glass transmits approximately 90 percent of visible light, reflects eight percent and absorbs 2 percent. Absorption is caused by iron oxide (approximately 0.1 percent) in the glass melt, which leads to the absorption of red light and gives a green colouration to the glass. The colour of the glass can be determined by the controlled addition of other metal oxides, which increases absorption at the expense of transmission. For example, grey-coloured glass transmits only about half of the light transmitted by clear float glass. With increasing glass thickness, the proportion of absorbed solar radiation increases and leads to the warming of the glass. Absorption can be reduced through the use of very pure silicon dioxide in the manufacture of clear *low-iron glass* – the glass appears colourless, and light transmission is almost independent of glass thickness. In an arrangement of strongly absorbing panes (e.g. in multiple-pane insulation glazing) it

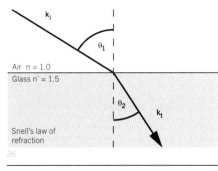

26

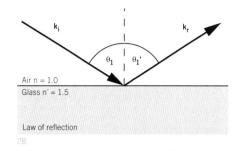

28

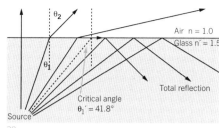

30

Material	Refractive index n
Air	1.00
Water	1.33
Plexiglass	1.49
Soda-lime glass	1.52
Lead crystal glass	1.60
Diamond	2.42

27

29

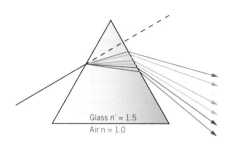

31

26 Light is refracted at a surface between transparent materials with different refractive indices in accordance with Snell's law: $n \sin\_1 = n' \sin\_2$.

27 Refractive index n for various transparent materials

28 Law of reflection: The angle of incidence equals the angle of reflection: $\theta 1$ (angle of incidence) $= \theta 1'$ (angle of reflection).

29 Refraction, reflection and absorption of light in an edge of a float glass ribbon

30 Total reflection: The percentage of reflected light increases for light striking a surface at an angle (see Fig. 27). From a critical angle (41.8° for glass), light attempting to pass through the interface plane between an optically denser material (glass) and an optically less dense medium (air) experiences total reflection and the rays are all reflected.

31 Refraction and dispersion of light in a prism

should be noted that the resulting transmittance is the product of the transmittances of each pane. Only with weakly absorbing glass can the absorptances be added to approximate to the total absorptance.

Specular reflection is a property of the boundary surface between two transparent media. Reflectance and therefore transmittance change with the angle of incidence. The flatter the angle at which the light strikes the pane, the greater the reflectance. Refraction also increases as the angle of incidence becomes flatter, i.e. the change in direction of the transmitted light at the surface boundary between glass and air increases. From a certain critical angle of incidence *total reflection* occurs at the side facing the light – none of the incident light is refracted and all the light is reflected. This effect, which depends on the various thicknesses and reflective indices of optical materials, can be neglected in relation to the light transmission by plan-parallel flat glass as the change in angle is reversed when the light exits the opposite surface of the glass. With non-parallel surfaces multiple refrac-

tions can result in a prism effect with the light being split into its spectral colours ____ Fig. 33. [**3.1/10**]

In terms of transmittance and reflectance, the surface quality of the glass has less influence on the radiation balance than it does on the ratio of direct, quasi-parallel light to indirect or diffuse, scattered light. With increasing roughness or texture of the surface, directional light becomes diffused on transmission, and specular reflection is reduced in favour of diffuse reflection. The image viewed though the glass and the reflected image become more and more indistinct until only a hazy outline can be seen on the surface of the glass. The transmission of diffuse light is called *translucence*. The transmission of direct light can be influenced by the cloudiness of the glass melt (opal or milk glass) as well as the texture of the glass surface produced by etching or grinding.

The proportion of diffused light from fire-polished transparent surfaces of float and drawn glass is extremely small and the incident light

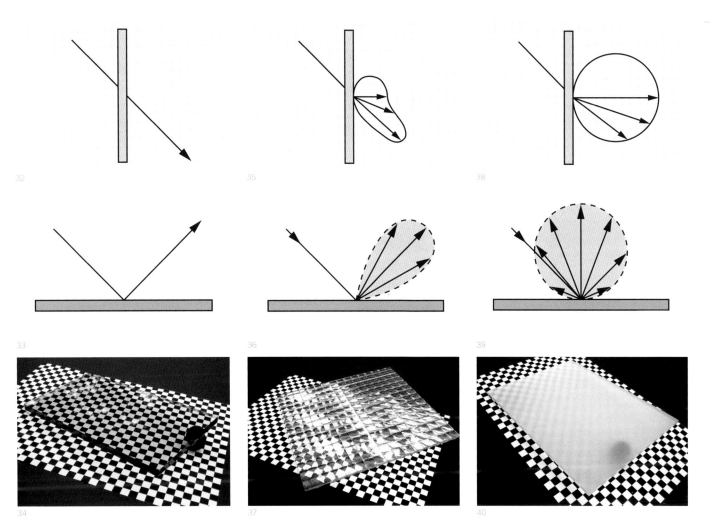

Transmission types:
32 Transmission of direct light at a perfectly smooth surface
35 Mixed transmission of direct and diffuse
    light at a textured surface
38 Scattering of light at a rough surface

Reflection types:
33 Specular reflection at a perfect surface
36 Mixed reflection at a textured surface
39 Diffuse reflection at a rough surface

34 The fire-polished, smooth surface of float glass

37 The textured surface of rolled glass

40 The rough surface of sand-blasted glass

rays follow the law of reflection. They leave the glass surface at the same angle to the perpendicular at which they entered.

___THERMAL AND ACOUSTIC PROPERTIES

Glass has a relatively high thermal conductivity. Thermal transmittance (U-value) can only be reduced to meet modern thermal insulation requirements by the multiple pane construction adopted for insulating glass units with the cavity between panes filled with an encapsulated layer of gas.

The use of unprocessed glass with unaltered properties as an enclosing element needs to be carefully considered with respect to fire safety requirements. Glass is non-combustible and does not contribute to the building's fire load but its low resistance to differential temperatures means glass can fracture on contact with hot combustion gases and therefore cannot be relied upon to provide a safe barrier to the entry of flames and hot gases. The fire-rating can be considerably increased by the use of tempered borosilicate glass, which has a lower coefficient of thermal expansion. Transparent glass-ceramics, which are different in that they have a partially crystalline microstructure, have excellent thermal resistance due to their very low coefficients of thermal expansion and are therefore used as fire-resistant glass. The transmission of heat radiation can be limited by laminated glass featuring fire retardant interlayers [3.1/11]

The wave-form propagation of sound is comparable with that of light. The reflection and absorption of sound waves depend upon on their wavelengths. Sound waves in the high frequency range are reflected from hard, smooth glass surfaces, an effect which may be to the detriment of local acoustics. Direct reflection can be reduced by texturing the glass surface. Sound absorption depends principally on the sound reduction index and can be increased by using thicker glass with higher mass and multiple laminated build-ups.

	Enclosing element (fire-resistant)	Enclosing element with reduced heat emission	Enclosing element with heat insulation (fire retarding, fire-resistant)
DIN 4102	G 30 G 120	–	F 30 F 120
EN ISO 12543	E 15- E 240	EW 30- EW 60	EI 15- EI 240

41

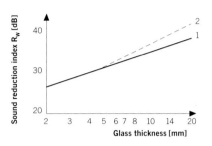

42

41 Fire protection classification in accordance
    with German and European standards

42 Graph of sound reduction index against glass thickness
    1 Monolithic glass
    2 Laminated glass

Body-tints from metal oxides	
violet	Manganese oxide
	Nickel oxide
blue	Copper(II) oxide
	Cobalt(II) oxlde
green	Iron(II) oxide
	Chromium(II) oxide
	Cobalt(III) oxide
yellow	Chromium(VI) oxide
	Tungsten oxide
yellow-brown	Iron(III) oxide
brown	Iron (III)oxide
	Nickel oxide
	Iron(III) oxide, Nickel oxide
	Manganese oxide
red	Copper(I) oxide

1   Glass batch materials being introduced
    into the melting bath

2   Float glass plant in Cologne-Porz, Germany
    The batch house and melting furnace can
    be seen in the bottom left of the picture

3   Ionic colorant range of glass colours produced
    by the addition of metal oxides

___ 3.2

BASIC GLASS – FLOAT GLASS, ROLLED GLASS AND DRAWN GLASS

Basic glass types have different production sizes and properties depending on their recipe and manufacturing process. Glass may be differentiated into *soda-lime* or *borosilicate* glass and *clear low-iron* or *body-tinted* glass. Flat glass is manufactured by the float glass, rolled glass or drawn glass processes. Float glass makes up over 90 percent of flat glass production and is the most important basic glass. The following section describes basic products and their importance for building skins and construction.

___ GLASS RECIPE

Soda-lime-silicate is the main type of glass used in buildings, whilst borosilicate glass is manufactured to a considerably smaller extent and used for fire-resistant glazing. Low-iron or clear soda-lime glass can be made to have very low absorption and a correspondingly high natural light transmittance that is practically independent of the glass thickness. The additional costs are between 15 and 25 percent, depending on the glass thickness. The use of colour formers (*colloidal colorants*) or metal oxides (*ionic colorants*) allows for the specific selection of the spectral transmittance and hence of the glass colour ___Fig. 3. The additives generally amount to less than 0.5 percent of the glass batch. Metal oxides produce a broad spectrum of colours. Noble metals, metal sulphides and selinides produce colloidal yellow and red colours depending on the manufacturing process. The colour of body-tinted glass can differ from batch to batch so that keeping a stock of replacement panes is recommended. [**3.2/1**]

4   The glass ribbon being formed by a pair of rollers

5   Float glass ribbon cut to jumbo panel sizes
    after cooling and visual inspection

6   View into a drawing chamber used in the
    Fourcault process

MANUFACTURING PROCESSES

____FLOAT GLASS

Float glass production is based on a process developed by Alastair Pilkington. At the heart of the plant is a molten bath of tin approximately 50 metres long on to which the 1 100 °C liquid glass melt flows out of the melting bath and floats until it solidifies at approximately 600 °C.

Today glass is manufactured by large corporations with a worldwide network of float glass plants. A factory can produce upwards of 750 tonnes (approximately 50 000 m²) of glass per day. The four leading glass manufacturers in the world – *Nippon Sheet Glass* (which took over Pilkington in 2005), *Asahi*, *Saint-Gobain* and *Guardian* – provide about two-thirds of global production of high quality float glass (approximately 25 million tonnes).

Float glass is usually manufactured in thicknesses between 2 to 19 millimetres and after cooling is cut into jumbo sheet stock sizes of 3.21 m x 6 m. Oversized jumbo- sheets are produced to a limited extent for the glass market. Some glass factories produce sheets up to 12 metres long for special purposes once a year. This is mainly in low-iron glass. Mass production limits the opportunities for modifications to the glass melt. In addition to low iron glass, body tinted glass is produced in bronze only up to a thickness of 12 millimetres and in grey, pink and green up to 10 millimetres. Borosilicate glass is produced in Jena by *Schott AG* in a micro-float glass plant in thicknesses up to 21 millimetres in a maximum sheet size of 2.30 m x 3 m.

____ROLLED SHEET GLASS

Rolled or "cast" glass is produced using the "overflowing tub" principle: A pair of forming rollers with patterned surfaces continuously pull a glass ribbon out of the melt, after which the ribbon is cooled and cut. Europe's largest rolled glass plant, with a capacity of 300 tonnes per day, is located in Mannheim, Germany.

Glass type	Optical characteristics	Stock sizes [mm]	Thickness [mm]		Advantages
Float glass	Smooth, transparent	Max. 3210 x 6000 oversized jumbo sizes in 0.5 m increments (cost premium)	2; 3; 4; 5; 6 8; 10; 12 15 19; (25)	±0.2 ±0.3 ±0.5 ±1.0	Mass-produced product, high quality, precise manufacture, (exact thicknesses)
		Borosilicate glass: max. 2300 x 3000 (thickness 5.5–9 mm)	3.8; 5; 5.5; 6.5 7.5; 8; 9; 11 13; 15 16; 17; 18; 19 20; 21	±0.2 ±0.3 ±0.3 ±0.5 ±1.0	
Rolled glass	Smooth / textured, light scattering, light directing	Max. 2500 x 4500 (product-dependent)	3; 4; 5; 6 8 10; 13; 15 Wired glass: 7; 9	±0.5 ±0.8 ±1.0	Large selection of colours and ornamentation even in small batch production
Drawn glass	Smooth / textured, slight draw lines	Max. 170 x 240 (product-dependent) Deviations of several 10 mm possible	< 1.8 (thin glass) > 19 (thick glass) 2; 3; 4 5; 6 8 10 12	Manufacture of special glass, large selection of colours ±0.2 ±0.3 ±0.4 ±0.5 ±0.6	

7

Product	Thickness [mm]	Dimensions [cm x cm]
Coloured glass *Imera*	2.75 ± 0.25	160 (2.5) x 150 (+10/-20)
Flashed glass *Opalika*	2.1–2.7 ... 5.0–6.0	140 x 160 240 x 160
Lead glass "RD 30" "RD 50"	6 ± 0.25 3.5 to 36	240 x 170 100 x 60 to 210 x 103

8

7   Stock sizes and features of basic glass types –
    the values for the borosilicate float glass are typical
    for Borofloat 33 produced by Schott AG.

8   Stock sizes of some special drawn sheet glass
    products manufactured by Schott AG

Rolled glass is also known as *ornamental glass* because of the ornamentation on one or both of its sides. *Wired glass* is produced in the rolling process by feeding wire mesh into the liquid glass. A multitude of standard patterns are available – some incorporating wire mesh – as well as customer-specific designs, if the cost and time frames allow for the fabrication of the rollers. In addition to clear glass, there are thirty different shades of brown, yellow, grey, violet and blue.

The maximum stock size measures approximately 2.50 m x 4.50 m, with smaller limits to size depending on the product and glass thickness. The commonly available thicknesses are 4, 5, 6, 8 and 10 millimetres, but thicknesses of 13, 15, and 19 millimetres can also be produced. Wired glass is made in similar sheet sizes in thicknesses of 7 and 9 millimetres. The thickness tolerance of rolled glass is approximately ±10 percent.

DRAWN SHEET GLASS

Mainly due to the short set-up times required for the drawn glass process *SCHOTT AG* in Grünenplan, Germany can produce special flat glass to specific recipes. The drawn glass process was developed at the beginning of the 20th century; today it sees use in the further developed *Fourcault process,* named after its inventor. The approximately 1.90 metres wide glass ribbon is drawn vertically out of the melt by a debiteuse (a slotted block of refractory material) and moved vertically up a drawing shaft by rollers, during which time it is annealed by cooling slowly to avoid in-built stresses.

Today, coloured glass is produced in more than thirty different basic colours, clear glass, thin (up to 1.8 mm) and thick (more than 19 mm) using the drawn glass process. The drawn glass process is also used to produce flashed glass, which consists of a clear basic glass overlaid with a thin layer of coloured or milky glass (white flashed opal glass, e.g. *Opalika*). The sheet widths of special glass are

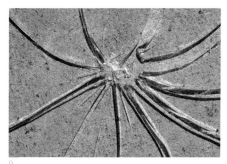

9   Fracture pattern of float glass

10   Oversized sheets of float glass: Shop window
     panes about 8 m long, New York

11   Fracture pattern of wired glass

12   Textured rolled glass surface with wire mesh

13   Machine-drawn white flashed opal glass *(Opalika)*

14   Visual distortions on the surface of drawn sheet
     glass due to the manufacturing process

between 1.4 and 1.7 metre, lengths are between 10 metres (2 mm thick) and 24 metres (8 mm thick) ____ Fig. 8. [**3.2/2, 3.2/3, 3.2/4**]

IMPLICATIONS FOR DESIGN AND CONSTRUCTION

The high dimensional accuracy and geometrical precision of float glass make it the only glass considered as suitable for use in buildings if it has to be further processed. The irregular thickness of rolled glass means that it is only about half as strong as float or drawn glass. All basic glass fractures radially from the centre of the break into acute-angled shards ____ Fig. 9. Wired glass has the lowest mechanical and thermal strength of any basic glass and its thermal shock resistance is only about 20 Kelvin.

IMPLICATIONS FOR BUILDING SKINS

Although the product portfolio of float glass is relatively small, nothing can compete with its high optical quality, so that float glass is the basic glass for all processing stages and is used in all areas of the building skin.

Rolled glass is flat and transmits light but it is not transparent. It is mostly used indoors where visual privacy is required. The deeper the pattern, the greater the degree of obscuration and diffusion. By combining colours and ornamentation, rolled glass can be produced with a wide range of optical effects, with the result that it also finds use as simple facade cladding. [**3.2/5**]

Drawn sheet glass can often be recognised by slightly uneven surface features called draw lines which can cause noticeable optical irregularities ____ Fig. 14. Drawn sheet glass has only a small scope of use, for example for special lighting applications. White flashed opal glass provides a diffused shadowless light and is mainly used in luminous ceilings ____ Fig. 13. The advantage of the drawn glass process is the large variety of different glass which can be produced.

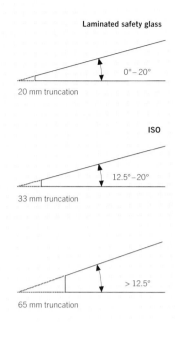

Laminated safety glass

0°–20°

20 mm truncation

ISO

12.5°–20°

33 mm truncation

> 12.5°

65 mm truncation

min. 30°

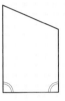

1 skewed edge
30% premium

Right-angled triangle
30% premium

Polygon
50% premium

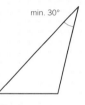

Triangle
50% premium

Parallelogram
40% premium

Trapezoid
40% premium

Radius
min. 10 cm

3 and 4 rounded corners
60% premium

Ø
min. 50 cm
max. 200 cm

Circle/sector
80% premium

1   Jumbo sheets before cutting

2   Price premium for cutting irregular shapes

3   Visual inspection prior to cutting

4   Truncation of corners required for triangular panes

FLAT GLASS AS A CONSTRUCTION MATERIAL   THE MECHANICAL PROCESSING OF GLASS

3.3

49

3.3

THE MECHANICAL PROCESSING OF GLASS – CUTTING, DRILLING AND GRINDING

Mechanical processing of this brittle material is done with multi-point tools (diamond or carborundum). Mechanical processing includes sawing, cutting, drilling, edge and surface grinding. Glass is usually mechanically processed before any other process to improve its properties takes place; therefore tempered glass may only be subsequently machined on its surface.

PROCESSES

Nowadays sawing, drilling and edge grinding is generally performed using CNC-controlled equipment, which is capable of carrying out several processing steps at once. Modern plants can machine 19 millimetres thick sheets up to the manufacturer's maximum stock size, weighing up to a maximum of 500 or even 1 000 kilogrammes.

All types of glass are cut fully automatically by a diamond-tipped cutting arm, with panels of the whole, half or a quarter ribbon width divided into final cut sizes with a cutting accuracy of up to 0.1 millimetres. The first stage in this process is the so-called *zero-cut*. Here the sheets are cut into stock sizes by trimming between 5 and 10 centimetres from all the edges whilst ensuring that the sheet is completely rectangular. Laminated glass cutting equipment can cut laminated glass up to 2 x 8 mm thick. The lower cutting speed and the greater amount of waste usually involved in cutting irregularly shaped sheets with one or more non-orthogonal angles or arcs result in them being

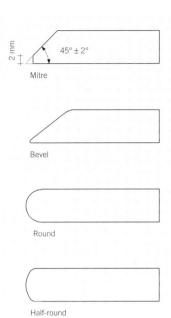

2 mm   45° ± 2°
Mitre

Bevel

Round

Half-round

5

6

Term	Description	Schematic representation
Cut	The cut, unfinished sides of the glass have sharp edges; slight waves (Wallner lines) can be seen running transversely to the edges.	
Arrised	The sharp cut edges have been broken off or bevelled with a grinding tool. (The dimensions of the bevels are not uniform).	
Ground (to required dimensions)	The glass has been shaped to the required dimensions by grinding the edge surfaces. The edges may be also cut or seamed.	
Fine ground	The edge is fully ground over its full surface. The edges may be also cut or seamed.	
Polished	The fine ground edges are finely polished. Polishing marks are permitted to some extent.	

7

5   Edge work and bevelling

6   Internal cut-outs produced using abrasive
    water jet cutting (Flow Europe)

7   Edge types and finishes

30 to 100 percent more expensive than rectangular sheets ——Fig. 2. Cuts meeting at acute angles are technically possible but should be cut back to prevent the point from being broken off during transport or installation ——Fig. 4. [3.3/1]

Workpieces up to 120 millimetres thick can be cut by abrasive water jet cutting, which uses a high pressure water jet up to 2.5 millimetres wide to which abrasive grains are added. With this method there are no restrictions on the cut geometry, even internal cut-outs are possible. The accuracy of the cut is higher than that of diamond cutting, although there may be angular inaccuracies at the cut edge, which may be up to 0.3 millimetres depending on the cutting speed. This time- and cost-intensive process is usually considered for only special applications.

Grinding and polishing the cut glass edges are performed using metal tools with a bonded coating of carborundum or diamond particles. The process may take place in several stages with decreasing grain sizes until the desired optical and mechanical properties are achieved. The first stage is the seaming, arrising and grinding of the cut edges. Subsequent flat grinding takes the sheet to the required dimensions but may result in blank (missed) spots on the edges. After fine grinding or smoothening, the edges of the glass have a flat, continuous matt appearance. The edges only become transparent after final polishing. In addition to straight edges it is also possible to create edge mitres up to 45°, bevelled, round or half round edges, stepped rebates, grooves etc., which are produced in small pane formats on a grinding line in a single process combining shape grinding and polishing. The amount of work required in grinding and polishing represents a significant cost factor.

Cylindrical, countersunk or undercut holes in non-tempered single or laminated glass can be made in the diamond drilling process by local grinding. More complex hole geometries must be made using the water jet process. To prevent the drill bit from breaking out of the opposite

8

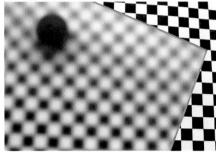

9

8 Detail of a sand-blasted glass surface

9 Detail of an etched glass surface

10 Laminated safety glass made from 2 x 10 mm low-
iron glass with external matt-etched surface,
Kunsthaus Bregenz, 1997, Arch.: P. Zumthor

10

side of the workpiece, drilling usually takes place from both sides. The misalignment of the holes in cylindrical hole components can be up to half a millimetre. Most equipment is capable of drilling holes of up to 70 millimetres in diameter, and in some cases even up to 150 millimetres. The tolerances for the positional accuracy of holes increase with the sheet dimensions and depend on the surface tolerances.

The glass surface can be given a matt, frosted finish by mechanical treatment, normally with a manually controlled sand blaster or in a wet grinding process by a frosting machine (max. width of glass approx. 2 m) – any previously applied coating being destroyed. Loose grains are used for this, unlike edge grinding. Compared with surface etching in an acid bath with hydrofluoric acid, the optical quality is less ——Fig. 8, and the rough surface texture attracts liquids, grease and other deposits, making external use not recommended even with a protective coating. The surface can be masked to produce a frosted finish on parts of the surface only.

___IMPLICATIONS FOR DESIGN AND CONSTRUCTION

Any form of mechanical processing leads to the removal of micro- and macroscopic flakes of material in the area treated and to a reduction in strength. The strength of the glass is directly dependent on the shape and quality of the treated edges and surfaces. For example, surface grinding or sand blasting to produce a matt finish reduces strength by up to 50 percent. Tempering a sheet after completion of this work mitigates the strength-reducing effects of mechanical processing.

The edges of conventionally cut glass have undulating waves (Wallner lines) and microcracks. Arrising the edges of glass reduces variations in strength because the glass is less prone to damage. Arrising is always carried out before tempering. Inward looking corners of recesses must also be rounded in order to avoid stress concentrations. The edges of glass intended for structural use typically have approximately 2 millimetres of material removed by fine grinding. In

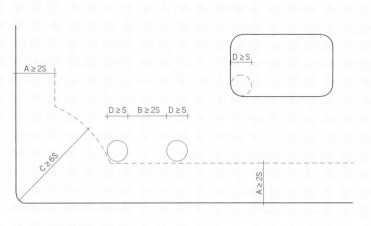

A   Edge distance
B   Distance between holes (hole edge to hole edge)
C   Distance to corner
D   Hole diameter
S   Glass thickness

11

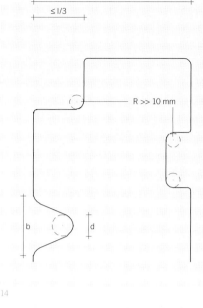

14

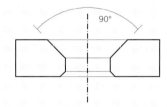

12

13

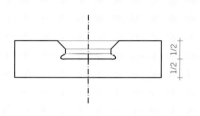

15

11   There are still no universally accepted
      rules for the positioning or dimensioning of
      drilled holes. The information given on the
      drawing is intended for guidance only.

Different hole shapes (12, 13, 15)
12   Cylindrical hole
13   Conical hole
15   Undercut hole

14   Standard recesses and notches: The radius of rounded
      corners should be at least 10 mm, laminated glass
      rounded corners at least 15 mm. Corner notches should
      not extend over more than a third of an edge length.
      The manufacturer should be consulted in advance
      if recesses are required on more than two edges.

forming butt corners, a tolerance on the mitre angle of ±2° has to be considered.

Cylindrical holes for bolted connections and conical countersunk holes for flush point fittings ___ Figs 12, 13 are most common in structural glass. The hole diameter should be at least equal to the glass thickness, preferably twice the glass thickness. The recommended distances between holes and edges are shown in ___ Fig. 11. Sheets with holes for structural use are usually tempered.

As the strength of edges cut by water jet are approximately 30 percent higher than conventionally machined glass, secondary processing is not always essential. [3.3/2]

___ IMPLICATIONS FOR BUILDING SKINS
Secondary processing is recommended for exposed glass edges in order to reduce the risk of damage and to create a consistent appearance. The glass edges become more transparent and reflective as the

quality of the edge treatment increases and the abrasive grain size decreases. In contrast a roughening of the surface has an antireflective effect, which scatters light and makes the glass look matt and translucent. A matt finish can be produced by mechanical means such as sand blasting or surface grinding or be chemically etched ___ Figs 8, 9.

___ COLD-FORMING GLASS
Its linear elastic deformation behaviour allows glass to be mechanically formed in the cold state. Clamp or point fixings allow a flat glass plate on a subconstruction to be forced into a curved shape. This process provides an inexpensive alternative to thermally deformed glass in achieving an irregularly curved building skin, although this method can only be used for single curved surfaces of up to half a degree per metre of curvature. The thicker and stiffer the glass sheet, the less it can be curved. For cylindrical curvatures the minimum ra-

Glass type	Tempered glass			Laminated safety glass made from tempered glass. Not heat treated			Laminated safety glass made from tempered glass. Heat treated		
Thickness [mm]	4	5	6	8	10	12	8	10	12
Radius [m]	2.4	4	6	5.2	8.4	12.3	2.7	4.8	7.2

17

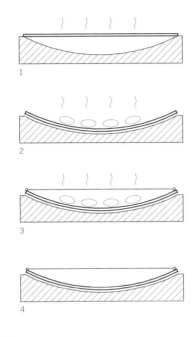

16

18

16 Production steps for cold bent glass
    arches ("Bogenglas")
    1 Place in form and heat to 70°C
    2 Apply load until the desired curved shape is achieved
    3 Fix the shape by installing ties
       (under load and temperature)
    4 Cool to room temperature and then remove the load

17 Table of approximate minimum bending radii for
    cylindrical cold-bent glass panes according to P. Kasper

18 2 m x 4 m cold bent glass elements functioning as a
    skylight, Main Bus Station, Heidenheim

dius for a given sheet thickness is many times larger than for hot deformed sheets ____Fig. 17. Between the fastening points, the edge curvature may deviate by up to ±10 millimetres from the specified line of curvature.

The German company *Maier-Glas* supplies prefabricated cylindrical curved segments of laminated safety glass, which are held in shape by tie rods. The manufacturing process is shown in ____Fig. 16. [**3.3/3, 3.3/4**]

Cold forming results in permanent tensile bending stresses in the component. The stresses increase with the size of the deformation and the tightness of the radius. These stresses apply in addition to the service loads. With approximately 60 percent of the total stress arising out of the curving process, cold-formed sheets have a lower load-bearing capacity than hot-formed sheets. The permanent nature of the loads supported means that only tempered glass with a high long-term strength can be considered for cold-forming. [**3.3/5**] Currently little is

known about the effects of permanent shear stresses on the seal of the edge zones of insulation glass sheets.

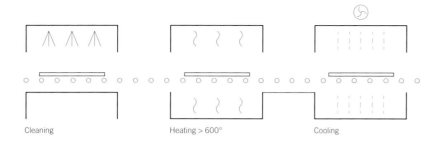

Cleaning   Heating > 600°   Cooling

1

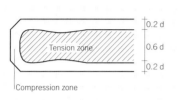

2

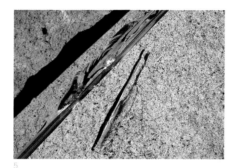

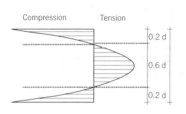

3

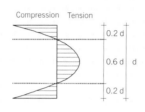

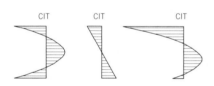

4

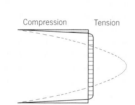

7

1   The manufacturing steps for tempering flat glass

2   Compression and tension zones in tempered glass
     cross-section (qualitative diagram)

3   Stress cross sectional diagram of fully tempered glass

4   Superimposed diagrams for thermal prestress and
     bending stress: bending stresses decrease compression
     in the bottom surface.

5   Typical needle-shaped edge damage of heat-treated glass

6   Stress cross-sectional diagram of heat-strengthened
     glass

7   Stress cross-sectional diagram of chemically
     strengthened glass

3.4

3.4

THE THERMAL TREATMENT OF GLASS – TEMPERING, ENAMELLING, BENDING AND SURFACE TEXTURING

The heat treatment of glass gives it greater resistance to mechanical and thermal loads. In this process the glass is heated to about 650 °C and allowed to cool with air blown over both sides. This process may also include enamelling, in which thin ceramic layers, usually coloured, are baked onto the surface. In a semi-fluid state at temperatures between 600 and 750 °C, the flat glass can also be bent and reshaped.

TEMPERING

___PROCESSES

The industry differentiates between fully *tempered* (toughened) *safety glass* and partially tempered *heat-strengthened glass*. Cooled more quickly from the same initial temperature, tempered glass has higher internal stresses than heat-strengthened glass. The glass is transported on a roller conveyor at the same time as it is heated to a uniform temperature approximately 100 °C above the transformation point, then nozzles blow cold air on to it. As cooling and stiffening takes place first on the surfaces of the glass, the delayed cooling and consolidation of the core leaves the sheet in a state of internal stress with a parabolic stress distribution across the section: the surfaces are in compression and the core is in tension. The glass must be at least 4 millimetres thick for this stress profile to be able to develop in the cross section. Tempered safety glass is produced in thicknesses up to 19 millimetres (occasionally 25 mm), heat-strengthened glass only up

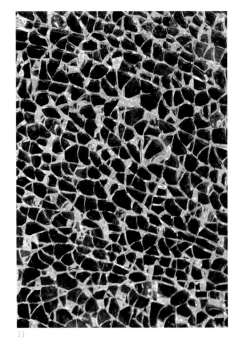

8

10

11

8   Fracture pattern of heat-strengthened glass

9   Heat-soak testing of tempered glass (at SGG Germany)
    as a certification procedure to detect nickel
    sulphide inclusions

10 Fracture pattern of heat-strengthened glass under high
    bending stresses: The initial break occurs two to
    three times the distance away from the edge of the glass.
    The fracture pattern is fine-grained like tempered
    glass because of the effect of the high stresses.

11 Fracture pattern of tempered glass:
    small glass fragments or "dice"

9

to 12 millimetres, as greater thicknesses currently present problems of quality control. The maximum production sizes depend on the manufacturer's tempering furnaces. Generally sheets of approximately 2.50 m x 4 m can be tempered, currently some glass treatment firms can temper sheets in the ribbon width of float glass (3.21 metres) and up to 6 metres long and beyond. Tempered borosilicate glass is available up to 15 millimetres thick and up to 1.60 m x 3 m in plan. Tempered sheets are generally identified with an enamelled stamp.

Thermal treatment is undertaken after all mechanical work on the glass is complete and can be carried out on all basic glass types except wired glass. Thermal treatment increases the dimensional and flatness tolerances.

The mechanical and thermal properties of tempered glass are summarised in ⎯ Fig. 12. Young's modulus is unaffected by the heat treatment.

⎯ IMPROVEMENT OF STRUCTURAL PROPERTIES

The compressive stress in the surface of the sheet caused by the thermal treatment compresses any surface defects, thus ensuring that they do not have any strength-reducing effect. Only if this prestressing is cancelled out by external loads can the surface defects have a strength-reducing effect. Tempered glass and heat-strengthened glass differ in the amount of induced stress. The lower surface precompression of heat-strengthened glass means that its characteristic minimum strength is only half that of tempered glass but twice that of annealed glass.

Thermal shock resistance is also significantly improved by heat-treatment. For tempered safety glass made from float glass this is approximately 150 Kelvin, for heat-strengthened glass 100 K and for tempered borosilicate glass (e.g. Pyran S) 300 Kelvin – compared with 40 Kelvin for annealed float glass.

The heat treatment also influences fracture behaviour. The large amount of energy stored in the glass causes a tempered glass pane to

	Stock sizes	Surface compressive stress [kN/cm²]	Fracture strength [kN/cm²]	Thermal shock resistance [K]	Risk of spontaneous fracture (NiS inclusions)	Can be cut
Soda-lime glass:						
Float glass	2 mm–21 mm 3.21 m x 6.0 m	–	4.5	40	no	yes
Heat-strengthened float glass	4 mm–12 mm 2.5 m x 5.0 m to 3 m x 6.0 m	3.5–5.5	7	100	no	no
Tempered float glass	4 mm–19 mm	10–15	12	150	yes	no
Rolled glass	4 mm–19 mm 2.5 m x 5.0 m	–	2.5	30	no	yes
Tempered cast glass	4 mm–19 mm 2.5 m x 5.0 m	10–15	9	150	yes	no
Borosilicate glass:						
Float glass	up to 21 mm 2.3 m x 3.0 m	–	2.5	90	no	yes
Heat-strengthened float glass	4 mm–12 mm 1.6 m x 3.0 m	3.5–5.5	7	200	no	no
Tempered float glass	4 mm–15 mm 1.6 m x 3.0 m	10–15	12	300	no	no
Chemically strengthened glass	up to 19 mm ca. 1.0 m x 2.0 m	Depends on depth of penetration and surface damage	(15)	250	no	yes–within limits

12

12 Mechanical and thermal properties of heat treated and annealed flat glass

break into many small glass dice ——Fig. 11. As the fractured pieces are blunt, tempered glass is also called "safety glass", although the fractured pieces may remain together in larger shards and if they fall out could lead to injury. In contrast, heat-strengthened glass breaks from the fracture centre outwards in larger shards and islands in a similar pattern to non-tempered glass ——Fig. 8. European standards EN 12150 and EN 1863 set out the precise requirements for the fracture patterns of tempered and heat-strengthened glass.

Thermally prestressed glass has tolerances of several millimetres, which must be taken into account in the detailed design ——Figs 13, 17. [3.4/1, 3.4/2, 3.4/3]

A phenomenon particular to tempered safety glass is *spontaneous fracture*, which is related to the gradual increase in volume of nickel sulphide (NiS) inclusions in the glass microstructure. As the increase in volume of nickel sulphide depends on temperature, impure sheets are filtered out using a destructive *heat-soak test* in which the finished

toughened glass sheets are kept warm for a specified period at a constant temperature. Sheets that have passed this test standardised in EN 14179 are appropriately labelled. NiS inclusions usually have no effect on heat-strengthened glass or borosilicate glass. [3.4/4, 3.4/5]

——DEFECTS IN OPTICAL APPEARANCE

The heat treatment process has a number of different effects on the optical quality of glass, which may be detrimental to its visual appearance. These effects include *anisotropy*, *roller-waves*, as well as extensive or localised distortions of the glass surface. These defects are more pronounced with tempered than with heat-strengthened glass.

It has been known for a long time that transparent homogeneous materials exhibit bi-refringence as soon as they enter a state of stress produced by internal or external forces. Anisotropic light, that is light which is linearly polarised at least partially, is necessary for this optical anisotropy to be seen. Under such light, coloured light or dark stripes

Edge length [mm]	t for d ≤ 12 mm	t for d ≥ 12 mm
≤ 2 000	± 2.5	± 3.0
2 000–3 000	± 3.0	4.0
> 3 000	± 4.0	± 5.0

13

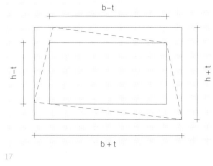

17

14

15

16

18

13, 17   Length tolerances for heat treated glass

14, 15   Looking through an insulating glass unit made from
tempered glass without (Fig. 14) and with a polarising
filter (Fig. 15), which shows the anisotropic effects.

16   Irregularities in tempered glass, Main Bus Station,
Hamburg, 2003, Arch.: Silcher, Werner and Redante

18   Example of use of chemically strengthened glass:
Structural glass dome at ILEK, Stuttgart University,
Eng.: Prof. W. Sobek and L. Blandini

or marks are noticeable on both sides of the glazing. Daylight is actually for the most part somewhat polarised but more so after being reflected off surfaces of glass or water ___ Figs 14, 15.

It is therefore not surprising that the anisotropy is more noticeable particularly in extreme lighting conditions, where there are multiple reflections, or near areas of water, with flat observation angles or with coated glass. However, anisotropy can be reduced by careful control of the cooling process. At the moment there is still no set of rules defining what is acceptable and what is classed as an optical defect in this context – great attention should be paid to this fact when selecting a glass processing company. [3.4/6]

The heat treatment of glass has a detrimental effect on its planarity. Physical distortions and roller waves can be seen as optical distortions when looking through the glass or in reflections. These defects occur when the heated glass "sags" between the transport rollers during transport in the tempering furnaces (normally with the narrow side to

the front). Industry standards alone are inadequate to limit these roller impressions for high quality architectural work; roller waves should be kept less than 0.15 millimetres for single pane and 0.07 millimetres for laminated glass in order to prevent noticeable lens effects.

Distortions occur through the differential cooling of the sheet surfaces, which causes the edges or the middle of the sheet to rise from the transport conveyor. Long sheets simply curve, square sheets form a dish shape.

___CHEMICALLY STRENGTHENED GLASS

Glass with a high sodium content can be prestressed chemically by immersion in a hot potassium chloride bath. Sodium ion exchange and the densification of the molecular structure create large compressive stresses in the surface. The small depth of penetration of this effect still leaves the glass highly susceptibility to surface defects. Chemically strengthened glass can be cut to a limited extent. The process is

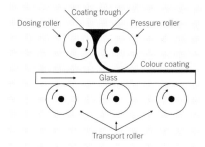

Coating trough

Dosing roller   Pressure roller

Colour coating

Glass

Transport roller

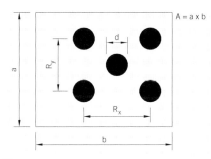

$A = a \times b$

20   Large-format screen printing machine
      at Glasid in Essen, Germany

21   Principle of roller-applied colour coating

22   Calculation of density of coverage:
      Coverage [%] = 50 πd^2 / $R_x R_y$

19   Translucent screen print. Finnish
      Pavilion, Expo Hanover, 2000

suitable for a wide range of thickness, including very thin and very thick glass, complex glass geometries and can maintain very high surface planarity ____ Fig. 18. A monolithic sheet of chemically strengthened glass is not safety glass. [3.4/7]

ENAMELLING AND PRINTING ON GLASS

Enamelled glass has virtually the properties of tempered or heat-strengthened glass. Ceramic pigments or frits are rolled, poured or *screen-printed* over one side before heat treatment, and are baked on to the glass during heat treatment so that they are permanently bonded to the glass surface. Enamelling and printing are carried out on final cut sizes after completion of all mechanical work. Only glass with a plane surface is suitable as the starting product for screen printing; patterned glass is unsuitable. However it can be enamelled in a "dry" process in which the ceramic colour is applied in powder form before being baked on. As the methods of colour application cause irregularities, all proposed uses should be discussed with the manufacturer beforehand. [3.4/8]

In the roller method a rubber printing roller transfers uniform colour on to one side of the glass, its homogeneity depends on the profile. Patterns can be applied with profiled rollers. In the pouring process the glass sheet passes horizontally through a "pouring curtain". On the other hand, any pattern or matrix can be applied in the screen printing process. Multicoloured patterns can be produced by further printing using different screens. Shades of colour (photographic originals) can be depicted using half-tone screen printing, in which the spacing and the diameter of the dots can be varied (screen). Four-colour half-tone screen prints can also be manufactured using ceramic colours by *Schollglas*. Standard formats go up to about 2 m x 4 m, some glass finishers offer fully automatic screen printing in sizes up to about 2.50 m x 6 m. In the further processing of insulating glass the enamel

23, 24   Bending and tempering line at a modern pivoting
         roller bending plant without forms ("zero-tooling")

will be protected from weather and UV radiation if facing the cavity. A combination of heat and solar protection coatings on the same surface is possible.

The mechanical properties of the glass surface are detrimentally affected by the ceramic frit. Enamelling reduces the bending strength of tempered glass or heat-strengthened glass by about 40 percent. As the enamel layer changes the adhesion (bond) properties, the printed glass surface of laminated safety glass is generally placed on the outside.

Glass with full or partial colour frits can be used to provide solar control, anti-glare or privacy glazing. Opaque, translucent or (semi-) transparent printing is available. Light transmittance depends on the pattern and the screen printed colour, glass type, thickness and above all on the density of *coverage* ___Fig. 22. [**3.4/9**]

THERMAL BENDING OF GLASS
___ PROCESS AND MANUFACTURE

Flat glass sheets can be bent in shape in the hot viscous state. Different bending processes can be used, depending on the quantity and the geometry. The time-intensive annealing process can be replaced by the forced cooling methods used for tempering and heat-strengthening.

The vertical bending process in which the glass is suspended and heated and then pressed in a mould is associated with large manufacturing tolerances and inferior optical quality and therefore nowadays is only used where extreme bending geometries are required. In the popular horizontal sag bending process, the sheet is heated in a furnace then either placed with its edges on a frame, where it bends under the action of its own weight or the sheet is allowed to sag on to a fire-resistant metal or ceramic form for better control of bending geometry. Full surface moulds require considerable tooling costs and

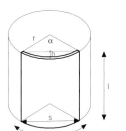

r: Radius
a: Girth
s: Chord length
α: Subtended angle
l: Length of straight edge
h: Rise

r₁: Radius 1
r₂: Radius 2
a₁: Girth 1
a₂: Girth 2
α: Subtended angle
β: Cone angle (max. 45 °)
l: Length of straight edge

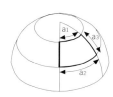

r: Radius of sphere
a₁: Girth 1
a₂: Girth 2
a₃: Girth 3

25

27

29

26

28

25 Geometry of cylindrical bending

26 Cylindrical laminated safety glass made from
    tempered low-iron glass with printed Concepta-
    special film, held in place with point fixings.
    La Tour de la Paix, St. Petersburg, 2003
    Arch.: Jean-M. Wilmotte, C. Halteri

27 Geometry of conical bending

28 Spherically curved glass on the
    passenger capsules of the London Eye,
    U.K., Arch.: D. Marks, J. Barfield

29 Geometry of spherical bending

are normally only suitable for mass production, for example in the automobile industry.

The minimum and maximum radii in sag bending depend on the weight of the sheet and thus its size and thickness. Several sheets placed one upon the other can be bent in a single process all at once, as long as they have not yet been prestressed, and can then be made into laminated safety glass.

Cylindrical bent and tempered glass is produced on roller bending plants with pivoting rollers to keep setting-up times short and allow efficient manufacturing. The glass is taken laying horizontally into the furnace and deformed there by pivoting and turning the transport rollers without a mould (zero-tooling) in sizes up to 4.20 m x 2.44 m ____ Figs 23, 24. [3.4/10]

Monolithic curved glass can be differentiated into cylindrical glass with a constant radius of curvature and conical glass with a linearly changing radius of curvature. Double curved glass may be spherical,

aspherical (e.g. parabolic) or saddle-shaped. With spherical bending the curvatures are all in the same direction and, unlike aspherical bending, of equal size; with saddle-shapes the curvatures are in opposite directions. It is recommended that in the design process the product profile, quantities and glass types are made clear to the manufacturer with the aid of an accurate specification of the shape (if necessary with 1:1 scale template). The bending geometry can be specified by reference to the girth, edge dimensions, internal and external radius, rise and subtended angle.

With standard cylindrical bending, the subtended angle may be up to 90°, for small sheet thicknesses even up to 180° (semicircle) and the cone angle up to 45°. Cylindrically bent float glass can be made in stock sizes with a rise of up to 1.50 metres. Curves with straight extensions on one or both sides ____ Fig. 37 and multiple curvatures in an S-shape or U-shape can also be manufactured. Tempered glass can be made in sizes up to about 2.50 m x 4.50 m and with a maximum sheet

Single pane, tempered glass

Laminated safety glass

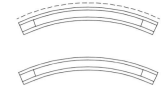

Multipane insulating glass

30, 32, 35 Further processing of bent glass into laminated and insulating glass: Bent glass can also be provided with low-E and solar control hard coatings.

31 Curved, tempered monolithic glass balustrade of the New Museum, Nuremberg, 2000, Arch.: V. Staab

33, 34 Single curved laminated safety glass: The glazed sides consist of 2 m wide laminated safety glass made from 2 x 6 mm float glass. Neglecting the membrane shell effect in the structural analysis the glass would have been required to be 2 x 12 mm thick. Skywalk Hanover, 1998, Arch.: Schulitz Architekten

36 Double curved insulating glass with solar control coating, Ford Research Centre Aachen, 1994, Arch.: J.L. Martinez

thickness of 15 millimetres. The maximum manufactured size of tempered borosilicate glass (*Pyran G*) is 1.50 m x 2.50 m. [**3.4/11**]

The subtended angle may be up to 30° for spherical glass. The radius of curvature is normally larger than 2 metres, smaller radii can lead to buckling and to folds at the edges. The control of bending geometry is a major challenge with freely formed sheets – generally numerous prototypes are required on a trial and error basis.

____IMPLICATIONS FOR DESIGN AND CONSTRUCTION
In the further processing of bent glass to laminated and insulating glass, adequate allowance must be made for the considerable dimensional deviations, which normally arise during deforming glass depending on the size, shape and thickness of the element. As there are yet no standards covering this, tolerances on edge length, girth, radius of curvature, straightness and distortion must be agreed with the manufacturer at an early stage ____Fig. 40.

After forming, the glass can be tempered or heat-strengthened. Uniform exposure to the cooling air is difficult to ensure with complex geometries. Bent glass can be further processed into laminated safety glass. If tolerances are high it must be bonded using a liquid resin. Drilling curved glass has high cost implications.

Single and especially double curvature stiffens the glass with the effect that it can act as a load-bearing shell element if the edges are fixed in position. Decreasing the radius of curvature also decreases bending moments and deflections, so that the required strength and stability can be achieved with thinner glass than would be the case with flat glass. [**3.4/12**]

____OPTICAL APPEARANCE
The surface planarity and optical quality of curved glass is extremely dependent on the individual processing steps. Reference samples of all the different geometries are essential in order to be able to judge

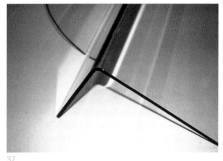

37

Thickness [mm]	min. R [mm]	max. R, Single pane glass [mm]
3	50	1 000
4	80	1 750
5	120	2 200
6	160	2 800
8	230	3 400

39

Description	Tolerances [mm]
Edge length l	
<2 000 mm	± 2
>2 000 mm	± 3
Radius r	
	± 3
Straightness	2/m float 3/m tempered/ heat-str glass
Distortion	3/m float 4/m tempered/ heat-str. glass

40

38

37 Example of bent glass with straight extensions

38 Bent laminated safety glass for showcase
    windows and sign band, shop window glazing
    Asprey Store, NYC, Arch.: Foster and Partners,
    Contractor: Glasbau Seele, Gersthofen

39 Minimum and maximum bending radii from manu-
    facturer's information provided by Glas Trösch AG.
    The values vary from manufacturer to manufacturer,
    as there is still no current uniformly applicable
    official standard.

40 Summary of average tolerances in mm for bent glass

the visual quality. Horizontal bending achieves better results than vertical; a full surface mould is preferable a perimeter frame for a distortion-free visual quality. Tempered and heat-strengthened glass can exhibit obvious surface distortions compared with stress-free annealed glass. This different quality is particularly obvious after further processing into laminated glass. As a result of the cooling process, the individual sheets cannot be bent one on top of the other. When the sheets are laminated, misaligned roller impressions produce a *lens effect*, which leads to distracting light reflexes.

Curved glass can be further processed into insulating glass units. When this is done it is important to bear in mind that only pyrolytic coated glass (hard coatings) can be curved and that the performance of this type of glass will not match that of glass with soft coatings with respect to thermal insulation, solar control or colour. These potential mismatches have to be considered at design stage ___ Fig. 38.

"TEXTURING" GLASS

Fusing means melting an additional layer of glass – normally coloured – on to the float glass. By re-heating the glass in a furnace, the float glass sheet takes on the shape and surface texture of the fire-resistant substrate, as occurs with traditional cast glass where the liquid glass melt is cast in a sand bed. In contrast to rolled glass, the surface relief is considerably more like *slumped* or *kiln-formed* glass. The sheets are heated up to 750 °C. Once the tempering or laminating processes have been completed, the surface relief can reach as much as 8 mm; finished sizes of up to about 1.50 m x 3 m are currently possible. An interesting idea from the point of view of the structural engineering design is that corrugation or folded features in the glass running parallel to the span direction would increase the structural depth and hence the bending stiffness. The expensive, mainly manual manufacturing process means that the product is most suitable for artistic, exotic, small production volume applications, internal or external. However,

41

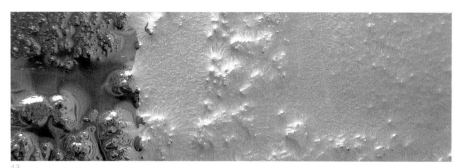

43

42

44

43 Texture of float glass re-formed on a sand
    bed in a furnace, Fusionglass Ltd., London

41 *Structuran* panel made from recycled clear
    glass, The Greenhouse Effect Ltd, UK

42 Example for use of *Structuran*, Eye Centre, Michelfeld,
    2003, Arch.: Heinle, Wischer und Partner

44 Textured float glass panels, the surface texture
    is produced in a furnace by heating and
    fusing the glass on a textured, fire-resistant
    substrate (Fusion Glass Design Ltd., London).
    Reception Tea Wharf Building, London

today's growing interest among architects has led to an increase in manufacturing capacity so that extensive use in building skins seems quite likely in the future.

A material with completely new properties is created when pieces of broken glass are melted together until they are partially crystallised (*sintered*). These types of glass ceramic with the product name *Structuran* are manufactured for different applications including cladding panels under a patent granted to *Schott AG*. The panels are normally 20 millimetres thick and can be manufactured in sizes up to about 2.75 m x 1.25 m. The material loses its transparency due to its partially crystalline microstructure. The raw material is broken and crushed automobile glass, which can be coloured by the addition of pigments.

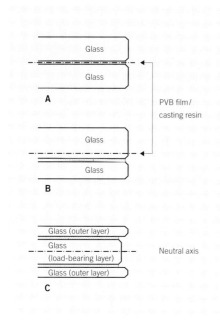

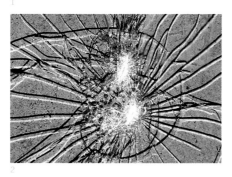

1   Build-ups of laminated glass and laminated safety glass:
    A   Symmetric build-up
    B   Asymmetric build-up
    C   Symmetric multipane laminated glass: The
        middle, load-bearing glass pane is recessed
        at the edges to protect it from damage; the
        outer layers act as sacrificial panes.

2   Laminated safety glass made from heat-strengthened
    glass: The shards remain bonded to the PVB film.

3   Laminated safety glass about to enter the autoclave

3.5

LAYERING AND BONDING OF PANES: LAMINATED GLASS AND LAMINATED SAFETY GLASS

Laminated glass consists of at least two glass or plastic glazing sheets bonded by interlayers. The materials used for the interlayers are *polyvinylbutyral* (PVB), *cast-in-place resin* (CIP), *ethylene vinylacetate* (EVA) and *SentryGlas Plus* (SGP) from Dupont. Full-surface bonding provides many opportunities to modify the mechanical and optical properties of glazing through the selection of the component layers, their sequence and thicknesses. *Laminated safety glass* remains as one piece when shattered and has an increased residual load-bearing capacity. [**3.5/1**]

MANUFACTURE AND FINISHING

PVB-laminated glass is made in two stages. First the individual sheets are washed, the film is layered in between them and the assembly is heated and pressed *(prelamination)* before the full-surface bond is created in an autoclave using high pressure and temperatures of about 140 °C. Prelamination can be done using the *roller process* or, in the case of bent sheets and multiple bonded layers, by the *vacuum bagging process*. The thickness of the interlayer is a multiple of the film thicknesses of 0.38 and 0.76 millimetres. Thicker films are used with heat treated glass to accommodate undulations. Specialist glass processing companies are able to laminate single and multilayer laminated sheets up to a jumbo panel size of 3.21 m x 6 m with a maximum total weight of 1 tonne, and in exceptional cases even up to 7 metres long with a total weight of 2 tonnes. For special glass applications, companies such as *Glasbau Seele* can produce laminated glass up to 12 metres long using the vacuum bagging process. The finished

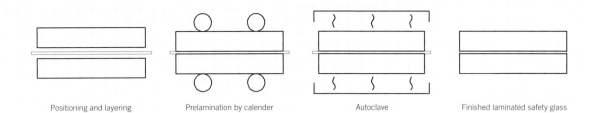

| Positioning and layering | Prelamination by calender | Autoclave | Finished laminated safety glass |

4

	Laminated safety glass	Glass-glass laminate	Glass-plastic laminate	Sound insulation	Embedded PV
PVB film	yes	yes	no	yes	Thin film cells
Cast-in-place resin	limited	yes	no	yes	Crystalline cells
EVA film	limited	yes	no	no	yes
PU film	limited	no	yes	no	limited

5

6

4   Schema of the two-stage production
    of laminated safety glass

5   Possible applications of laminated materials

6   Positioning the PVB film   7   Automatic placement of the top next glass layer   8   Prelamination

sizes of glass components made from heat treated glass are normally limited by the dimensions of the heat treatment furnaces. [3.5/2, 3.5/3]

The considerably stiffer SGP interlayer is processed into laminated safety glass in an autoclave in a similar way to PVB. In contrast to PVB, the material is not applied by roller but comes in sheets in standard thicknesses of 1.52 and 2.28 millimetres. At the moment the manufacturing width is limited to 2.50 metres, the standard sheet length is 3 metres.

In the manufacture of casting resin laminated glass, a process which is not fully automated, the resin is introduced into the 1 to 2 millimetres wide gap between the sheets, the edges of which are sealed with transparent double-sided adhesive tape. This method also allows sheets with large thickness deviations to be laminated. The finished sizes are only limited by the size of the tilting table and can be up to 3 m x 8 m. [3.5/4]

Laminated glass made from glass and polycarbonate (PC) is manufactured under various product names (Scholl-Leichtglas, Sila-Carb, Rodurlight, etc.). They usually consist of a PC sheet as the core with thin heat treated glass sheets on the outside faces ___Figs 15, 17. Polyurethane (PU) is able to accept the large thermal expansion of PC, achieves good adhesion and is resistant to chemicals, but is relatively expensive. Like PVB, PU can be applied as a film or in liquid form. Liquid polyurethane is pressed between the sheets, which are sealed at their edges, and there are hardly any limits on the shape of the laminated element. [3.5/5]

Schollglas manufactures a laminated glass called Gewe-composite, in which a special casting resin with high bond strength is used; like SGP, this allows the sheet thickness to be reduced.

9

10

11

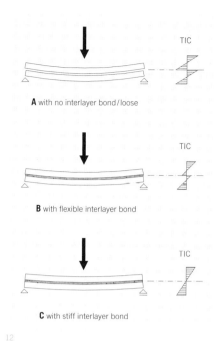

A with no interlayer bond/loose

B with flexible interlayer bond

C with stiff interlayer bond

12

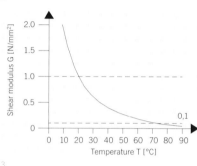

13

12 Stress distribution diagram on a cross
    section of laminated glass:
    A: with no interlayer bond
    B: with partial interlayer bond
    C: with full (stiff) interlayer bond and composite action

13 Approximation curve showing the relationship between
    shear modulus G and temperature T (laminated safety
    glass)

9   Roof glazing with SGP and Pilkington Planar, Yorkdale
    Shopping Center, Toronto, Canada

10 Residual load-bearing capacity of laminated safety
    glass made from tempered glass: Shortly after breakage
    the laminated safety glass is still relatively stiff; as the
    load duration increases it sags like a "wet blanket".

11 Delamination of laminated safety glass as a result of
    a manufacturing defect

IMPLICATIONS FOR DESIGN AND CONSTRUCTION

By laminating glass into composite elements, the load-bearing behaviour, post fracture integrity and robustness can be substantially improved. Glass fragment retention, full and residual load-bearing capacities depend on the strength of the individual sheets and above all on the composite action effect of the interlayers.

The detailed design should take into account the larger manufacturing tolerances associated with laminated glass. The lamination process with PVB or SGP can result in a misalignment of up to 2 millimetres at the edges of the glass or the walls of the drilled holes; as the glass is heat treated, grinding the edges to compensate for the misalignment is not an option. The actual external dimensions could deviate by as much as 4 millimetres from the original ____Fig. 18. By manual adjustment of the sheets in the casting resin lamination process, smaller edge misalignments than those experienced with the PVB process can be achieved. Casting resins are mainly used for the man-

ufacture of laminates made from sheets with large planarity deviations or from curved or textured sheets.

____LOAD-BEARING CAPACITY

The position of the interlayer within the stressed cross section is relevant to its load-bearing capacity. With outer layers of equal thickness in a symmetrical laminated section, the interlayer lies at the neutral axis and in an intact system is subject to shear stresses only. The stiffer the film, the greater is the composite action effect and the smaller are the resulting deflections. As PVB is a viscoelastic thermoplastic, the shear modulus is particularly dependent on the ambient temperature and the load duration. These interdependencies make it advisable to carry out computer analyses of different load cases as suggested in draft standard EN 13474. The full composite section shear stiffness can be assumed to be effective for short-term loads such as wind or impact. On the other hand for permanent loads such as dead load

14

15

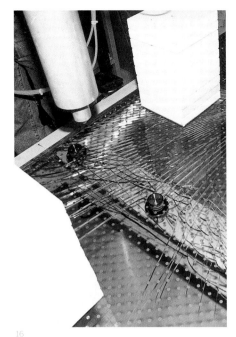

16

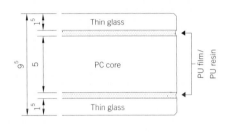

17

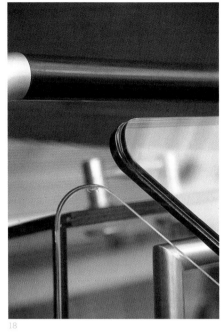

18

	Glass-glass laminate	Glass-polycarbonate laminate
Thickness [mm]	40	24
Weight [kg/m²]	90	38
U-value [W/m²K]	4.47	3.95

19

14, 16 Component test of a multi-leaf laminated safety glass
unit for glazing subject to foot traffic:
For short-term loading, such as a hard impact (here
simulated by a steel torpedo), the composite stiffness
is high, but it is low for medium-term and long-
term loads, as is also the case for the residual load-
bearing capacity of broken panes under self-weight
and foot traffic loads (here simulated by a block).

15 Multilayer construction of SILA-CARB security glazing

17 Build-up of a glass-polycarbonate laminate to the anti-
intruder classification P6B in accordance with EN 356

18 Production methods may result in edge misalignments
in laminated safety glass of up to 4 mm.

19 Comparison of a glass-glass laminate and a
glass-polycarbonate laminate of the same
resistance class (anti-intruder classification
P8B in accordance with EN 356)

only the stiffness of the individual sheets may be considered. At temperatures below 23 °C medium-term loads can be assumed to act on
a section with partial composite stiffness. Above 80 °C the PVB film
starts to separate from the glass *(delamination)*. [3.5/6, 3.5/7]

EVA and CIP have similar rheologic material properties to PVB.
Their stiffness at room temperature is only about half that of PVB, although at temperatures of 60 °C the reduced stiffness is substantially
higher. No composite effect can be assumed in the case of sections
with interlayers of soft casting resin that have been optimised for
sound insulation.

A structural interlayer of SGP, originally developed for glazing in
hurricane-prone areas, has a stiffness up to 100 times higher than
that of PVB, casting resin or EVA. High permanent temperatures (up
to 70 °C) hardly change the mechanical properties. Full composite
action can be assumed even for permanent loads and thus the sheet
thicknesses and weights can be substantially reduced. Instances of
use of SGP as structural glasswork now include the stairs for Apple
stores, where fittings are laminating into glass surfaces to avoid un-
sightly mechanical connections. As the thermal expansion of SGP is a
number of times that of glass, it is particularly necessary to consider
long-term temperature stresses.

—POST-FRACTURE INTEGRITY, RESIDUAL LOAD-BEARING CAPACITY
The ability of glass to hold its broken fragments together and retain
some residual strength once broken is most important in terms of health
and safety building regulations, and is the main factor in assessing its
classification as laminated safety glass. Over 95 percent of all laminated
safety glass incorporates PVB film. Standard EN ISO 12543 sets out the
minimum requirements of laminated safety glass. The values are oriented towards the properties of PVB, however SGP interlayers exceed
these requirements. CIP resin, EVA and PU film can also be optimised
for their post-fracture integrity.

20

Nominal total thickness [mm]	Pane 1	Thickness [mm] Glazing cavity	Pane 2	Total weight [kg/m²]	Sound reduction index [dB]
With standard PVB film					
9	44.2	–	–	20	34
12	64.4	–	–	25	35
13	66.2	–	–	30	36
15	66.6	–	–	30	37
With special PVB film (*Trosifol Sound Control*)					
9	44.2	–	–	20	37
29	44.2	16	4	30	39
31	44.2	16	6	35	41
33	44.2	16	8	40	43
39	66.3	16	10	55	46
38	44.2	16	66.3	50	48

23

21

22

Thickness [mm]	Colour	Light transmittance [%]
0.38	Colourless	88
0.76	Colourless	88
1.14	Colourless	88
1.52	Colourless	88
0.38	Clear	71
0.38	Clear-translucent	65
0.38	Light turquoise	73
0.38	Ocean blue	71
0.38	Medium bronze	52
0.38	Grey	44
0.38	Light brown	55
0.38	Mid-brown	26
0.38	Dark brown	9

24

20   Example of use of laminated safety glass with Trosifol Sound Control, Airport Cologne-Bonn

21   Samples of laminated safety glass with coloured PVB films (Stadip Color by SGG)

22   Sample of laminated safety glass with a printed film interlayer (Sentry-Glass Expressions by Dupont)

23   Sound reduction index R_w for a selection of laminated safety glass configurations: A build-up designated 44.2 means a laminated safety glass unit comprising two 4 mm panes and two interlayers of PVB film, each 0.38 mm thick

24   Light transmittance of various coloured PVB films (Trosifol MB)

The residual strength of laminated safety glass depends on the type and thickness of film and the fracture pattern of the individual leaves. Tensile stresses build up in the film following the breakage of one or more sheets and therefore it is the tearing resistance and extension at break of the interlayer which determine the remaining period of serviceability. The residual load-bearing capacity of PVB laminates can be improved by using greater film thicknesses. The use of SGP can significantly reduce deformation after breakage. Research at the Institute for Lightweight Structures and Conceptual Design (ILEK) at Stuttgart University has shown that residual load-bearing capacity can be significantly improved by the incorporation of fibre or fabric in the laminates.

Once all the leaves have broken, the residual load-bearing capacity is mainly determined by the fracture pattern. Annealed or heat-strengthened glass breaks into shards that remain interlocked with one another, so that a certain amount of integrity is retained – in contrast to laminated safety glass made from tempered safety glass, which deforms like a "wet blanket" ____ Fig. 10.

IMPLICATIONS FOR THE BUILDING SKIN

____ OPTICAL PROPERTIES

The interlayers are almost indistinguishable from glass in terms of their refractive index, with the effect that they are not apparent when looking through the glass. PVB and CIP resin layers absorb almost all of the UV light. With thicker PVB and casting resin layers (from about 1.5 mm) laminated clear glass shows a slight yellow hue, whilst SGP remains completely colourless, similar to polycarbonate. In certain lighting conditions refraction can occur on the casting resin sheets at the edges of the adhesive tape. The edge stability of PVB laminates is less than those incorporating SGP but normally good enough so that, even with edges exposed to the weather, there is no delamination or colour change.

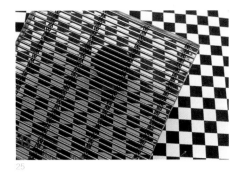

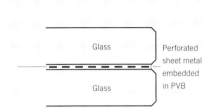

25 Sample of laminated glass with a decorative interlayer

26 Build-up of glass-perforated sheet metal laminated glass

27 Simulation of a self-supporting suspended facade constructed with laminated glass incorporating perforated sheet metal (preliminary design: Chr. Lueben, M. Mertens)

28 Spherically curved laminated safety glass with special safety requirements, passenger capsule, London Eye, 1999 (contractor: Hollandia)

29 Laminated safety glass with translucent PVB films, SGG Stadip with Trosifol MB PVB film, Visitor Galleries Turbine Hall Tate Modern, London, 2000, Arch.: Herzog & de Meuron

The appearance of laminated safety glass can be modified by the use of coloured PVB film. The film manufacturer can supply a range of transparent and translucent basic colours, which can also be combined with one another. The film widths depend upon the colour and pattern; basic colours are manufactured in the width of the float glass ribbon of 3.21 metres. Further design possibilities are gained by incorporating PE or PET laser printing film (patterned film). Digital four-colour printing can also be applied directly to the PVB film. [3.5/8, 3.5/9]

Casting resin can be given any colour from the full spectrum or impregnated with any material, although most will have a detrimental effect on the mechanical properties. Precise pattern specification and reproducibility of the decorative effects are not always possible.

___SECURITY

Laminated safety glass can provide active security when used as an enclosing element. There are various categories: EN 356 covers anti-

vandal and anti-intruder, EN 1063 bullet-resistant and DN EN 13541 explosion-resistant glass, all of which can be further divided into different resistance classes.

The extremely high impact toughness and strength of PC in laminates improve their anti-intruder performance. The covering layers of glass ensure good scratch resistance. For the same resistance class, a glass-PC composite is thinner and lighter than a glass-glass laminate.

___ACOUSTIC PROPERTIES

The build-up of laminated glass around a soft interlayer is similar to a sound-damping mass-spring-mass system. Special PVB films with a soft core have been developed to provide optimum sound insulation. They are available up to the manufacturer's stock size standard width of 3.21 metres. Casting resin is often used in sound insulating glass, although the necessary elasticity of the interlayer means that these units usually do not satisfy the requirements for post-breakage integ-

30 Laminated natural stone-glass panels create unusual optical effects (laminated glass comprising 12 mm tempered glass, 1.5 mm casting resin and 10 mm marble). Christ Pavilion at Expo 2000, Arch.: gmp, glass: Wendker & Selders

31 View of laminated glass with integrated HOE film: The incident light is dispersed into its spectral colours.

rity. The higher stiffness of SGP results in poorer sound insulating properties ___ Fig. 23.

___ SPECIAL LAMINATED GLASS

Sheets can be bonded to other flat materials using casting resin or PVB to achieve a decorative effect. Thinly sawn translucent slices of natural stone can be laminated into supporting glass sheets to show off the texture of the stone *(e.g. Fiberglass, GreinTec)*. The natural stone layers are between 15 millimetres (marble or onyx) and 1 millimetres (granite) ___ Fig. 30.

Other decorative or functional layers can be integrated into PVB or casting resin laminates. Seasonal solar control can be provided by inlaid wire, mesh, fabric or perforated sheet metal. In order to be suitable for integration into PVB laminates, the materials must have enough perforations or allow sufficient penetration to permit the formation of an adhesive bond ___ Fig. 25.

Another possible application is to embed films with *holographic optical elements* (HOE), which can be used to deflect direct or diffuse natural light to act as a transparent screen for back projection or provide a coloured light effect ___ Fig. 31. [**3.5/10**]

Thermotropic, electrochromic and *electro-optic* laminated glass with variable radiation transmittance have been under development for some time now. Laminated glass with *liquid crystal* (LC) layers embedded between PU film is currently the only product on the market. The crystals become aligned by the application of an electric field and the glass switches from translucent to transparent. Its light transmittance remains almost unchanged (approximately 75%). This electro-optic glass is classified as laminated safety glass and is available in sizes up to about 1 m x 2.8 m. [**3.5/11, 3.5/12**]

Laminated glass consisting of heat treated leaves with fire-retardant filler material introduced into the gap between them can be used as room-defining elements and restrict the spread of heat. The mate-

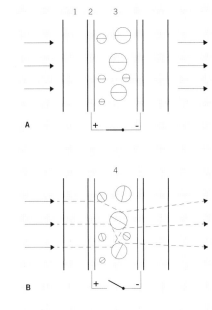

32   Solar modules integrated into the glass skin of the
College of Further Education, Herne, 1998
Arch.: Jourda & Perraudin Architectes with HHS Planer

33   Curved laminated safety glass panes with coloured
cast-in-place resin installed as overhead glazing:
The uncoloured sealing strips and the streaks
in the surface impair the appearance.

34   Electro-optic glass – how it works: A translucent glazing
unit (B) becomes transparent (A) when an electric
field is applied.
1   Glass
2   Transparent electrode layer
3   Polymer layer with aligned liquid crystals
4   Polymer layer with randomly oriented liquid crystals

rial may be waterglass or a salt-containing hydrogel. In the event of fire, the side of the glass subject to the fire load breaks and the fire retardant filler foams to completely block the path of the radiated heat. The maximum size of sheet is approximately 1.35 m x 2.70 m.

The integration of photovoltaic (PV) cells is a very significant development for building skins. In contrast to separate "add-on" systems in which the solar cells are embedded in EVA and Tedlar film attached to the rear side of a glass sheet, the cells in PV systems are integrated into the roof and facades of a building and are protected in the centrally positioned unstressed interlayer of symmetrical build-ups of laminated glass. The covering sheets are normally low-iron glass. Front and rear sheets are heat-strengthened glass to resist the high temperatures created as solar energy is absorbed. The maximum finished size is approx 3.2 m x 2 m.

On the basis of efficiency and appearance they are classed as mono-, polycrystalline or amorphous cells. Crystalline cells are thicker and are therefore preferably embedded in casting resin (layer thickness about 2 mm), whilst the 100 times thinner amorphous cells (thin film modules) can be embedded in a PVB laminate. The best efficiency is achieved by blue, dark-blue to black monocrystalline solar cells (efficiency about 16%). However, polycrystalline cells are normally used because of their durability and the lower amount of energy consumed in their manufacture. The cells, which are square and manufactured with edge lengths of 10, 12.5 and 15 centimetres, can be positioned anywhere in a module. [3.5/13]

Sheets with embedded PV cells are normally not classed as laminated safety glass as their intact and residual load-bearing capacities are too low.

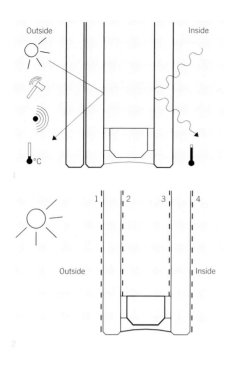

	Processes	Product
Hard coating		
Resistant to heat and mechanical damage, suitable for further processing, can be used as monolithic glazing, and in Pos. 1–4 in insulating glazing	Online spray (pyrolysis)	Low-emission glass
		Solar control glass
		Mirrors
		Self-cleaning glass
	Dip coating for baking temperatures > approx. 600 °C	Non-reflective glass
Soft coating		
Not resistant to mechanical damage, often not heat-resistant, limited suitability for further processing, and used only in Pos. 2, 3 in insulating glazing	Magnetron sputtering	Low-emission glass
		Solar control glass
	Dip coating for baking temperatures < approx. 600 °C	Dichroitic glass
Online		
Limitations on coating materials and number of coatings, limited performance	Online spray (pyrolysis)	Low-emission glass
		Solar control glass
Offline		
Flexibility on coating materials and number of coatings, high performance	Magnetron sputtering	Low-emission glass
		Solar control glass
		Non-reflective glass
	Dip coating	

1   The various protective functions of insulating glass
    units: Thermal insulation, solar protection, sound
    insulation and resistance against intrusion

2   Identification of the positions of coated
    glass surfaces in a double glazing unit

3   Summary of coating types

_____ **3.6**

COATING THE PANES AND SEALING THE EDGES: INSULATING GLASS

The final stage in the further processing of float glass is the combination of single or laminated panes into a multipane insulating glazing unit. Insulating glass is of prime importance in heat insulation but is increasingly used in a multifunctional role by integrating solar control, anti-glare and noise insulation functions ____Fig. 1. The properties of insulating glass are determined by the coatings on the individual leaves, the method of sealing the edges and the overall construction.

SURFACE COATINGS

The hard, durable and smooth float glass surface is an ideal substrate for the uniform application of material during or after the manufacture of the glass. The mechanical properties remain generally unaffected by the coating process. [**3.6/1**]

Thin film coatings for solar control and insulating glass are applied by spraying, sputtering or dipping. *Thick film coatings* include printed or rolled colour coatings and cast laminate layers (see Section 3.5).

Coatings are called *hard* or *soft* on the basis of their resistance to mechanical, thermal and chemical influences. Hard coatings are mostly baked on to the hot glass surface *(pyrolysis)* as an online coating sprayed on immediately after the forming of the glass. The industry is currently developing pyrolytic hard coatings with improved properties and heat-resistant soft coatings. The more delicate offline coatings are applied to the cooled glass. Multiple coatings and flexible layer construction produce higher-performance coating systems Fig. 3. [**3.6/2**]

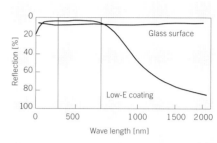

	Visible light [%]			Total radiation [%]		
Reflection colour	τ_v	ρ_v	α_v	τ_e	ρ_e	α_e
Pyrolytic (online)						
blue-grey	54	19	27	38	16	46
bronze colours	18	17	65	29	14	57
green	26	32	42	19	17	64
Magnetron sputtering (offline)						
intense silver	08	42	50	06	37	57
silvery	32	13	55	26	14	60
grey	40	10	50	37	09	54
intense blue	08	30	62	08	25	67
blue	50	07	43	45	08	47
strong green	07	30	63	04	17	79
green	26	11	63	15	08	77

4   Magnetron sputtering

5   Optical properties of various solar control coatings

6   Lighter test for coating detection: The flame is
reflected at each glass surface, a colour distortion
of reflected image marks the position of a coating
(here the low-E coating at position 3).

7   Reflection curve for a low-E coating: The reflectivity in
the visible light range is low but very high in the IR range.

____PYROLYTIC VAPOUR DEPOSITION COATINGS

Pyrolytic hard coatings, which are also suitable for thermal processes such as bending, tempering and enamelling, are used as coatings for solar control, thermally insulating and self-cleaning glass.

A coat of metal oxide is applied on clear or coloured glass, which reduces the amount of light and energy transmitted through the glass either selectively or across the whole solar spectrum. In reflected light the panes may appear to have a colour-tinted metallic sheen. To improve the heat insulating effect, a layer of tin oxide can be applied, which reduces the *emissivity* (heat radiation) of the glass from about 90 to about 15 percent *(low-E coating)* ____Fig. 7.

The effect of self-cleaning glass *(e.g. SGG Bioclean, Pilkington Activ)* is based on a hydrophilic coating on the outside of the glass, which reduces surface tension and allows rainwater to flow off evenly. The formation of droplets and dirt residue is prevented. Furthermore a photocatalytic effect accelerates the breakdown of organic residues

on the glass. Silicone sealant must not be allowed to contaminate the surface, as silicone impairs the efficiency of the coating ____Fig. 10.

____MAGNETRON SPUTTERING

To the construction industry, high-performance soft coatings applied by magnetron sputtering for solar control and heat insulation are the most important coatings ____Fig. 4. The coating is either applied on to jumbo sized sheets or on to customer-specific final cut sheets: in this case any tempering, drilling or cutting out is executed before the coating is applied, then the glass may be laminated. In modern plants, up to fifteen different coatings can be applied one after the other. The maximum clearance height of these plants is limited to 16 millimetres. Single sheet glass with standard coatings can normally be produced in thicknesses up to 10 millimetres.

Coating systems with layers of silver have lower external reflection (approx. 12%) and a neutral reflection colour and therefore a high

8, 9   New coating technology for abrasion- and
        weathering-resistant chromium mirror coatings,
        which are applied not over the full surface but only
        on parts of it (SGG *STADIP* made from *Planilux
        Diamant* and the PVB film *Trosifol* MB), Lentos
        Museum of Art Linz, Arch.: Weber and Hofer

10   Effects of SGG *Bioclean*:
        Wet float glass surface, with (right) and
        without hydrophilic coating (left)

11   Colour effect of dichroic coated glass samples

selectivity. The noble-metal coating has a high transmittance in the visible light range and a high reflectance in the UV and infrared range. With the help of a double silver coating system, it is possible to achieve a light transmittance of up to 70 percent with a total solar energy transmittance of only 35 percent and a selectivity close to the physical limit of 2. The heat emissivity of the glass can be reduced to as low as 2 percent, so that it provides effective thermal insulation as well as solar control. Early generations of these *high-performance coatings* showed unnatural reflected colours.

___DIP COATINGS

Special offline coatings are applied to both sides of the glass in the *sol-gel dip coating process*. These coatings are classed as soft or hard depending on the temperature of subsequent heat treatment (between 400 °C and 650 °C). Interference effects on the applied metal coatings reduce reflection – normally 8 percent with float glass – to around

1 percent (e.g. *SCHOTT Amiran*). Anti-reflective glass is usually available up to 12 millimetres thick, with a maximum sheet size of 1.80 m x 3.80 m. [**3.6/3**]

Multiple coatings, up to forty, as required in the manufacture of *dichroitic* glass, can be applied by using different immersion baths ___Fig. 11. The layers are made of different oxides with high and low refractive indices arranged in such a way that a system of interference layers is created and light is dispersed by a colour effect filter into the spectral colours. Certain wavelengths of visible light are transmitted, complementary wavelengths are reflected. The colour effect depends on the coating thickness, the angle of incidence and intensity of the light and the position of the observer. They cost around 150 times as much as normal flat glass. [**3.6/4, 3.6/5**]

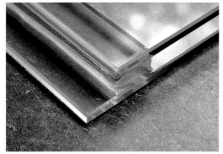

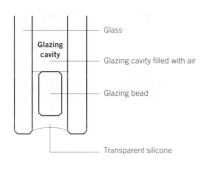

Glass

Glazing cavity

Glazing cavity filled with air

Glazing bead

Transparent silicone

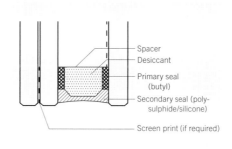

Spacer

Desiccant

Primary seal (butyl)

Secondary seal (poly-sulphide/silicone)

Screen print (if required)

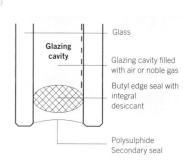

Glass

Glazing cavity

Glazing cavity filled with air or noble gas

Butyl edge seal with integral desiccant

Polysulphide Secondary seal

12   Forerunner of modern insulating glass: Insulating glass unit with a soldered all glass edge seal

13, 14   Sample provided by *Glasbau Hahn* and build-up of a full-glass edge seal

15   Standard two-pane insulating glazing unit with an aluminium spacer

16   Sample of a stainless steel edge spacer (edge seal from *Interpane*)

17   Build-up of a standard edge seal

18   Sample of insulating glazing unit, *Thermur* HM with climate film from *Fischer Glas*

19, 20   Sample provided by *Scholl Glas* and build-up of a TPS edge seal

3.6

THE BUILD-UP OF INSULATING GLASS

An insulating glass unit complying with the European standard EN 1279 consists of at least two panes, which are joined linearly along their edges so as to seal the air- or gas-filled gap between them, the *glazing cavity*. A standard insulating glass unit consists of two panes and a high-efficiency insulating glass unit consists of three. The specific properties of the insulating glass depend on the type of glass used, the type and position of any coating(s), the size of the cavity, the gas filling and the type of edge seal.

In principle, all types of glass can be processed into insulating glass, including curved glass, fire-resistant glass, rolled or "cast" glass and, within certain limits, wired glass. Of course, if a facade is to have a uniform appearance, the same construction should be used throughout. The quality and thickness of the glass is dependent on the structural requirements. Laminated glass and laminated safety glass are used for sound insulation and intruder protection.

Coatings improve the building physical properties of insulating glass. To describe the position of a pane surface in an insulating glass unit, the surfaces are numbered from the outside (Pos. 1) to the inside (e.g. Pos. 4). Soft coatings are only applied in positions 2 and 3, which are sheltered within the glazing cavity. Solar control coatings are intended for use on the outside, whilst low-E coatings go on the room-side ___ Figs 2, 6.

The glazing cavity in standard insulating glass is normally 12 to 16 millimetres and is filled with the rare gas argon or less often krypton, rather than dry air, to reduce thermal conductivity ___ Fig. 22. The cavity can be increased up to 40 millimetres to integrate shading or light-deflecting devices. When used in combination with solar control or solar control coatings in the glazing cavity, the devices must not come into contact with the soft coatings. Triple glazing (with a correspondingly thicker overall cross section) offers the best performance. The coatings and devices can be positioned in separate cavities ___ Fig. 23.

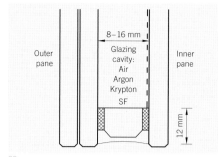

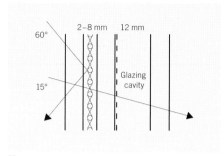

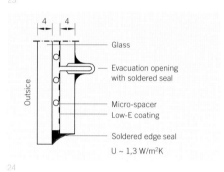

22   Typical build-up of a standard gas-filled insulating
      glazing unit

21   Cold-bent perforated sheet metal integrated
      into the glazing cavity, Mediathek Vénissieux,
      2001, Arch.: D. Perrault

23   Build-up of a triple insulating glazing unit with
      enclosed steel fabric to provide seasonal solar
      control, with noble gas filling and thermal
      insulating coating in a separate glazing cavity

24   Construction of a vacuum-filled insulating glazing
      unit with a U-value of about 1.3 W/m²K
      (Spacia from Nippon Sheet Glass)

The bonded edge seal of a standard insulating glass unit features a continuous, approx. 12 millimetres wide, shear-resistant glued aluminium rectangular hollow spacer bar. As a complete vapour seal cannot be guaranteed, the spacer is filled with a fine-grained desiccating agent *(molecular sieve)* to absorb any penetrating moisture and prevent condensation from forming. To avoid corrosion of soft coatings, the coatings are mechanically removed from the edges of the individual sheets before they are joined. A two-stage sealing system is generally used, in which the first stage is a *butyl* seal between the profile and the glass. The second stage is a permanently elastic seal made from *polysulphide*, *polyurethane* or *silicone*, applied to the outside faces of the spacer frame ____Fig. 17. Polysulphide achieves better gas-tightness than silicone but it is not UV-resistant and therefore should not be used for an exposed edge seal such as is found in structural glazing.

New types of edge seal systems such as spacers made of roll-formed stainless steel strip or plastic reduce the cold bridges in the edge area (warm-edge systems), which improves the U-value of the whole glazing unit by between 0.1 to 0.2 W/m²K. With *thermoplastic edge seals (thermoplastic spacer, TPS)* the edge spacer consists of a desiccant-containing extruded butyl compound with a thermal conductivity 1000 times less than aluminium ____Figs 19, 20. [**3.6/7**]

Evacuating the glazing cavity minimises thermal conductivity. One product currently on the market, *Spacia*, has a 0.2 millimetres vacuum layer, the sheets are connected by micro-spacers and the glass edges are hermetically sealed. The maximum pane size is about 2.40 m x 1.35 m. A U-value of 1.3 W/m²K can be achieved with a Low-E coating ____Fig. 24. [**3.6/6**]

IMPLICATIONS FOR DESIGN AND CONSTRUCTION

The detailed design must take into account the high self-weight of the units. The edge seal and the hermetically sealed glazing cavity contribute to a series of special mechanical characteristics which influ-

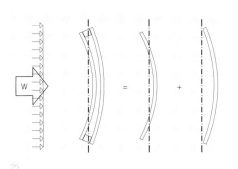
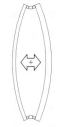

min. 6 mm
max. d_2 + 2 mm   min. 5 mm

d_1 ≤ 16 mm d_2

+

Poss. heat-
strengthened or
tempered glass;
not wired glass

Solar control glass, coloured glass

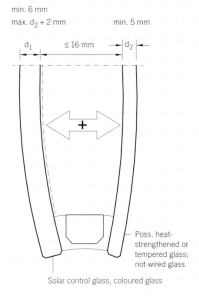

25 Schematic representation of the cushion
    effect: Both panes are loaded even if the unit
    is loaded from one side only, e.g. by wind.

26 Insulating glazing on a high-rise in New York: The
    optical distortions show up the bowing inwards or
    outwards of the panes in response to climate loads.

27 Bowing out with falling temperatures or barometric
    pressure (left) and bowing in with rising temperatures
    or barometric pressure (right) – the thinner pane is
    at most risk of breaking if deformations are large.

28 Stiff panes, such as small format insulating
    glazing units with standard pane thicknesses,
    are at particular risk of breakage.

29 With solar control and coloured glazing units at
    higher risk of breakage, the pane thicknesses
    (d1, d2) should not differ by more than 2 mm,
    and the thinner pane should be heat treated.

3.6

ence the load-bearing behaviour of the insulating glazing. Among these is the so-called cushion effect, the bowing and arching of the sheets in response to climatic loads and the stiffening effect of the spacer. Temperature and climatic stresses can make the use of tempered glass necessary.

The term "cushion effect" is used to describe the mechanical connection of the glass (with an intact edge seal) through the glazing cavity under bending loads at right angles to the plane of the glass. The loaded pane "supports" itself through the enclosed volume on to the indirectly loaded pane so that each pane carries about half the applied load.

Climatic loads occur though the "preservation" of the barometric pressure at the production factory in the glazing cavity when the sheets are sealed together. Pressure differences occur as a result of changes in the weather or altitude at the installation site, which lead to deformations. Increasing temperature or falling air pressure causes the sheets to bow outwards due to overpressure in the glazing cavity. The opposite climatic conditions create an underpressure and the panes arch inwards towards one another. The bowing of the panes is directly proportional to the width of the glazing cavity. As a rule of thumb, this climate load leads to a deformation of about 10 percent of the cavity width. Solar control glazing in particular is subject to considerable climate loading due to the way it heats up. A temperature difference of 3 °C can cause a climate load of approximately 1 kN/m² ___ Fig. 27.

The internal stresses produced depend on the stiffness of the installation fittings and the build up of the panes. Point fixings and very stiff insulating glass (small, thick panes) triangular or curved panes, which only permit slight deformations, increase the risk of breakage of individual panes. In asymmetric units, the thinner pane is at most risk of breakage. Wired glass should only be used with glazing cavities of about 10 millimetres width. The risk of breakage of single panes can generally be reduced by the use of tempered glass.

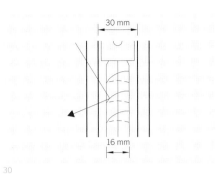

30

31

32

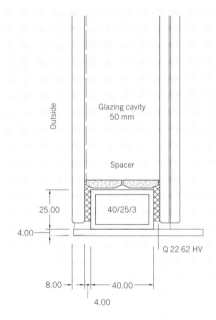

33

30 Construction of an insulating glazing unit
    installed as vertical glazing with integrated,
    adjustable microlouvres to provide flexible solar
    control, anti-glare and privacy functions; the
    big glazing cavity leads to high climate loads.

31 Sample panel

32 Failure of an insulating glazing unit with
    integrated louvers due to climatic loads.

33 Sketch showing the continuous support of individual
    panes of an insulating glazing unit by the structural
    bonded edge spacer made from stainless steel

The continuously bonded edge seal creates a shear connection of the panes along their edges. Normally the aim is to keep the shear stresses in the edge seal as low as possible in order to avoid any loss of function. Therefore the self-weight of both panes in vertical and inclined glazing should be supported directly and not through the edge seal.

Stiff and adequately dimensioned spacers made from stainless steel or glass fibre reinforced plastic (GFRP) and a structurally bonded connection with high shear stiffness are essential to achieve a suitable seal ___ Fig. 33. [**3.6/8**]

IMPLICATIONS FOR BUILDING SKINS
___THERMAL INSULATION

The heat loss of an insulating glass unit by *heat radiation* from the glass surface (emission), *thermal conductivity* and *convection* in the glazing cavity is expressed by the thermal transmittance coefficient or U-value ___ Fig. 35. Modern requirements for thermal insulation call for the U-values of building components made from glass to be 1.5 or better. While the insulating air or gas layer reduces the flow of conducted heat between the outer and inner panes, an insulating coating reduces heat emission. On the other hand, heat loss due to convection rises with increasing gas volume and increasing inclination from the vertical of the installed insulating glass unit.

An 8 millimetres pane of float glass has a U-value of approximately 5.8 W/m²K. Filling the glazing cavity with argon, providing a thermal insulating coating and a warm-edge seal, reduces the centre-pane U-value of a double insulating glazing unit to about 1.1 W/m²K, for a triple glazing unit the figure is 0.7 W/m²K ___ Fig. 34. To save weight, a "heat mirror film" can be used as the middle pane in highly insulating triple glazing units ___ Fig. 18. [**3.6/9**]

To improve the thermal insulation properties of a triple glazing unit, the inner glazing cavity can be filled with a transparent thermal insula-

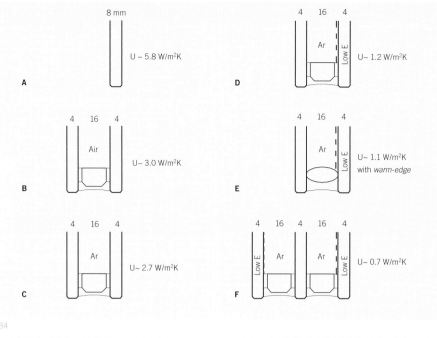

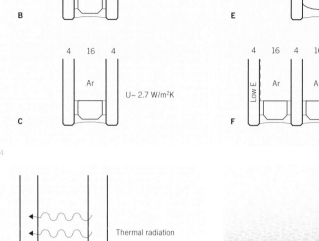

34

34 Comparison of U-values of single panes
    and insulating glazing units
    A   Single pane glazing 8 mm
    B   Air-filled insulating glazing
    C   Argon-filled insulating glazing
    D   Double glazing with low-E coating and argon filling
    E   Insulating glazing with warm-edge seal
    F   Triple glazing with argon filling

35 The physical causes of heat loss from and through an
    insulating glazing unit: Thermal radiation between the
    glass surfaces, conduction through the gas filling and
    the edge seal, and convection in the glazing cavity.
    Two-thirds of the total heat loss is radiated
    (emitted) by the glass panes.

36 Light-transmitting capillary mats can be integrated into
    a separate glazing cavity of triple glazing to improve
    thermal insulation (e.g. *Kapilux* from *Okalux*)

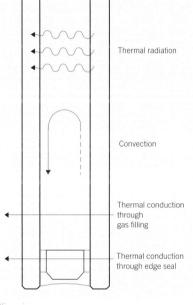

Thermal radiation

Convection

Thermal conduction through gas filling

Thermal conduction through edge seal

35

36

tion, which could be a cell or capillary structure made from glass, polycarbonate or Plexiglas ____Fig. 36. In addition to thermal insulation, another advantage of transparent thermal insulation is the uniform and glare-free dispersion of daylight, which is enhanced by the clear capillary structures and, where used, a woven fibre backing. [**3.6/10**]

____SOLAR CONTROL

An effective reduction of the solar gain can be achieved by a reflective solar control coating on one surface of a pane of the insulation glazing unit (see p. 76). Coloured or tinted glass also reduces direct transmission, however it gives off its absorbed energy into the room through heat radiation.

Solar gain can be further reduced by integrating fixed or mobile microlouvres, perforated sheet fabrics, mirror arrays and prismatic panels into the glazing cavity of a triple glazing unit. The geometry and shape of these elements allow them to admit more or less light from certain angles and therefore provide seasonal solar control. In this way the light transmittance in summer can be a minimum with a high solar altitude and an angle of incidence of approximately 60° and maximum in winter with a low solar altitude (approximately 7°) ____Figs 37, 38. High-energy light from the southern sky can be completely blocked by suitably shaped mirrored longitudinal and transverse lamellae of micro-grillage elements. [**3.6/11**] Research is currently ongoing into *gasochromic* insulating glass, the transparency of which can be controlled by the chemical reaction of an introduced gas with the coated inner surfaces ____Fig. 40. [**3.6/12**]

____ACOUSTIC PROPERTIES

The multipane construction of an insulating glass unit and the natural frequency of the mass-spring-mass system considerably improves its sound insulation index for certain frequencies. For increased sound insulation, thicker panes and/or laminated glass can be used for the

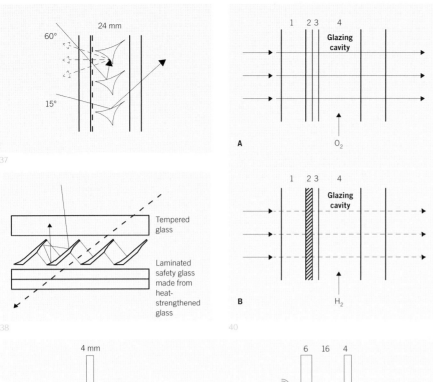

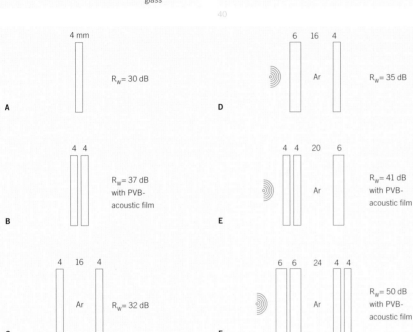

37 Construction of an insulating glazing unit with integral, fixed microlouvres for directing light and solar control

38 Build-up of an insulating glazing unit with integrated micro-mirror louvres installed as overhead glazing (developed by Chr. Bartenbach with Siemens AG). Mirror-finished plastic lamellae run transversely to the direct light and act as reflecting surfaces. The lamellae are attached one below the other to vertical strips; direct light is reflected, diffuse light is allowed to pass.

39 Weighted sound reduction index R_W for a selection of glass construction types. Glazing cavity filled with krypton gas rather than argon can further improve the sound reduction index for certain construction types.
A Single pane glazing
B Laminated safety glass with PVB acoustic film
C Insulation glazing with two equal-thickness monolithic panes
D Insulation glazing with monolithic panes of unequal thickness
E Insulation glazing with a laminated safety glass outer pane
F Insulation glazing with laminated safety glass of unequal thickness

40 Gasochromic glazing – how it works: Hydrogen generates a blue tint (B), decolouration follows the introduction of oxygen (A).
1 Glass
2 Tungsten oxide coating
3 Catalyst
4 Gas-filled cavity

41 Different optical effects exhibited by insulating glazing: Distortion of reflections caused by bowing out of the panes, bank building on Pariser Platz in Berlin, 1999, Arch.: F. O. Gehry

inner or outer panes ____ Fig. 39. The construction must be designed for the noise conditions specific to the installation site. [3.6/13]

____APPEARANCE

The optical appearance of insulation glass arises from the superposition of transmission and reflection of the different glasses and coatings with different refraction indices. The appearance will differ from time to time, depending on the distance, observation angle, quality of the reflected object and the difference in brightness between the surroundings and the inside of the building [3.9/15]. Only a reference sample facade can give some idea of how it looks in changing light conditions.

The bowing out and in of the glass under climate loads are particularly noticeable as pronounced distortions when there are strong reflections in the outer panes. Having a stiffer outer pane in relation to the inner pane reduces this effect. [3.9/16] An associated prism effect occurs with light from the rising or setting sun striking the glass at a very flat angle and shows itself as local dispersal of the light into its spectral colours. As a double pane effect it is responsible for the characteristic appearance of insulation glass. The optical anisotropy of heat treated glass has been discussed earlier (see Section 3.4). [3.6/14]

4

DESIGN
AND
CONNECTIONS

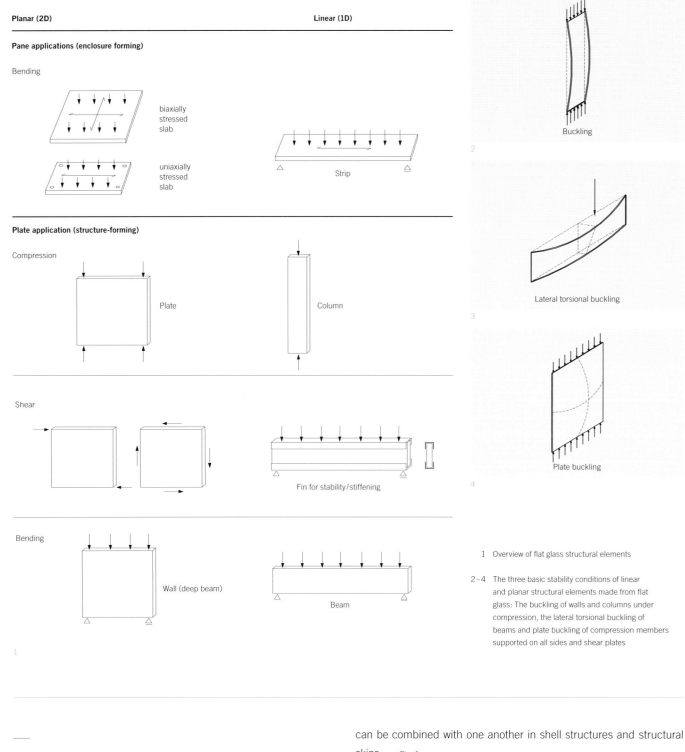

Planar (2D)   **Linear (1D)**

Pane applications (enclosure forming)

Bending

biaxially
stressed
slab

uniaxially
stressed
slab

Strip

Plate application (structure-forming)

Compression

Plate

Column

Shear

Fin for stability/stiffening

Bending

Wall (deep beam)

Beam

Buckling

Lateral torsional buckling

Plate buckling

1   Overview of flat glass structural elements

2–4   The three basic stability conditions of linear
and planar structural elements made from flat
glass: The buckling of walls and columns under
compression, the lateral torsional buckling of
beams and plate buckling of compression members
supported on all sides and shear plates

4.1

DESIGNING WITH GLASS

FLAT GLASS AS A BUILDING SKIN AND CONSTRUCTION ELEMENT
Glass differs from all other construction materials in that it is brittle: when glass components break they generally do so without warning. In order to be able to use construction elements made of glass, in addition to its load-carrying capacity when intact, the designer must also take into account its ability to carry loads in the fractured state, i.e. its *residual load-bearing capacity*.

Glass for use in structures can be generally classified as panes, plates and beams, based on their shapes. Pane and plate elements can be combined with one another in shell structures and structural skins ——Fig. 1.

The use of glass in pane or panel form as an *enclosing element* is inseparably linked with the traditional protective role of the building skin. Wind or snow loads acting transversely to the plane of the glass are resisted by the bending stiffness of the pane and transmitted to the supporting edges. Even if damage to tertiary structural elements (glazing in facades or roof surfaces) has no consequences for the overall stability of the structure, the requirements for residual loadbearing capacity must still be fulfilled in the case of overhead, accessible and safety barrier glazing. Plates or beams of glass are loaded in their planes. Compared with its strength when used as panes, the greater load capacity of glass plates or beams means that they are *structure-forming*, i.e. they allow system loads to be transmitted in a predictable way from the loaded surface to the ground. There are very few design or construction standards that can be applied to these new glass ap-

5   Example of a pane application: Vertical panes
    supported by point fixings, Sony Center Potsdamer
    Platz Berlin, Arch.: Murphy Jahn, 2000

6   Example of a plate acting as a load-bearing wall panel:
    Temple de l'Amour, Burgundy, 2002, Arch.: D. J. Postel

7   Example of a plate acting as a shear
    plate: Suspended glazing Zeppelin-Carré,
    Stuttgart, 1998, Arch.: Auer + Weber

8   Example of a glass column, detail of
    pillar foot, installation in public space
    Göttingen, 2004, Arch.: M. Hägele

9   Example of a stiffened glass fin as part of a facade post,
    New Museum Nuremberg, 2000, Arch.: V. Staab

10 Example of a linear element acting as a glass beam, roof
    of the Judenbad in Speyer, 1999, planning: W. Spitzer

plications. Plate-shaped components include compression members, shear plates and walls (deep beams), linear-shaped components include columns and beams.

These structural elements are usually very slender and hence have a cross section that tends to deflect laterally under load, so that stability criteria generally limit load-bearing capacity. Compression members tend to buckle, shear plates bulge, beams undergo local buckling or lateral torsional buckling —— Figs 2–4.

Transmission of system loads requires the designer to consider the modes of failure and safety measures of the system. Whilst the fracture of a single shear plate stiffening the load-bearing structure (acting as a secondary structural member) will not directly lead to the failure of the whole structure, the breaking structural glass components that are part of the primary structure break may lead to the collapse of further parts of the building.

CONNECTIONS

The brittleness of glass presents a major challenge when connecting glass construction components. Connection techniques should be based on a glass-conscious "construction kit" of various solutions designed to suit different stress conditions, which can be combined and modified.

In all cases there must be a uniform force transfer between glass and connecting elements by means of suitable intermediate layers. Glass to glass or glass to metal contact must be prevented. The hardness, stiffness and durability of the intermediate layer have a large effect on the behaviour under load of panes and plates. The load transfer layer should combine a low modulus of elasticity similar to that of glass with good durability and as high a compressive strength as possible.

Pane or plate structural elements can be supported on their edges, corners or surfaces at points or on their edges linearly or by a

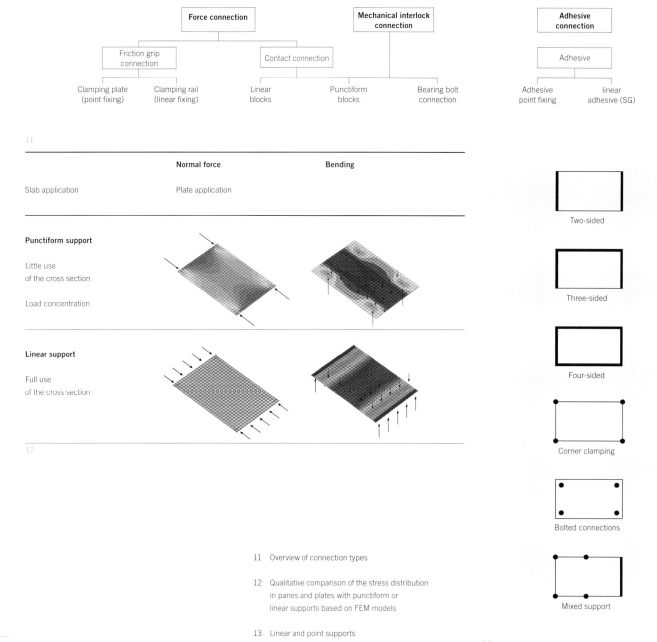

11   Overview of connection types

12   Qualitative comparison of the stress distribution
     in panes and plates with punctiform or
     linear supports based on FEM models

13   Linear and point supports

combination of the two methods ____Fig. 13. The form of loading transfer has a great effect on the stress distribution in brittle glass. Point or unevenly distributed load transfers produce concentrated load effects and do not make efficient use of the glass cross section ____Fig. 12. [4.1/1, 4.1/2] As well as varying in the number and size of the point fixings, systems also differ in relation to the way loads are transferred and behaviour on breakage. Whereas button, countersunk and glued point fixings support the glass surface, edge clamp fixings or clamping plates attach to edges or corners. The stress at the support points can be up to three times the general stress level, making it usual to have to use thermally treated glass point fixings are able to accommodate construction tolerances well but the engineering design of the support points is complex. The calculations required can be time- and cost-intensive.

Depending on the mechanism of force transfer they are classified as mechanical interlock, force or adhesive connections. The force connections used in glass construction include friction grip and contact connections, mechanical interlock connections include bolted and bearing bolt connections. Adhesive bonded connections have many and diverse roles in glass construction and are given special consideration in the sections below ____Fig. 11.

____ADHESIVE CONNECTIONS

An adhesive connection is one in which the joint is made using an adhesive, non-metallic material which achieves its properties only after undergoing some additional processing. The load-bearing mechanism of an adhesive connection relies on the load path linking joined part, boundary and adhesive layers ____Fig. 16, in which the adhesion forces in the boundary layer (boundary layer adhesion) and cohesion forces in the adhesive layer (strength of the glue) play separate roles. The main advantages of adhesive connections stem from the fact that selecting an adhesive for its mechanical properties opens a universal

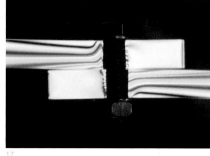

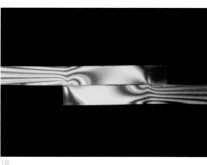

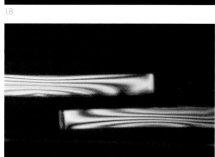

Criterion for use	Form interlock connection	Force connection	Adhesive connection
Connecting different materials	+	++	++
Connection can be structurally designed, connection strength depends on temperature, static load causes creep	++	0	+/0
Thermal strains	++	++	++
Occupational health aspects e.g. chemical emissions	+	++	+/-
Sealed connection	-	0	++/+
Corrosion	0	0	+
Time between installation and achievement of required strength	++	++	+/0
Temperature resistance	++	+/0	+
Ease of dismantling	++	+	0

++ = very good, + = suitable,
0 = limited suitability, - = unsuitable

— Joined part 1
— Boundary layer 1
— Adhesive layer
— Boundary layer 2
— Joined part 2

14 Bonded glass components in furniture

15 Qualitative comparison of mechanical interlock, force and adhesive connections

16 The sequence of loaded components of an adhesive connection

17–19 Optical display of stress distribution
17 Stress peaks in the area of the drilled holes of a threaded connection under load
18 Stress peaks in the ends of a lapped connection formed with a hard adhesive
19 Uniform distribution of stress in a connection formed with a thick, elastic adhesive

4.1

spectrum of use. Depending on the joint width and stiffness, forces can be transferred very evenly ____Figs 17–19, various materials joined and compensation made for thermal movements and dimensional variations in the joined parts. The bonded joint can fulfil further technical functions, such as sealing.

In comparison to force and interlock connections, the designer needs to take into account that the strength of an adhesive connection in service can be influenced by a large number of factors. Its strength depends on the mechanical characteristics of the system and the type and duration of loading, the geometric shape of the adhesive joint, the quality of its installation and the surface quality of the joined parts, as well as environmental influences such as UV light, moisture and temperature.

The strength of a bonded connection may be affected by many influences: the build-up of strength during curing and the degeneration of strength in service due to environmental influences, ageing and shrinkage, creep under long-term loads and fatigue under high rates of change of loading after curing ____Figs 21–23. Several different test procedures give information about the ageing process of adhesive systems under the influence of temperature, UV light and moisture, so that their long-term durability can be demonstrated by calculation. [4.1/3, 4.1/4]

Experience in the automobile, aircraft and ship-building industries, where structural adhesives have long played an important role, shows that bonded connections can find general application with the correct choice of adhesive system, when designed and installed in a manner suitable for requirements. New product developments allow the huge potential of adhesive technology, increasingly so also in the field of structural glass, to be used for a whole range of new possible applications of transparent bonded connections of edges and surfaces ____Fig. 24.

Adhesive systems can be differentiated according to their moduli of elasticity and shear into flexible, tough-elastic and hard or brittle

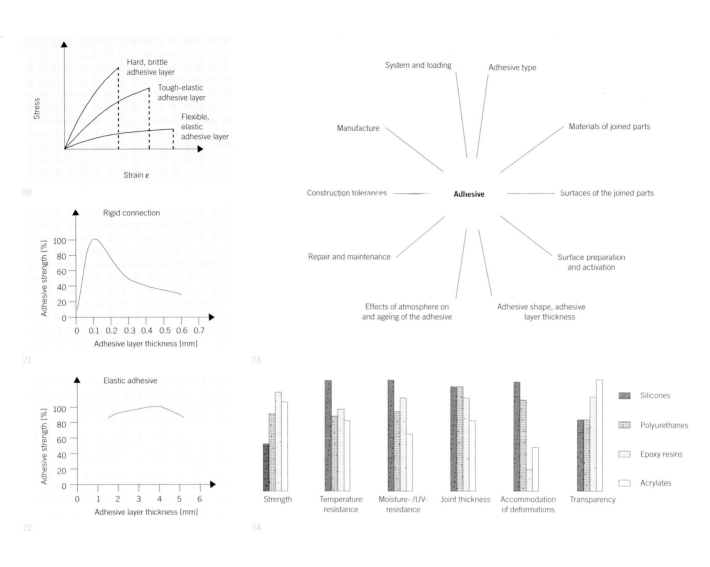

20   Stress-strain graph for various adhesive systems

21   Graph of strength against layer
     thickness for a hard adhesive

22   Graph of strength against layer thickness
     for an elastic adhesive

23   Factor influencing the strength of an adhesive
     connection

24   Qualitative comparison of various adhesive systems

adhesive systems ___Fig. 20. Silicones, MS polymers (modified silicones) and polyurethanes (PUR) are some of the flexible systems. Flexible adhesives normally have a strength in excess of 1 N/mm² and an elongation at break of more than 150 percent and are therefore suitable for linear bonded joints. With a joint thickness of approx. 5 millimetres, an elastic adhesive fills gaps and equalises stresses ___Fig. 22. The flexible connection is very suitable for accepting dynamic loads, damping sound transmission between the components and functioning as a seal. Compared with hard adhesives, it is more feasible to repair or take apart a connection made with an elastic adhesive. The high tear resistance provides a favourable fracture pattern with no sudden loss of strength. The pronounced tendency to creep means that values of short-term strengths are several times those of long-term strengths.

Epoxy resins and acrylates are usually considered as hard adhesives and at thicknesses of between 0.1 and 0.5 millimetres they have a very low elongation at break ___Fig. 21. At the optimum thickness they have extremely high strengths but do not accommodate construction tolerances nor do they equalise stresses, therefore they are mainly suitable for connections with point fixings. Imposed strains such as may arise as a result of their high thermal expansion coefficients must be taken into account. Hard adhesives fail through brittle fracture without warning.

Joints with an intermediate layer of *Sentry Glass Plus* (SGP) developed by DuPont for manufacturing laminated safety glass with a high composite strength are now taking on a special role. Recently SGP has been successfully used to form an adhesive connection with the glass surface for point and edge fittings under pressure and temperature in the autoclave or vacuum bag processes. SGP produces a relatively hard bonded connection even at thicknesses of between 1.5 and 2 millimetres, making it important to take into account the different coefficients of thermal expansion of glass and SGP.

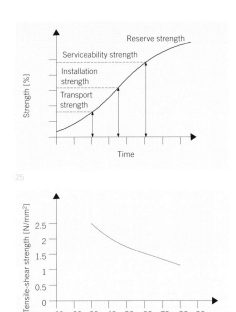

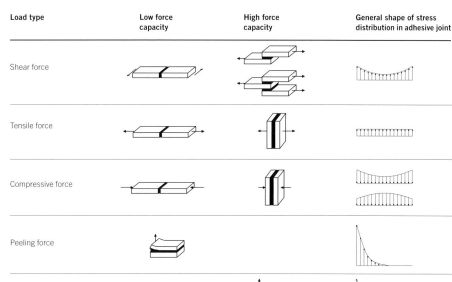

Load type	Low force capacity	High force capacity	General shape of stress distribution in adhesive joint
Shear force			
Tensile force			
Compressive force			
Peeling force			
Tearing force			

25

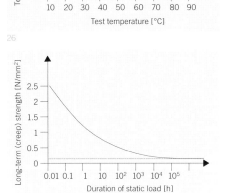

26

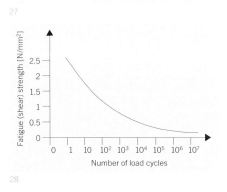

27

28

29

25 Qualitative graph of increase in strength
    of an adhesive with time after installation

26–28 Factors influencing the long-term
    strength of a flexible PUR adhesive
26 Influence of temperature

27 Influence of duration of load (static) –
    the curve approaches the limiting value of
    long-term strength with increasing duration
    of load.

28 Influence of alternating load (dynamic)

29 Adhesive joint geometries and load types

DESIGN CALCULATION PROCEDURES

CONSTRUCTION REGULATIONS

The procedures for design and approval of glass construction are de-termined by regulations governing construction in the country in which the project is being built and the standards applicable to products, construction and design calculations in that country. Work on stand-ards progresses only slowly because of questions of safety associated with brittleness and therefore lags significantly behind the possibilities of the material. [4.1/5] In addition, approval procedures often differ on a continental, national or regional level. The following section gives a simplified general overview of the regulations governing construction in Europe.

There is a distinction made between *construction products* and *construction types*. The various basic glass products and processed flat glass products are classified as construction products. Each coun-try has implemented its own national or European product standards

covering regulated construction products, such as EN 572 for float and rolled glass, EN 12150 for tempered glass, EN 1863 for heat-strengthened glass or EN ISO 12543 for laminated safety glass. These documents give the requirements relating to manufacturing process-es, dimensions and tolerances, as well as properties such as mechan-ical strength. Compliance of the construction product with the stand-ards must be attested by a manufacturer's declaration of conformity or a certificate from an accredited testing body. In the European Eco-nomic Area this is acknowledged with the CE mark. [4.1/6]

By construction type we refer to the ways and means in which the construction product is used and assembled. At the European level there are no implementation standards for glass construction, although a standard for the design of glass components is in the course of prep-aration. Few standards exist even at national level. Germany simply has regulations for the use of ventilated external wall cladding, *linearly supported glass* and *safety barrier glass* (the last two are known as the

Guidelines for European Technical Approval (ETAG) Dated 01/2005				Construction	Approval
No.	Part	Title			
002		Geklebte Glaskonstruktionen *Structural sealant glazing systems*		Vertical or overhead glazing on point supports, not supported in accordance with TRPV (Technical rules for the design and construction of point-supported glass)	abZ, ZiE
	01	Gestützte und ungestützte Systeme *Supported and unsupported systems*	SSG	Structurally bonded, glazing	ETA, abZ, ZiE
	02	Beschichtete Aluminium-Systeme *Coated aluminium systems*			
	03	Systeme mit thermisch getrennten Profilen *Systems incorporating profiles with a thermal barrier*	>1,20 m	Linear overhead glazing, not supported in accordance with TRLV (Technical rules for the design and construction of linearly supported glass)	ZiE
	04	In preparation: Beschichtete Verglasung *Opacified glazing*		Glazing subject to restricted foot traffic with point or linear supports	abZ, ZiE
				Safety barrier glazing, not in accordance with TRAV (Technical rules for the use of safety barrier glass)	abZ, ZiE
				Compression members	ZiE
				Shear plates	ZiE
				Walls (deep beams) and beams	ZiE

30

30 Guidelines for European technical approval

31 Overview of the technical approval procedures for non-regulated construction types (in Germany)

abZ: National technical approval, granted by DIBt (Deutsches Institut für Bautechnik)

ETA: European technical approval granted by the European Organisation for Technical Approvals (EOTA)

ZiE: Approvals on a case by case basis are granted by the federal construction supervisory body in Germany

31

4.1

TRLV and TRAV rules respectively in Germany). A draft version of technical rules for the design and construction of *point-supported glass* is available (October 2006). [4.1/7, 4.1/8, 4.1/9]

As in most cases the usability of a glass product or construction cannot be demonstrated by means of currently applicable technical construction rules; a manufacturer's approval for the construction product or type must be available, e.g. in the form of a nationally applicable approval such as a national technical approval, which may be granted in Germany by the *Deutsche Institut für Bautechnik* (DIBt) Berlin, or a *European Technical Approval* (ETA), which is issued by the European Organisation for Technical Approvals (EOTA) in consultation with the relevant national authorities. Applications for approval are assessed using European Technical Approval Guidelines (ETAGs) or specially agreed assessment criteria. One example of an ETAG is the Guideline for European Technical Approval of Structural Sealant Glazing Systems (ETAG 002) ___ Fig. 30. [4.1/10]

When a construction product or type is not regulated by technical rules, approvals or manufacturer's test results, the usability of this kind of special construction must be demonstrated on a case by case basis. The responsibility for executing and controlling this demonstration of usability is not regulated on a uniform pan-European basis. In Germany clients must obtain an individual approval known as a *Zulassung im Einzelfall* (ZiE) from the highest construction approval authority in the relevant federal state. In addition to proofs of stability and performance, there may also be the need to demonstrate impact resistance and residual load-bearing capacity by a recognised specialist test house. [4.1/11, 4.1/12]

Today, the majority of structural glass applications still fall into the category of special constructions, meaning that complex computer analyses or tests are frequently required ___ Fig. 31.

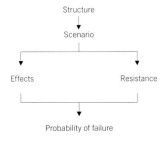

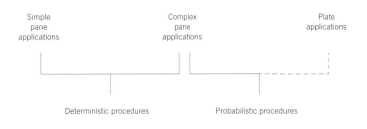

32

33

Glass type	Use	Characteristic bending strength [N/mm²]	Permissible stress [N/mm²]	Global safety factor γ
Tempered float glass		120	50	120/50 = 2.4
Tempered rolled glass		90	37	90/37 = 2.4
Enamelled tempered float glass		70	30	70/30 = 2.4
Annealed glass	Overhead glazing	45	12	45/12 = 3.8
	Vertical glazing	45	18	45/18 = 2.5
Rolled glass	Overhead glazing	25	8	25/8 = 3.1
	Vertical glazing	25	10	25/10 = 2.5
Laminated safety glass made from annealed glass	Overhead glazing	45	15 (25)*	45/15 = 3.0
	Vertical glazing	45	22,5	45/22,5 = 2.0
Heat-strengthened float glass		70	29	70/29 = 2.4
Enamelled heat-strengthened float glass		45	18	45/18 = 2.5

32 The principal steps in investigating the safety of a
    structural element; it is advisable to examine possible
    damage scenarios when working with brittle materials.

33 Appropriate application of deterministic
    and probabilistic procedures

34 Overview of parameters relevant to structural
    design calculations using the deterministic
    procedure in accordance with the German
    TRLV rules (heat-strengthened glass is not
    yet regulated in construction approvals)

*permissible for the insulating glass bottom pane of overhead glazing in the scenario „Failure of top pane"

34

____COMPUTER ANALYSIS

For most structural applications the dimensioning of glass components is not or only inadequately regulated, due to the lack of design standards. Some aspects of the calculation of stresses are unclear, e.g. how to realistically model the systems using the finite element method (FEM) and how to interpret and assess the results. The technical rules in Germany, the *American Standard* ASTM E 1300, the *Australian Standard* AS 1288 and the withdrawn draft version of EN 13474 are based on different deterministic and probabilistic assumptions. [4.1/13, 4.1/14] In the case of deterministic procedures – described for example in the German rules for linearly supported glass – the variations in material properties and loads are covered by a global safety factor which depends only on the glass type and use.

In contrast, determining the probability of failure in accordance with the probabilistic safety concept on which the draft version of EN 13474 is based uses partial safety factors arrived at in a differentiated way involving statistical variations as well as aspects such as materials (strength) and loads (wind, snow). On the material side, influences such as the type and duration of load, dimensions and location of the pane and environmental conditions such as air moisture content can be taken into account. Special application-related issues such as the composite performance of laminated safety glass over time and under different temperature conditions and the variations in the distribution of prestressing forces over the surface of the heat treated pane can also be addressed. [4.1/15, 4.1/16, 4.1/17, 4.1/18, 4.1/19] Limit states for load-bearing capacity and performance can also be formulated with the aid of failure scenarios ____Fig. 32.

Whilst the deterministic method makes a safe-side estimate of the influence factors and therefore provides a user-friendly and practical process for calculating simple pane sizes at the cost of cross sectional optimisation, the more complex and detailed probabilistic method more realistically models the physical behaviour of the glass and is

Construction	Experimental verification	Criterion
Safety barrier glazing	Pendulum impact test with soft impact body (Twin tyres in accordance with EN 12600)	Glazing not penetrated, does not become loose from fixings, no dangerous shards fall down
Overhead glazing	Residual loadbearing capacity verified with impact load and additional load	Minimum residual resistance time e.g. 24 hours
Overhead glazing subject to restricted foot traffic for cleaning purposes	Drop test with soft impact body (glass ball sack, 50 kg) and drop test with hard impact body (steel ball, 4 kg) under loading with concentrated load	Glazing not penetrated, does not become loose from fixings, no dangerous shards fall down, minimum residual resistance time e.g. 30 mins
Glazing subject to unrestricted foot traffic	Drop test with hard impact body („Torpedo", 40 kg) under loading with concentrated load	Glazing not penetrated, no dangerous shards fall down, minimum residual resistance time e.g. 30 mins
Other loadbearing glass components e.g. beams, columns	Load tests to calibrate computer analysis	Depends on specific application, residual load-bearing capacity always required
Glass fixings which cannot be verified with structural calculations	Determination of load-bearing capacity of the fixings by pull out tests and under transverse load, determination of long-term adhesion of fixings (salt mist spray test), tests of the interlayers used	Depends on specific application

36

35

37

35 Overview of demonstration of compliance by testing: Requirements for various construction types

36 Pendulum impact test with two pneumatic tyres to verify the performance of safety barrier glazing

37 Ball drop test to verify the impact resistance of overhead glazing

therefore more suitable for the design of special pane applications and above all for structure-forming plate and beam applications ____Fig. 33.

____THE USE OF TESTS IN ANALYSIS

The use of tests in analysis normally involves destructive testing of original construction components. In many cases they are unavoidable as there is inadequate knowledge of load capacity for many non-regulated construction products or types and dynamic effects cannot yet be fully modelled by computer ____Fig. 35. Tests cover impact resistance, load capacity and residual load-bearing capacity. Destructive tests have further uses, for example heat soak tests for tempered glass and quality control. [4.1/20]

In the proof of adequate impact resistance of, for example, attack-resistant or safety barrier glass the distinction is made between a *soft* and a *hard impact*. Safety against a collision with a soft body with a high mass (soft impact) is proven for safety barrier glazing using the pendulum impact test in accordance with EN 12600. Two pneumatic tyres swing from a specified height against the glazing so as to cause the maximum load on the support and glass ____Fig. 36. Now the dynamic load effects of a soft impact can also be modelled by computer. The resistance to the collision of a hard object with a relatively low mass (hard impact) with overhead or accessible glazing for example is proven in accordance with DIN 52338 by a ball drop test ____Fig. 37 or a standard steel torpedo projected against the weakest point of the test object. Glazing is normally considered to have passed these destructive tests if it does not slip from its supports, the pane has not been penetrated and no dangerous fractured pieces become detached.

Proof of load capacity can be obtained from a load test on original components using the specified loading and appropriate factors. Loading to fracture gives information about the actual level of safety of the construction. Strain gauged tests can also be used to calibrate and benchmark the results of computer analyses. [4.1/21]

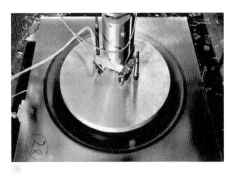

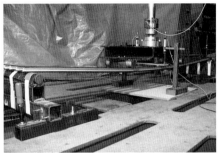

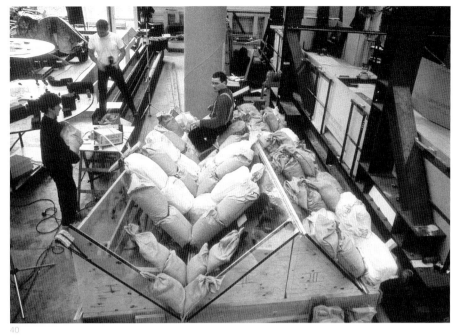

38   Double ring test to determine the fracture
     strength of a pane of rolled glass

39   Four-point bending test of a sandwich
     of heat treated glass panes

40   Load and residual load-bearing capacity
     tests on a folded plate structure

41   Float glass samples for testing and quality
     assurance

Residual load-bearing capacity tests demonstrate that the construction retains adequate strength for a prescribed period of time even after breakage and that there is no danger from glass components or shards falling out. As the possibility of glass fracture can never be fully excluded, one or more or all of the panes in the glazing must provide a period of residual protection until collapse, even after breakage. This period depends on the use and the maintenance interval
——Fig. 38–40.

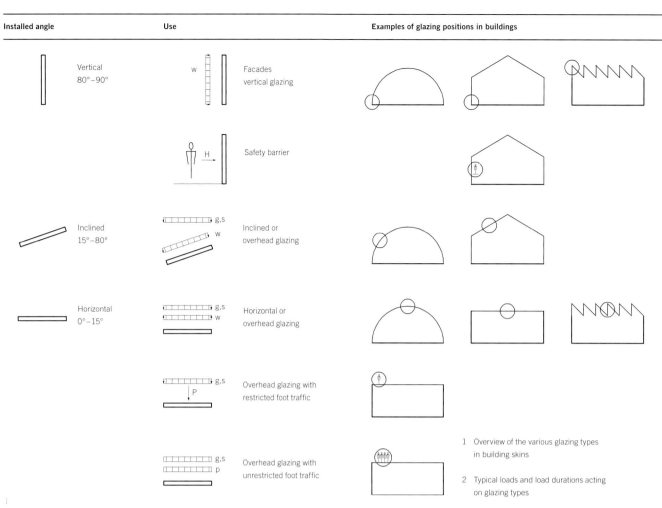

Installed angle	Use	Examples of glazing positions in buildings

1 Overview of the various glazing types
  in building skins

2 Typical loads and load durations acting
  on glazing types

1

	Very short-term effect		Short-term effect		Medium-term effect		Permanent effect		
	Hard impact	Soft impact	Wind	Snow	Barrier load	Foot traffic	Climatic load	Self-weight	Altitude
Vertical glazing			X				poss.		poss.
Vertical glazing with a safety barrier role		X	X		X		poss.		poss.
Horizontal and inclined glazing	poss.		X	X			poss.	X	poss.
Glazing subject to unrestricted foot traffic	X	poss.	X	X		X	poss.	X	poss.

2

4.2

THE USE OF GLASS PANES IN BUILDING SKINS

Depending on the installed position of the glass panes in the building envelope, they may be classified as vertical, inclined or horizontal glazing according to the relevant national standards. German standards for example define vertical glazing as inclined at up to ten degrees to the vertical; horizontal glazing at up to 15 degrees to the horizontal ____Fig. 1.

The installed position of the glazing determines the type and duration of the loadings and the associated potential danger ____Fig. 2. As inclined and horizontal glazing represent a particular danger over traf-

ficked areas, they are dealt with together as 'overhead glazing' to which special requirements for residual load-bearing capacity apply. Vertical glazing in public circulation zones and glass floors carrying restricted or unrestricted foot traffic or vehicular traffic must have special safety characteristics and fulfil additional requirements for robustness and residual load-bearing capacity. Detailed descriptions of glass pane applications can be found in numerous publications including the "Glass Construction Manual". The following section summarises the requirement profiles for different glazing types and methods of support. [4.2/1]

5 Safety barrier glazing: Café in the Tate Modern
with a view over the Thames, 2001,
Arch.: Herzog & de Meuron

3 *Dorma*-Spider point fixings on vertical glazing

4 Pendulum impact test on safety
barrier glazing

6 Frameless vertical glazing made from tempered
glass presents the danger that fragmented glass
dice, which are still attached together in a shard,
may fall down and cause severe injury.

GLAZING TYPES

_____VERTICAL GLAZING AND GLASS BARRIERS TO *PREVENT* FALLS FROM HEIGHT

Short-term wind pressure and suction forces act out-of-plane to the glass surface. Self-weight, which acts in-plane to the glass, surface must be transferred by shims and setting blocks or bearing connections to the supporting framework. The most important safety objective in the event of failure is to ensure that trafficked areas below are protected against falling glass shards ___Figs 3, 6. When supported along all edges and away from human contact even glass products that break into large pieces such as annealed or rolled glass may be used. If not supported in this way, safety glass must be used. Laminated safety glass must also be used for vertical glazing that has to resist medium-term live loads (e.g. accumulations of snow on shed roof glazing). Edge supported glazing is normally guided or regulated by national standards such as the German "Technical rules for linearly supported glazing (TRLV)". [**4.2/2**]

Vertical glazing that protects people on adjacent circulation areas from a drop of height and from falling is described as *safety barrier glazing* ___Fig. 5. Storey-high glazing with or without safety rails or transoms at the proscribed barrier height has to satisfy a number of different requirements. In general laminated safety glazing made up of heat strengthened glass is most appropriate for safety barrier glazing.

In addition to load capacity under line loads applied from the rail, another important criterion for safety barrier glazing is its resistance to an impact by a human body and its residual load-bearing capacity on breakage. Proof of impact resistance by computer modelling or experimental derivation using a pendulum impact test ___Fig. 4 may not be necessary if the dimensions and support conditions comply with national guidelines, such as the German "Technical rules for the use of safety barrier glazing (TRAV)". [**4.2/3**]

8 Non-regulated overhead glazing made from bent
tempered glass, the trafficked surface below must
be protected from falling pieces of broken glass by a
tensioned net: Overhead walkway Neue Messe Leipzig

9 Overhead glazing with structurally bonded panel
edges, all glass components are constructed
from laminated safety glass and therefore have
adequate residual load-bearing capacity. Entrance to
underground train station, Buchanan Street, Glasgow,
2003, Eng.: Dewhurst Mcfarlane and Partners

7 The shape and arrangement of point fixings have
most effect on the determination of the residual
load-bearing capacity of overhead glazing, in this
example: Neue Messe Leipzig, 1996, Arch.: gmp

___OVERHEAD GLAZING

The self-weight of overhead glazing represents a permanent out-of-plane load; therefore laminated safety glass must be used for single glazing or the inner pane of insulating glass units. In domestic applications wired glass can also be used with an adequate glazing rebate for spans of up to 700 millimetres. The use of laminated safety glass incorporating only tempered glass is inadvisable because of its poor residual load-bearing capacity. With glass supported on two opposite edges in contrast to all four edges, even with laminated safety glass there is the risk of folding in the centre of the pane, therefore the German technical rules for linearly supported glazing, for example, recommend support on all sides and a maximum side length ratio of 3:1 for spans greater than 1200 millimetres. Linearly supported glass with drilled holes or notches and glazing made from rolled or curved glass are not covered by the regulations ___ Figs 7–9.

___GLAZING SUBJECT TO RESTRICTED OR UNRESTRICTED FOOT TRAFFIC

Overhead glazing may require to be temporarily accessed by trained personnel carrying out cleaning or maintenance. Health and safety requirements and, where applicable, professional/trade association regulations need to be taken into account. Risk to public safety can be avoided if access to the zone underneath the glazing is blocked off during cleaning or maintenance work. The necessary load-bearing capacity to support restricted foot traffic and robustness to prevent falling-through are demonstrated by drop tests. [4.2/4, 4.2/5]

Glass panels subject to unrestricted foot traffic such as stair treads, landings and transparent or translucent illuminated floors have to be designed to support concentrated and uniformly distributed pedestrian loads. There are currently no standards for the design and construction of such glass floors. However, some manufacturers supply glazing systems for point and linearly supported glass floors subject to

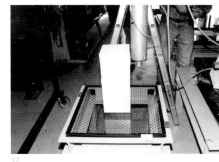

10 Example of use of SGG *Lite-Floor*:
Private house Antwerp, Belgium

11, 12 Load and impact tests as part of the
testing for obtaining National Technical
Approval (abZ) for SGG *Lite-Floor*

unrestricted foot traffic (e.g. SGG *Lite-floor*, ___Figs 10–12). [**4.2/6**] The load-bearing capacity under uniformly distributed pedestrian load (e.g. 5 kN/m²) and a concentrated load applied in the most adverse position are generally investigated. Impact resistance is demonstrated by drop tests using a steel ball or torpedo and followed up by a residual load-bearing capacity test. With all leaves of the laminate broken the specimen must provide a residual strength commensurate with its use (minimum 30 minutes, up to 48 hours). [**4.2/7, 4.2/8**]

Glazing carrying full pedestrian loading is normally made up of laminated safety glass of at least three panes, possibly combining tempered, heat-strengthened and annealed glass. The top pane is usually tempered glass for better impact-resistance, however heat-strengthened glass is less rewarding to vandals. It is considered a wear layer and often disregarded in the structural analysis. The glass must have anti-slip properties suitable for its use, possibly provided by screen printing, sand blasting, a top layer of patterned glass etc.

Support on all sides enhances residual load-bearing capacity ___Figs 12, 13. The glass is evenly supported on elastomer gaskets of adequate thickness and width. The supports on the lateral edges of the panels should allow free movement so that the system is statically determinate. Spacer blocks are used to prevent uncontrolled relative lateral displacement and the panels may require restraint against uplift. In the case of two-edge support it must be ensured that the panel cannot slide off the supports after breakage, for example by providing countersunk bolt fixings ___Fig. 14.

RESIDUAL LOAD-BEARING CAPACITY OF PANES

The residual load-bearing capacity of damaged glass panes is determined by examining various fracture scenarios in which a single, several or all leaves of a laminated panel are broken.

If one leaf is broken the residual load-bearing capacity depends on the bending resistance of the remaining intact leaf or leaves. The

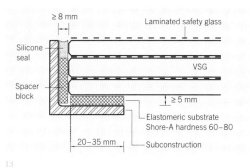

Max. support spacing [mm]	Laminated safety glass construction top to bottom [mm]	Minimum thicknes of the PVB film [mm]
700	8 HST / 15 TEM / 8 HST	1.52
1 400	8 HST / 19 TEM / 8 HST	2.28

13

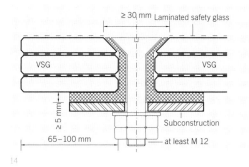

Max. length [mm]	Max. width [mm]	Laminated safety glass construction top to bottom [mm]	Minimum glass embedment [mm]
1 500	400	8 HST/10 ANN/10 ANN	30
1 500	750	10 HST/12 ANN/12 ANN	30
1 250	1 250	10 HST/10 HST/10 HST	35
1 500	1 250	10 HST/12 HST/12 HST	35

14

Residual load-bearing capacity on breakage of all panes	Low	Medium	Good	Very good
Laminated safety glass made from ANN				x
Laminated safety glass made from TEM	x			
Laminated safety glass made from HST			x	
Laminated safety glass made from HST and TEM		x		
Wired glass		x		

15

Residual load-bearing capacity on breakage of all panes	Low	Medium	Good	Very good
Four-sided supported				x
Two-sided supported	x			
Point supports with button fixings			x	
Point supports with countersunk fixings		x		

16

13　Schematic of the construction of a glazing unit linearly supported on all sides and subject to unrestricted foot traffic and examples of glazing components
　　HST: heat-strengthened glass
　　TEM: tempered glass
　　ANN: Annealed glass

14　Schematic of the construction of a glazing unit linearly supported on two sides and subject to unrestricted foot traffic and examples of glazing components

15　Residual load-bearing capacities of various types of glass

16　Residual load-bearing capacity of laminated safety glass with various types of support

resulting high stresses mean that heat-treated glass is recommended for use here. Broken leaves in the compression zone can still transfer loads through the interlayer. [4.2/9]

If all leaves are broken, the residual load-bearing capacity is determined by the type of support and fracture pattern. As a general rule, panes that break into large pieces (annealed glass or heat-strengthened glass) have a considerable better residual load-bearing capacity than glass that breaks into fine pieces and dice, like tempered glass, as the glass shards interlock to contribute to the transfer of loads in the tensile zone. Laminated safety glass made from tempered glass only exhibits large deformations, as the tensile forces are transferred by the film alone ＿Fig. 15. As a general rule, a pane with linear supports on all sides has a higher residual load-bearing capacity than a pane supported on two or three edges, as after breakage the pane mobilises membrane forces, which tend to stiffen the element. When larger deformations occur there is the risk of the pane slipping from its supports.

The residual load-bearing capacity of point-supported glass depends on the type of fixings. Depending on the stiffness of the broken glass and the design of the fixings, high stresses may occur at the fixing points, which may in extreme cases lead to the countersunk bolt fixings tearing out of the glass. Articulating bearings improve control of these stresses after breakage. The interlock of the bolts with the glass element ("nailing") gives a better overall residual load-bearing capacity than a pane supported on two edges ＿Fig. 16.

CONNECTIONS

＿MECHANICAL INTERLOCK: COUNTERSUNK AND BUTTON FIXINGS

Point fixings or bolted bearing connections such as countersunk or button fixings allow the glazing elements to be decoupled from the main structure, but additional conditions must be fulfilled to ensure restraint-free support in-plane and out-of-plane of the glass.

For a restraint-free assembly, first it must be ensured that the con-

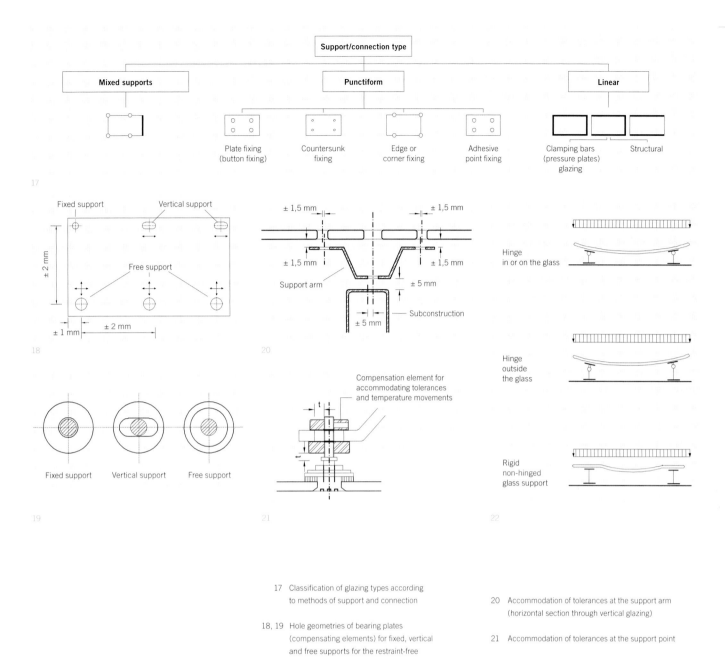

17 Classification of glazing types according to methods of support and connection

18, 19 Hole geometries of bearing plates (compensating elements) for fixed, vertical and free supports for the restraint-free accommodation of tolerances and temperature movements

20 Accommodation of tolerances at the support arm (horizontal section through vertical glazing)

21 Accommodation of tolerances at the support point

22 The articulating bearings support the glass transversely to its plane in restraint-free manner.

nection elements ("Spider" fittings or similar) can accommodate all the misalignments resulting from the construction tolerances between the subconstruction and the glass panes ____Figs 20, 21, the fittings should allow for an adjustment of at least ± 10 mm for a steel-framed building. [4.2/10] These compensating elements also allow the support system to be statically determinate in-plane and tolerate temperature movements to some extent. Fixed bearings are installed as precise locating holes, vertical or horizontal bearings as slotted holes and free bearings as larger diameter oversized holes ____Figs 18, 19.

Restraint-free, statically determinate support out-of-plane is provided by articulating fixings. The greater the distance between the ball or elastomeric joint and the plane of the pane, the greater are the imposed strains arising from the eccentricity of the joint and, with that, the required glass thickness. Rigid connections can lead to very high local stress peaks ____ Fig. 22. [4.2/11] The skin is made weatherproof by wet-sealing the joints with permanently elastic silicone sealant. The

structural silicone around the glass edges also has a beneficial effect on residual load-bearing capacity.

A *button fixing* (plate fixing) consists of two clamping discs of up to 70 millimetres diameter which are pressed on to the glass surface by a stainless steel bolt ____ Figs 27, 28. The glass bearing width is normally 12 to 15 millimetres. The wind forces are transmitted by contact between the glass surface and the clamping disc; the stresses depend on the compressive surface stiffness of the interlayer. The dead load of vertical or inclined glazing on the other hand is carried by the contact between the bolt and the cylindrical bearing hole. The material for sleeves and bushes should be as flexible as possible so that it is able to accommodate construction tolerances and misalignment of the drilled holes. The typical misalignment of approximately two millimetres between the heat-treated leaves of a laminated safety glass may be accommodated by adopting oversized holes and by injecting a fast curing resin or mortar into the chamber between bolt and bearing

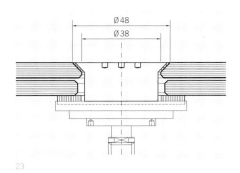

23

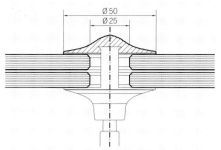

27

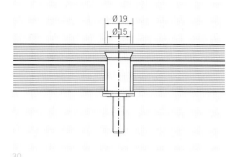

30

24

28

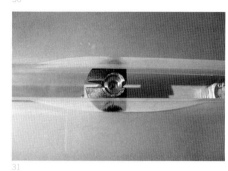

31

25

29

26

27–29 Plate and button fixings
28 *Rodan* button fixing
29 Plate or button fixings interrupt the flow of
rainwater on overhead glazing.

23–26 Countersunk fixings
23, 24 Common forms of construction
25 *Dorma* support arm (spider) for connecting
the glazing to the subconstruction
26 Countersunk fixing for the *Dorma* Manet
Construct system

30, 31 Special fixing with greatly reduced head
size and correspondingly lower load capacity
30 Undercut anchor from the SGG *Point-*
XS system for laminated safety glass
31 Joint fixing from *Pauli und Sohn* at glasstec 2004

hole. The larger the glass bearing width and disc diameter, the greater is the residual load-bearing capacity. [**4.2/12**]

The *countersunk fixing* consists of a countersunk bolt head flush-fitted into the glass surface and a clamping plate on the internal glass surface ____ Figs 23–26. The conical hole allows better accommodation of construction tolerances within the hole diameter. Self-weight and wind suction forces are transferred by a plastic or aluminium sleeve between the hole and the countersunk bolt. In spite of the mechanical interlock connection, the countersunk arrangement achieves only a poor residual load-bearing capacity, as the risk of the fixings tearing out of the glass is considerably greater than with the button fixings. The system has therefore only limited suitability for suspended overhead glazing.

A special form of point fixing is the *undercut anchor* (e.g. SGG Point XS), which does not completely penetrate the glass and thus leaves the outside face undisturbed ____ Fig. 30. The fixing has a diameter of approx. 20 millimetres. It is generally used for vertical single pane tempered glass and has only about half the load-bearing capacity of an ordinary point fixing. When applied to overhead glazing using laminated safety glass made from heat-strengthened glass, the residual load-bearing capacity is even less than with countersunk fixing systems. [**4.2/13, 4.2/14**]

____CLAMP FIXINGS AND PRESSURE PLATES: FORCE CONNECTION

Clamp fixings are point supports at the panel edge (edge clamp fixing) or corner (corner clamp fixings). Out-of-plane loads are transferred by mechanical interlock, in-plane loads (for example self-weight of vertical glazing) by setting blocks and brackets. Clamping plates result in wider joints, but can accommodate more construction tolerances. The embedded depth should be a minimum of 25 millimetres and the clamped surface area of the glass should be at least 10 cm² per fixing. The larger the clamped surface area and glass embedment, the greater the

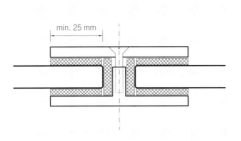

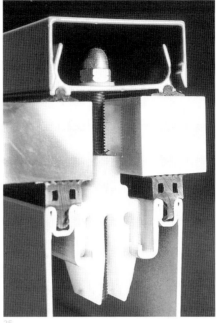

32 Principle of the clamp plate fixing

33 Interior view of overhead glazing with external suction clamp plate fixings at the nodes

34, 36 Clamping bar glazing on an inclined roof, the free flow of rainwater is interrupted.

35 Cross sectional model of clamping bar glazing

residual load-bearing capacity. The sealing of the panel edges is made more difficult by the connection elements in the joint ___Figs 32, 33.

With *clamping bar glazing* the edges of the panels are clamped with suitably stiff pressure plates and cover profiles between rectangular or profiled EDPM gaskets on a framing system of mullions and transoms. With vertical and inclined glazing the self-weight must be carried by suitable setting blocks in horizontal joints, elastic spacer blocks fix the pane in the frame. The rebate must be drained to counter the risk of penetration by moisture.

Numerous manufacturers offer stick systems for clamping bar glazing made from steel profiles or aluminium extrusions. To ensure restraint-free support the deflection of the framing members should be limited to approximately 1/200 of its span or a maximum of 15 millimetres. Residual load-bearing capacity should be investigated for overhead glazing supported only on two edges with a span of over 1.20 metres or a side ratio of over 3:1. In normal circumstances a glazing rebate of 15 millimetres will prevent a broken unit supported on all four edges from sliding from the framing members and will not compromise the ability of the panel edges to twist freely in use ___Figs 34–36.

___STRUCTURALLY BONDED POINT AND LINEAR FIXINGS: ADHESIVE CONNECTION

With *structural sealant glazing* (SSG), the linear bonding of facade and roof panels onto a frame is normally performed with silicone; the adhesive joint does not only provide the seal but also transfers the loads into the supporting structure. The system has been used in the USA since 1963.

In Europe, SSG is regulated by the Guideline for European Technical Approval of Structural Sealant Glazing Systems (ETAG 002). The ETAG presently covers three areas of regulation in accordance with which European Technical Approval (ETA) can be granted (see section 4.1, ___Fig. 30). The guideline generally limits the design life of such

37

38

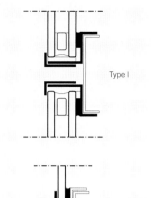

Type I

Type II

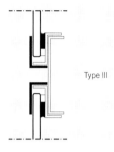

Type III

Type IV

40

Manufacturer	Product	Tensile strength [N/mm²]	All. tensile stress (short-term)	Shear strength [N/mm²]	All. shear stress (static) [N/mm²]	Tear resistance	Temperature in use	Colour
Dow Corning	2-part silicone DC 993	0.95	0.14	n. k.	0.011	130%	-50°C to 100°C	Black
Sika	2-part silicone SG 500	0.95	0.14	0.8	0.0105	160%	-50°C to 100°C	Black
Sika	1-part PUR SikaTack-HM	approx. 8	application-related	approx. 4.5	application-related	approx. 400%	-40°C to 90°C	Black

39

37 Example of an SSG facade type 2

38 Structural glazing with 2-part silicone

39 Comparison of the properties of two structural
    glazing silicones with a PUR adhesive system

40 Types of SSG facades in accordance with ETAG 002

41 *Citroën* Centre de Communication Paris, prototype
    special roof glazing with twisted geometry and
    integrated pyramid elements with structural
    sealant glazing, 2005, facade construction:
    Gartner, Arch.: Manuelle Gautrand

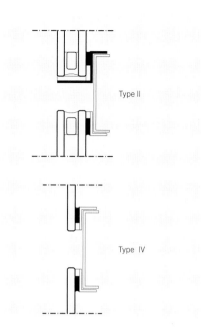

41

constructions to twenty-five years and is based on the use of silicone as an adhesive and sealant.

Part 1 of ETAG (Supported and unsupported systems) lists four construction types classified according to the type of load transfer ___Fig. 40. For types 1 and 2 only short-term wind loads are transferred by the adhesive, for types 3 and 4, which are approved only for single glazing, the permanent dead load is also taken by the structural bond. Types 1 and 3 have additional mechanical safety systems in the event that the adhesive fails.

As silicones are elastic even at low temperatures and adhere very well to glass and common frame materials, they are extremely suitable for structural glazing systems. Two-component systems like *DC 993* from Dow Corning and *Elastosil SG 500* from Sika are in common use and have been tested in accordance with the EOTA guideline for SSG applications.

Silicones have long-term weather resistance and are temperature-resistant between -50 °C and 150 °C (some special silicones as high as 300 °C) and have good chemical resistance. Low cohesive stresses mean that its tensile strength is about 1 N/mm², the permissible tension for short-term loads is ten times less and for permanent loads approximately 100 times less ___Fig. 39. [**4.2/15, 4.2/16, 4.2/17**]

The joint thickness is between 6 and 8 millimetres, the ratio of joint depth to thickness is usually between 1:1 and 3:1. The best arrangement is a bond on two parallel surfaces. The minimum depth of the joint is calculated from the governing load case.

Structurally bonded connections using PUR can achieve higher strengths than those made with silicone. The *Sika-Tack Panel System*, which uses a high-modulus windscreen adhesive to bond facade panels of various materials on to an aluminium subframe, is classified as a type 4 product in accordance with the ETAG, in which the dead load is transferred by the adhesive without need for a mechanical safety system. The adhesive joint runs vertically over the height of the pane.

42

45

43

46

42, 43, 45   Adhesive point fixing from the *Delo-Photobond* 4468 system by *Hunsrücker Glasveredelung Wagener*

44   Comparison of properties of brittle and viscoelastic adhesive systems (manufacturers' instructions)

46   Load test of a glass louvre structurally bonded with an acrylate adhesive

Manufacturer/ adhesive system	Product/ use	Tensile strength [N/mm^2]	Shear strength glass-glass/ glass-Al [N/mm^2]	E-modulus [N/mm^2]	Temperature in use (long-term) [°C]	Elongation at break (tearing) [%]	Colour
Huntsman/ 2-part epoxy resin	Araldite 2020 *internal use only*	n.k.	26/n.k.	- 2500	up to 40	n.k.	Colourless/clear
Delo/ acrylate adhesive	Photobond GB 368 (UV-cured) *furniture*	20	23/23	900	-40 to 120	17	Colourless/clear
	Photobond PB 4468 (light-cured) *point fixings*	12	22/24	250	-40 to 120	200	Colourless/clear
	Photobond PB 493 *internal/ linear adhesive connections*	12	10/12	80	-40 to 120	280	Colourless/clear
	Photobond PB 4496 *linear adhesive connections*	6	6/4	–	-40 to 120	300	Yellow/clear

44

__ADHESIVE POINT FIXINGS

With structurally bonded point fixing, the glass is obviously not weakened by drilled holes, but additional means of carrying self-weight in-plane and ensuring adequate residual load-bearing capacity are often required. The systems are unsuitable for suspended overhead glazing. If the adhesive is an acrylate or 2-component epoxy resin then it should not be exposed to the effects of the weather. The load-bearing behaviour depends on the adhesive thickness and the radius of the fixing plate. The design calculations must take into account the stress peaks at the perimeter of the fixings. [**4.2/18**, **4.2/19**]

Delo, a leading company in the modification of acrylates for use in construction, has a range of light- and UV-curing single component acrylates for rigid and tough-elastic glass-to-glass and glass-to-metal connections ____ Figs 42, 43, 45. [**4.2/20**]

Acrylate used for high strength glass-to-glass bonded connections can be modified in relation to layer thickness, viscosity, elongation at break and curing time. Light-curing acrylates with an elongation at tear of up to 300 percent and layer thickness of up to three millimetres are used for full-surface or linear bonded connections between different materials. In comparison with silicones, acrylates are about ten times stronger but have lower temperature resistance and moisture stability. Even with a degradation of strength of about 30 percent after 42 days in the climate chamber, some acrylates almost comply with the requirements of ETAG and are therefore suitable for outside use ____ Fig. 44. Embrittlement, the decrease in elongation at break and tensile strength over time, and the yellowing of the adhesive can be controlled in modern acrylate adhesive systems.

1–3 Sculpture „Big Blue" by Ron Arad in Canada Square,
Canary Wharf, London 1998, Eng.: Arup.
A disc of glass fibre reinforced plastic with a diameter
of approx. 14 m fully seated on a ring of curved glass
panels. The dead load of about 7 t and wind pressure
and wind suction forces are fully carried by the glazed
wall panels. The glazing provides overhead light to the
underground shopping mall below the square and acts
as a safety barrier. The panels consists of 2 x 15 mm
tempered glass (class ESG-H), the force of about 30
kN per connection is transferred by a balance beam
into bearing bolt connections in the glass plates.

4 The glass arch „Glasbogen 1" with a
span of 10 m, 1998, W. Sobek and M.
Kutterer, ILEK, Stuttgart University

4.3

THE USE OF GLASS PLATES AND BEAMS IN STRUCTURES

PLATES LOADED IN COMPRESSION

The brittleness of the material scarcely reduces the strength of plate elements under compression. Glass plates can be used as wall panels, struts and shell elements. Examples of projects in which load-bearing wall panels are designed to support the roof structure include the Sommerakademie in Rheinbach ——Figs 53–56, the "Temple de l'Amour" at Noyers in Burgundy ——Fig. 12 and "Big Blue", a sculpture by Ron Arad in Canary Wharf, London ——Figs 1–3. Struts are used in externally prestressed tie systems and in trusses ——Figs 5, 6. The special load-bearing capabilities of plates under in-plane compression are best demonstrated by self-supporting glass arches and shells ——Fig. 4.

The load-bearing and failure mechanisms of compression members depend above all on the support conditions. Point supports produce stress concentrations and transverse tensile stresses at the point of load transfer and hence lead to fracture before any stability failure can take place. The transverse tensile forces between the lines of compressive stress in rest of the plate surface are small and are not the determining factor in the analysis ——Fig. 15.

However, stability considerations are more important in the case of plates with linear forms of load transfer. Plates with unsupported edges in the direction of load transfer may buckle about the weak axis. Warning of plate buckling under increasing load is often preceded by a gradual increase in lateral movement of the plate cross section until

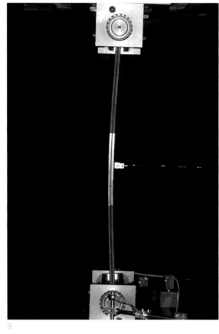

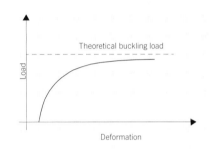

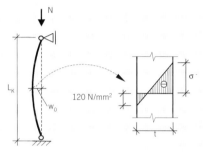

5, 6 Large pane format, truss-like glass structure externally
prestressed with *Rodan* tie rod system manufactured by
Dorma, glass roof Schloss Juval, 1998, Arch.: Robert Danz

7, 9 Buckling test of laminated glass pane at EPFL
Lausanne by Andreas Luible: Both ends of the
glass member are held in the test apparatus by
articulating bearing heads so that the force is always
aligned with the longitudinal axis of the member;
left: Unloaded glass, right: Loaded, deformed glass.

8 Load-deformation graph of a glass loaded in
compression: As the theoretical buckling load
is approached the lateral deflection of the member
sharply increases.

10 The buckling deflection creates bending stresses:
Failure of the pane results when the effective
tensile bending strength is exceeded.

it results in an initial break in the middle third of the plate on the side subject to tensile bending stresses _____ Fig. 8. The value of the critical buckling load does not therefore depend on the compressive strength but rather on the tensile bending strength of the glass _____ Fig 10 Numerous other factors are involved, such as the geometric slenderness of the component, whether the edge supports are hinged or rigid, the presence of initial imperfections and deformations distributed throughout the glass thickness, the eccentricity of the load transfer and, in the case of laminated safety glass, the composite action effect. [4.3/1, 4.3/2]

It is important that compressive forces are introduced into the glass plate in an even and controlled manner under all conditions of loading and imposed deformation. In particular for stiff roof constructions it is essential that the imposed deformations are accommodated by bearings and articulated connections at the support points _____ Fig. 55. Compression forces can be transferred by contact, bolted or friction grip connections.

SHEAR PLATES

Glass has been used as a stiffening element in glasshouses since the 19th century. The panes were supported in a bed of putty, which not only braced the whole structure, it also stabilised the wrought-iron ribs, which were prone to buckling, with the result that there was no need for diagonal struts or rigid corner connections _____ Fig. 11.

The following description by John Claudius Loudon, the great pioneer of glass construction, provides an impressive account of the glasshouse built at Bretton in 1827: *"No rafters or principal ribs were used in addition to the wrought-iron glazing profiles to stiffen the roof. This caused some concern, as at the moment when the iron structure had been erected but not yet glazed the slightest wind put the whole thing in motion. But as soon as the glass had been put in place, one could see that the structure completely stopped moving and became quite firm."* [4.3/3]

Today the shear stiffness of a glass plate and its potential to stiffen steel and timber frame buildings, is mainly exploited in small-scale and

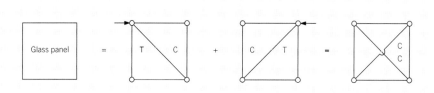

11   Kibble Palace, Glasgow, built around 1870: The glass
panes supported in a bed of putty stabilise the
domed surface.

12   "Temple de l'Amour" at Noyers in Burgundy: Wall
plates made from laminated heat treated glass support
the roof and stiffen the structure against wind forces.

13   The theoretical structural model of a glass
plate idealised as a pin-jointed frame with edge
tensile members and crossing diagonals.

14   Methods of providing shear-resistant support to
a glass panel:
    A Without a frame, with diagonally opposed blocks
    B With continuous perimeter frame and diagonally
      opposed blocks
    C With continuous perimeter frame structurally
      bonded to the edges

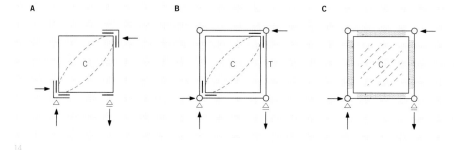

often experimental structures such as in the pavilion "Temple de l'Amour" ___ Fig. 12. Here the wall panels provide longitudinal and lateral stiffening in addition to bearing the roof loads. The suitability of flat glass as a structural shear plate is demonstrated by recent experience in the automotive industry, where fixed glazing is used to stiffen vehicle body shells. [**4.3/4, 4.3/5**]

In accordance with the current state of technology, glass shear panels could be used extensively to replace rod-shaped diagonal members within lattice structures such as trusses and grillages and thus reduce the apparent number of components ___ Figs 17, 18, 20, 21.

The structural behaviour of a shear plate under horizontal loads, e.g. wind forces can be explained in a simplified model as tensile forces along the edges between nodes with complementary diagonal compressive forces. If the panel is embedded in a structural framework, the profiles along the edges will take these tensile forces ___ Figs 13, 14.

The shear forces can be conducted to the panel edges by diagonal arrangement of setting blocks, bolted or friction grip connections in the corner areas or by structurally bonded connections. A linear transfer of shear forces can also be achieved by interlocking the parts of a connector with the help of corrugated profiles or knurling of the edge fittings and the glass edge, and by filling the cavity in between with an injection mortar.

Contact blocks on both sides of a corner can transfer a diagonal compressive force into the glass plate in two components. By truncating the corner, the force then acts at right angles to the glass edge surface, which gives rise to lower surface stresses and transverse tensile stresses ___ Figs 15, 16, 19. [**4.3/6**]

Point supports may lead to failure due to the local effective tensile bending stress being exceeded near the fittings. Shear and compression stresses in the centre of the panel can lead to buckling of plates that are also restrained along their sides.

With increasing load, the ratio of the side lengths becomes stead-

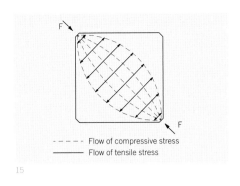

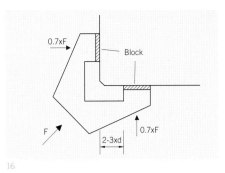

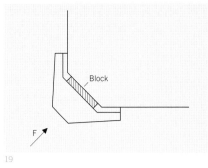

15

16

19

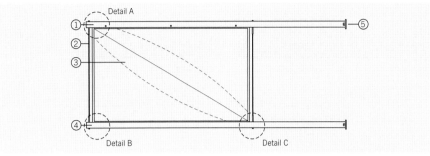

17

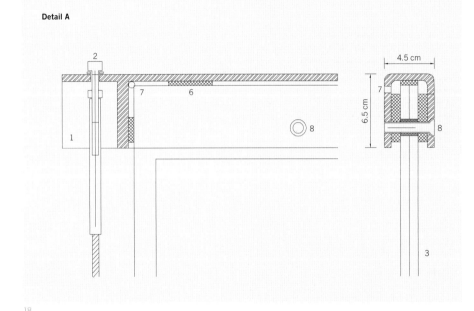

Detail A

18

15 Force flow with diagonally opposite blocks:
The transverse tensile stresses between
the lines of equal compressive stress are
quite small due to the efficient distribution
of the forces in the plane of the glass.

16, 19 Application of the diagonal compressive force by
division into two components (diagonally opposed
blocks) or by truncating the corner of the panel

17, 18, 20 Heat treated 1 m x 1.75 m laminated safety glass
panel with HOE elements for back projection,
Karman-Auditorium RWTH Aachen, concept and
design: C. Kielhorn, A. von Lucadou
1 Top chord stainless steel U-profile 65/45/6
2 Stainless steel cable 8 mm
3 Laminated safety glass consisting of 2 x 8 mm
heat-strengthened glass and HOE film
4 Bottom chord as item 1
5 Top chord plate / 2 M 16 high strength anchor
6 Elastomeric bearing as an aid to installation
7 6 mm hole for injection of HILTI HY 50
8 M 8 bolt in plastic sleeve

After breakage occurs, the residual load-bearing
capacity is ensured by the stiffness of the steel
chords. The tensioned rope and interlock (bolts)
prevent the pane from slipping out of the frame.

ily more important to buckling. After the theoretical buckling stress
has been exceeded or the supercritical load situation is reached, initial
fracture occurs on the edge which in turn produces an almost explo-
sive breakage of the glass on the tensile bending side —— Fig. 34. [**4.3/7**]

To ensure the support is as restraint-free as possible, all sources of
imposed forces or strains, such as temperature deformations, shrinkage or swelling effects must be considered and accommodated. Non-
linear analysis of the important principal tensile stresses using an FEM
model must also take into account the type and size of initial panel
deformations, deformations of the construction and the shear stiffness
of the viscoelastic interlayer of laminated safety glass.

Adhesive connections in glass with linearly bonded edges can resist the effects of imposed forces and strains. Permanent loads should
be avoided due to the creep behaviour of viscoelastic and elastic adhesives. Flexibly bonded joints will fail at a load below the theoretical
buckling load.

Compressive shear stiffness and the geometry of the structurally
bonded joint must be optimised for each specific application. Stiff
PUR systems have a proven record of success in automobile body-
shell glazing.

21 Steel-glass composite system: Glass fins between the
vertical chords stabilise the facade posts, New Museum
Nuremberg, 2000, Arch.: V. Staab, Eng.: Verroplan

22 Modular construction system of the full-glass pavilion:
The load-bearing structure is formed by columns, beams
and stiffening walls and roof panels, all made from
glass. Concept and design: U. Knaack and W. Führer,
Lehrstuhl für Tragkonstruktionen RWTH Aachen, 1996

COLUMNS, GLASS FINS AND BEAMS

____COLUMNS

Brunet & Saunier developed a glass column, which was used for the
first time for the internal courtyard of the St. Germain-en-Laye mu-
nicipal building. The column has a cruciform, buckling-resistant cross
section made up of several slender plates (see also Section 4.1
____Fig. 8). On the other hand their slenderness and associated risk of
buckling mean that one-piece, strip-form glass columns have only a
limited load-bearing capacity ____Fig. 22. Their load-bearing behaviour
is similar to slender compression members (see Section 4.3.8).

____GLASS FINS

Vertical glass fins have been used from around 1950 to stabilise shop
windows. In facades, glass fins only act as stiffeners and carry wind
positive pressure and suction forces, with the effect that laminated
glass does not have to be used for storey-high glazing. Fins are normally suspended and any movements in the primary structure are accommodated at the bottom support to the fin. For multi-storey facade
construction, multipart glass fins connected to one another by friction
grip can also be used.

Multi-flanged posts or beams can have long glass web bracing
members fitted between their flanges. The bracing members behave
as shear plates, with buckling loads dependent on their slenderness.
This type of steel-glass composite system was installed in the New
Museum in Nuremberg for some 16 metres long facade posts ____Fig. 21.
[**4.3/9**]

____BEAMS

Since the end of the 1980s short- and medium-span glass beams
have been increasingly used in roof structures.

In comparison with glass fins, glass beams used in glass floors or roofs
subject to unrestricted foot traffic (see. Section 4.2) generally have to

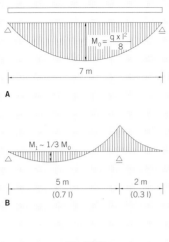

$$M_0 = \frac{q \times l^2}{8}$$

7 m

A

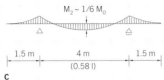

$M_1 \sim 1/3\ M_0$

5 m (0.7 l) 2 m (0.3 l)

B

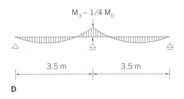

$M_2 \sim 1/6\ M_0$

1.5 m 4 m (0.58 l) 1.5 m

C

$M_3 \sim 1/4\ M_0$

3.5 m 3.5 m

D

$M_4' = 4 \times M_0$

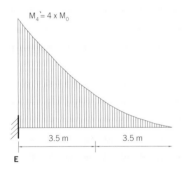

3.5 m 3.5 m

E

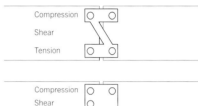

Compression
Shear
Tension

Compression
Shear
Tension

23 Comparison of various support conditions for beams:
   A Single-span, simply supported beam, span
      7 m, max. bending moment Mo = q*l²/8
   B A cantilever projection reduces the span,
      which means the support and span bending
      moments are only about 1/3 M₀.
   C A cantilever projection on both sides reduces support
      and span bending moments to about 1/6 M₀.
   D A two-span continuous beam has a maximum
      support bending moment of 1/4 M₀.
   E A cantilever beam with a 7 metre span has a support
      bending moment four times greater than M₀.

24 Buckling test of a slender glass beam at EPFL Lausanne

25 Principles of transfer of forces at a longitudinal splice
    joint in a beam: Bending moments are transferred
    by tensile and compressive forces in the splice
    plates and bolt pairs at the bottom and top edges of
    the beam. To transfer shear in addition to bending
    stresses, the splices must either be connected to
    one another or must have an additional bolt.

carry higher live loads as well as medium- and long-term loads. The span of individual beams is limited by the available manufactured sizes of glass to between 6 and 7.50 metres.

Glass beams are loaded in bending about their strong axis. Bending stresses in a beam depend on the span and the type of support. The moment of inertia increasing with the width and above all with the height of the cross section resists the bending moment. The bending moment generally creates linearly distributed tensile and compressive bending stresses across the section. [**4.3/10**]

Depending on the types, numbers and arrangements of supports, the beam may act as a cantilever, a simply supported single span with cantilever extensions, or as a continuous beam and therefore influence the shape of the bending moment diagram ___Fig. 23.

The bearing capacity of a beam is limited by local and lateral torsional buckling as well as tensile bending stresses. The low torsional stiffness of the slender cross section makes it prone to undergo lateral

deformation whilst twisting ___Fig. 24. Buckling occurs when the tensile bending stress on the glass surface exceeds the effective tensile strength of the glass. The design of slender glass beams prone to buckling must consider reduction factors which take into account slenderness, actual glass build-up, shear stiffness of the PVB interlayer, type of loading, effective tensile bending strength and the presence of any inherent deformations.

In the case of non-slender beams, the design strength is usually determined by stress concentrations at the load transfer points and the edge strength in the tensile bending stress zone. [**4.3/11 – 13**]

A fork support, often in the form of a shoe fabricated from flat plate, offers a simple way of providing an articulating bearing for the beam. In-plane shear forces are transferred by edge contact pressure, stabilization against buckling is provided by the elastic restraint of the beam ends and, where present, a structurally bonded shoe connection [**4.3/14**]

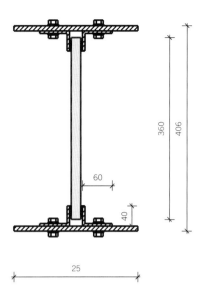

26

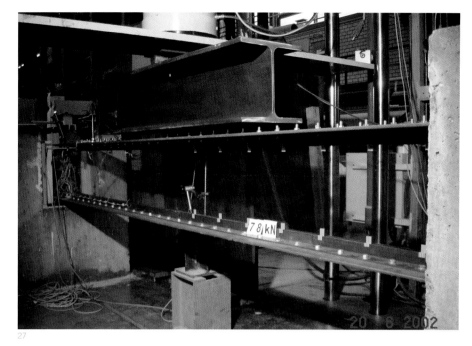

27

26, 27 Prototype of a fabricated steel-glass composite
beam: The flanges of the I section carry
tensile and compressive bending forces and
are joined to the glass web by angle sections
attached by a shear-stiff connection.

28 Glass pavilion RWTH-Aachen: From a structural
engineering viewpoint the columns and beams do
not form a frame. The column foot has a fixed joint.
The beams are pin-jointed to the column heads
thus exerting only vertical forces on the column.

28

Rigid corners and lapped or butt joints in beams should be positioned close to points of zero moment in order to keep the bending stresses on the joint as low as possible. Friction grip connections in glass beams that for reasons of residual load-bearing capacity have to be made of laminated safety glass are scarcely ever considered suitable, therefore moment connections are normally designed as bearing bolt connections (see the section entitled "Connections").

Each pair of bolts is subject to the compressive or tensile bending stresses along the top and bottom edges of the glass. If the connection must also transmit shear forces, then normally each pair of bolts has to be connected with a further bolt to prevent twisting of the fixings ____Fig. 25.

Currently experiments are being carried out with bonded lap joints transmitting the bending forces. The more elastic is the adhesive, the higher are the stresses on the bonded joint but the stresses on the glass are reduced. Frank Wellershoff of the Lehrstuhl für Stahlbau at RWTH Aachen developed a beam with an I-shaped cross section ____Figs 26, 27. The web member is glass; the flanges are steel. Therefore the steel transfers compressive and tensile forces and the glass is mainly required to take the shear forces. The connection is provided by L-shaped steel sections, which are structurally bonded to the glass surface with a high modulus PUR windscreen adhesive and bolted to the steel flange.

Experimental studies have been carried out with discontinuous glass segments at TU Delft as part of the ZAPPI research project. The glass elements were connected to one another by thin sheets of polycarbonate and a UV-curing acrylate adhesive in order to improve the residual load-bearing capacity of the beam ____Figs 31, 32. However, in none of these cases has the creep behaviour of the polymer adhesive been conclusively researched.

Glass type outer	Glass type inner	
ANN	HST or TEM	The load-bearing capacity of the annealed glass is critical to the design strength, therefore large cross sections; the residual load-bearing capacity with intact heat-strengthened or tempered glass is good.
HST	TEM	The load-bearing capacity of the heat-strengthened glass is critical to the design strength, the residual load-bearing capacity with intact tempered glass is good.
TEM	HST	The loadbearing capacity of the heat-strengthened glass inner pane(s) is critical to the design strength, the impact strength and residual load-bearing capacity with intact tempered glass are good.
TEM	TEM	Very good load-bearing capacity, at failure all panes break; other measures are necessary such as a high-tensile cable along the underside; good impact resistance due to tempered glass

29

31

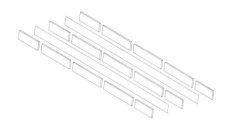

32

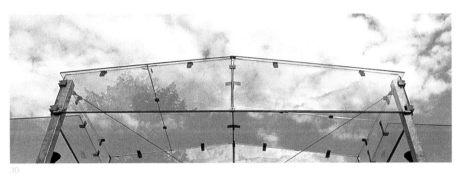

30

33

29 The initial and residual load-bearing capacity of glass beams depends on the combinations of glass types in the laminated safety glass composite.
ANN: Annealed glass
TEM: Tempered glass
HST: Heat strengthened glass

30, 33 The steel flat along the bottom edge of the glass beam carries the tensile bending forces and ensures adequate residual load-bearing capacity is provided, stairwell roof of University guest house, RWTH Aachen, 2002, Arch.: Feinhals, Eng.: Führer Kosch Jürges

31, 32 ZAPPI research project at TU Delft: Laminated beams were built with staggered butt joints and bonded polycarbonate plastic films to improve residual load-bearing capacity.

RESIDUAL LOAD-BEARING CAPACITY OF GLASS

The residual load-bearing capacity of glass plates and beams depends on the failure scenario, the build-up of the laminate and its support conditions. In the event of breakage the stability both of the individual broken element and of the whole structure has to be secured. [4.3/15]

The design must ensure that all the leaves in a laminated glass member cannot break at the same time. If all the glass layers in a laminated safety glass are broken then the residual load-bearing capacity has to rely solely on the thickness and tear resistance of the interlayer. There is the danger of the PVB film tearing along the edges under tensile stress and the glass element then splitting in two.

A stability failure by local or plate buckling must be prevented, because if all leaves fail simultaneously in a supercritical area as due to impact failure, the fracture pattern is very fine-grained, even with heat strengthened glass, and the component has little or no residual load-bearing capacity ____ Figs 34, 36.

When individual leaves break as a result of imposed strains or impact, the stresses on the remaining intact leaves increase substantially. To prevent a progressive fracture, the load-bearing capacity of the damaged element must be at least as large as at the time of the initial fracture. Hence the arrangement, dimensioning and quality of the glass layers within a laminated safety glass plate or beam are of fundamental importance.

For an increased residual load-bearing capacity, at least one of the leaves in the laminated glass panel should be made of glass that breaks into large pieces. As the stresses are too high for annealed glass, this is normally provided as heat-strengthened glass. To achieve a desired symmetrical build-up, a triple laminated safety glass is used which has both outer leaves of heat-strengthened glass with a middle leaf of tempered glass. This arrangement ensures adequate residual load-bearing capacity after breakage of the outer panes ____ Figs 29, 37.

[4.3/16]

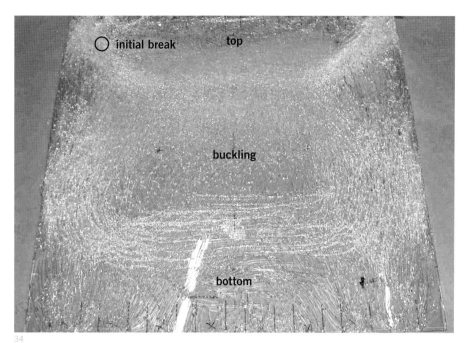

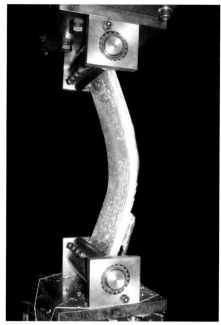

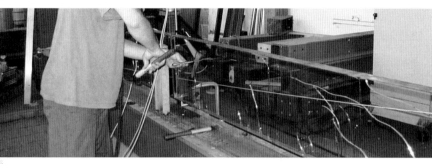

34, 36 Plate load-bearing elements exhibit a fine-grained fracture pattern even with the use of laminated safety glass made from heat-strengthened glass, with the result that they have almost no residual load-bearing capacity; left: Shear plate after plate buckling failure; right: Compression member after buckling failure.

35 Residual load-bearing capacity test of a glass beam made from heat-strengthened glass: Under load the composite glass beam is gradually taken to failure and the stresses and deformations measured.

37 A glass beam made from three-pane laminated safety glass exhibits good residual load-bearing capacity if each pane is designed to carry the full design load.

To prevent all layers of a triple pane laminated safety glass panel from breaking as a result of a hard impact on the edges, the inner load-bearing leaf can be recessed.

The residual load-bearing capacity of a beam can be improved by reinforcing the tensile zone, for example by inserting a steel cable in the edge recess of a triple laminated safety glass or by placing a steel flat along the underside of the beam (Figs 30, 33).

CONNECTIONS

CONTACT CONNECTIONS

Contact connections transfer the compressive forces by edge pressure into the plane of the plate. Especially with arch and shell constructions, the size of the compressive surface stress can exceed the tensile bending strength of the glass by up to ten times __ Figs 40, 42. Point or linear block supports to the panel edges create a force connection through intermediate load transfer layers. An increase in the block length minimises stresses in the area of the supports but places higher demands on the evenness of the supporting substructure and on ensuring the edges of the panel run parallel. Contact blocks must be kept a distance of between two and three times the glass thickness from glass corners, which are frequently prone to damage __ Fig. 16. Compromised planarity of the contact surfaces must be avoided as they lead to twisting and slipping of the fixings.

As with all mechanical connections, the properties of the layers between the glass and the fixing elements are extremely important. Linear connections are best constructed with materials that can be cut or punched out of sheet material. Among these are elastomers with a Shore-hardness of at least D 80, hard-elastic fibre gaskets from the field of plant engineering (such as *Klingersil*, __ Fig. 38) and strips of pure aluminium.

Machined or moulded parts of a hard-elastic plastic such as *polyoxymethylene* (POM) and hybrid injection mortars are suitable as load

	Material	Compressive strength [N/mm²]	Stability	Standard thickness [mm]
Klingersil C-4430	Synthetic fibres, bonded with NBR	39 [16h/175°C] (DIN 52913)	8% (thickness reduction at 23°C und 50 N/mm²)	0.5/1/1.5/2/3
Klingersil C-4500	Carbon fibre with special highly temperature-resistant additives	35 [16h/175°C] (DIN 52913)	10% (thickness reduction at 23°C und 50 N/mm²)	0.5/1/1.5/2/3
Hilti HIT	Hybrid mortar	10 [recommended]		max. 4

38

39

40

41

43

42

38 Technical data for block materials and fibre gaskets

39, 41, 43 Contact block supports using *Hilti-HIT HY 50:*
39 Example of Tetra glass arch (see Section 7.3)
41 Filling with injection mortar using a mould
43 After curing of the mortar and removal of the mould the inlet and vent openings are still visible.

40 Contact edge connection of a folded vault structure, Lehrstuhl für Tragkonstruktionen RWTH Aachen,1997

42 Contact connection: A block length of approximately 500 mm can support a load of up to 7 kN.
"Glasbogen 2", ILEK Stuttgart University

transfer block supports for laminated safety glass in particular. By changing the proportion of organic and inorganic materials the compressive strength and the elasticity of the mortar can be adjusted. The injection mortar *Hilti HIT-HY 50* has been sucessfully used in glass construction over the last decade. The layer thickness of the materials, in the cured condition after injection, can be up to 4 millimetres. Manufacturing tolerances, for example on edge misalignment in laminated safety glass and assembly tolerances, can be compensated for in this way. [4.3/17]

The application of the mortar in a semifluid state requires the fittings to be specially designed. The chamber-like void between the fixing element and the edge of the glass must be sealed on all sides. Inlet openings for the mixing nozzle of the dispenser device of about 6 mm and venting openings of about 3 millimetres must be provided ____Figs 39, 41, 43.

____FRICTION GRIP AND CLAMP CONNECTIONS

Friction grip connections have a proven record in structural steelwork for transferring large forces, in glass structures they have been in use since about 1960. It is a pure force connection, normally involving double-shear: two spice plates are pressed against an intermediate glass plate by a prestressed bolt connection so that high adhesion forces are created at the contact surfaces ____Fig. 44. For loads in-plane of the glass the friction forces resist the shear forces between the components of the joint. The magnitude of the normal, shear and bending stresses that a friction grip connection can carry depends directly on the contact pressure and the friction coefficients of the surfaces. By the use of special friction layers very high forces can be transferred into the glass surface; friction grip connections normally have a greater load capacity than bearing bolt connections. Bolt groups and multiple bolt connections are typical for friction grip connections ____Figs 45–48. The most effective way to transfer compressive

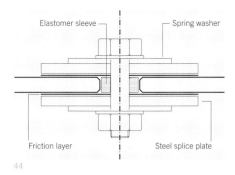

Elastomer sleeve ⎯⎯ ⎯⎯ Spring washer

Friction layer ⎯⎯ ⎯⎯ Steel splice plate

44

45

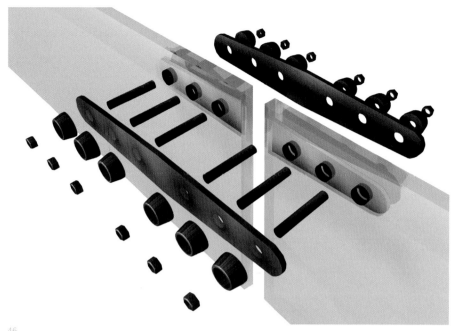

46

44–48 Friction grip connection:
   44 The forces are transferred by friction
      in the plane of the glass.
   45 External lapped butt joint at the Educatorium
      Utrecht: The arrangement of bolts is
      typical for friction grip connections.
   46 Model of a friction grip connection in laminated
      safety glass: In the area of force transfer the tough-
      elastic interlayer must be replaced with stiff inserts.
   47 Internal splice plate design of a friction
      grip connection, Sony Center Berlin
   48 Friction grip connection with more
      than one individual splice plate

47

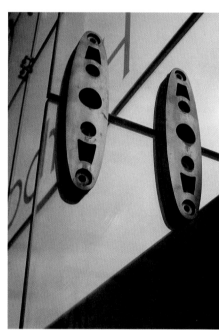

48

and tensile bending stresses in multipart beams is to locate the fittings close to the edges. As the forces are not transferred by bearing bolts, tolerances are simply accommodated by adopting oversized holes. In contrast to bearing bolt connections there are no deformations in the hole area and therefore no stress concentrations if very stiff clamping plates are used. The geometric shape of the splice plates can control stress concentrations on the edge of the fitting ⎯⎯Fig. 48.

The contact surfaces must be finely machined and flat. Surface undulations in machined steelwork, above all in the area of the bolt holes, must be prevented, otherwise the very high contact forces which are generated in friction grip connections could lead to stress concentrations on the glass surface and to fracture.

Friction grip connections are normally used only with monolithic heat-treated glass. In normal circumstances friction grip connections cannot be used with laminated safety glass because of the creep be-haviour of PVB, cast-in-place resin or even SGP unless they are lo-cally replaced in the areas of load transfer by inserts of a stiffer mate-rial such as aluminium sheet – a condition which is technically very challenging ⎯⎯Fig. 46.

⎯⎯BOLTED AND BEARING BOLT CONNECTIONS

In a bearing bolt connection a shear-resistant steel pin in a precise locating hole transfers a concentrated force into the connected plate by means of a mechanical interlock with the hole in bearing. The bear-ing force is then distributed at an angle of approximately 120° in the plane of the plate ⎯⎯Fig. 49. Bolted connections are widely-used in structural timber and steelwork but their application in structural glass presents specific challenges because of the lack of plastic behaviour of glass. The use of heat-treated glass is necessary because stress concentrations occur in the hole, which are about three times greater than those occurring in a ductile material like steel ⎯⎯Fig. 51.

In recent decades extensive research has been undertaken on the

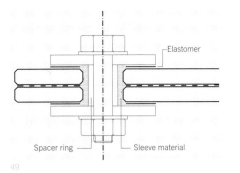

Elastomer

Spacer ring — — Sleeve material

49

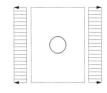

51

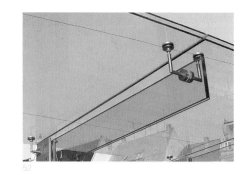

52

49–52 Bearing bolt connections:
   49 The loads are transferred into the plane
      of the glass by contact between suitable
      interlayers and bolt bearing surfaces.
   50 Bearing bolt connection Sony Center Berlin
   51 Stress concentrations in the drilled hole
      in a bearing bolt connection
   52 Bearing bolt connections in a cantilever
      beam, bus-stop shelter, Anger in Erfurt

50

influences hole geometry, edge quality, properties of the sleeve materials and bushes and support types have on bolted connections.

The ultimate breaking stress depends on the number and diameter of the bolts, forces of up to about 30 kN and more per bolt can be transmitted. To prevent restraint forces, the number of bolts should be reduced in favour of larger bolt diameters. The use of single shear connections, which consist of a single splice plate, should be avoided, due to load eccentricities.

Fine ground circular holes with a 45° chamfer on both sides are generally used for bolted connections (see Section 3.3 ___ Figs 11–13). The quality of the edge treatment of the hole is critical for good load transfer capacity. It should be smooth and free of scores. The edge misalignment of two parts of an aligned bolt hole should be as small as possible as polishing out an off-set is not feasible from an economic point of view. A uniform application of stress can only be ensured if the hole diameter is at least the thickness of the plate.

Prefabricated plastic sleeves placed on the sides of the bearing bolt adjust themselves under load to the surface of the connected piece. Stiff sleeve materials such as nylon or aluminium have small load distribution areas and therefore lower fracture loads than those of softer POM (polyoxymethylene) sleeves. Sleeve inserts are simple to install but allow for small tolerances only. Inaccuracies in the diameter and position of the holes of ±2 millimetres must be compensated for by slotted holes in the fittings or by the use of precisely drilled POM discs or aluminium double eccentric rings. Cast sleeves of epoxy resin, polyester or PUR with proven compatibility with PVB must be used for heat-treated laminated safety glass panels, which may have edge misalignments of up to 3 millimetres.

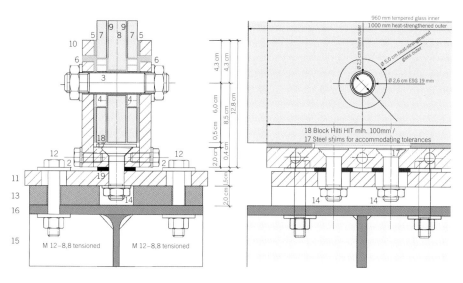

54

55

56

53

53 Bearing bolt connection at the base of a load-bearing
wall panel in the system used at the Sommerakademie
Rheinbach and the Glass Pavilion Düsseldorf
1 M 20 bolt
2 M 10 bolt
3 Aluminium sleeve
4 Eccentric ring, aluminium
5 Klingersil C-4500
6 Bedding mortar Hilti-HIT HY 50
7–9 Laminated safety glass made from 10 mm heat-
strengthened glass and 19 mm toughened glass
10 Steel shoe
11 Steel support bracket
12 M 12 bolt (8.8, tensioned)
13 Spacer plate d = 20 mm
14 2 No. M 16 bolts
15 Steel web stiffener
16 HEA 180
17 Steel shims for accommodating tolerances
18 Hilti-HIT HY-50, in the area of the blocks

54 Here the glass roof is fully supported by the glass load-
bearing wall plates. Sommerakademie Rheinbach, 2000,
Arch.: Marquardt and Hieber, Eng.: Ludwig and Weiler

55 An articulating connection shoe between roof
and wall plate provides restrain-free support

56 Eccentric ring for the wall plate connection

ADHESIVE CONNECTIONS

There are two types of structurally bonded connections: *hybrid adhesive connections*, in which point or linear metal fittings are bonded to the glass surface or edge during manufacture and *all glass adhesive connections*, in which adjoining glass surfaces or edges are bonded directly with one another. Viscoelastic adhesives with enhanced silicones, PUR, acrylates or high performance adhesive tapes such as VHB from 3M are the main materials considered suitable for hybrid or mixed structurally bonded connections, which are increasingly important in the design of composite materials. Flexible adhesive connections are very suitable for the transfer of small, permanently acting shear, tensile or moment forces or for stiffening or stabilising structural elements ____ Figs 57, 59.

In glass construction there is still only limited experience with the transfer of permanent loads by high-strength, stiff adhesive connections, mainly because their creep behaviour is not yet adequately understood. Stress concentrations at the edges of the adhesive must also be considered with shear connections and hard adhesives. Acrylates and hot glues come into consideration particularly for structurally bonded butt joints in an all glass assembly (*end-bonded joints*) of folded plate structures where only small compressive, tensile and shear forces are transferred through the joint.

Structurally bonded connections are usually designed to act as an overlapping shear connection to transfer large forces in-plane of the glass. Using a lap or a face joint connection increases the effective bonding area, which in turn allows the connection to transfer more force and/or the use of a more elastic adhesive. Single face connections are used for transmitting small forces. For larger forces, four workpiece surfaces form a two-face bonded connection ____ Fig. 60. New studies show that a three-face bonded connection does not necessarily lead to better load transfer performance. [4.3/18]

Out-of-plane forces can be transferred into the glass by bonded-

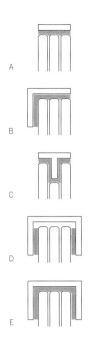

57

59

60

58

57 Adhesive bonding of an aluminium edge
fixing with silicone, Prof. B. Weller, Thomas
Schadow, Dresden University

58 The „Glass Cube" at glasstec 2002, J.
Knippers, S. Peters, Stuttgart University

59 Linear adhesive connection with 2-part epoxy
resin applied with pneumatic mixing gun

60 Cross section of a linear adhesive connection
A   One-faced adhesive connection (end face application)
B   Two-faced adhesive connection (L-shaped application)
C   Mortise and tenon adhesive connection
D   Parallel two-faced adhesive connection
E   Three-faced adhesive connection
(U-shaped application)

on patch fittings with the adhesive connections loaded in tension.
These arrangements should be designed to avoid peeling and splitting
load effects, such as those that pull joint components off the glass
surface or open out an adhesive connection, so that connections do
not tear as a result of stress peaks on the edges of the adhesive (see
Section 4.1 ____Fig. 29).

Glass can make a considerable contribution to stiffening a structure, particularly when positioned in the compressive stress zone of a
composite section, as documented by the *Glass Cube* presented by
the *Institut für Tragkonstruktionen und Konstruktives Entwerfen* (Institute for Structural Systems and Structural Design) from Stuttgart University at the glasstec 2002. The exhibition pavilion had a roof of large
glass plates stabilised by glass fibre reinforced plastic (GFRP) ribs attached to the glass by structural silicone ____Fig. 58.

5

FUNCTIONAL
REQUIREMENTS

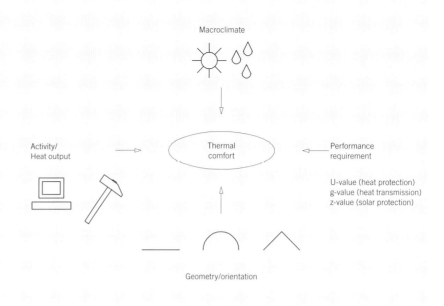

Thermal

Comfort

Acoustic   Visual

1

Macroclimate

Activity/   →   Thermal   ←   Performance
Heat output   comfort   requirement

U-value (heat protection)
g-value (heat transmission)
z-value (solar protection)

Geometry/orientation

2

1   Thermal, acoustic and visual aspects
    influencing the feeling of comfort.

2   Factors involved in the thermal comfort of a glass hall

3   The glass roof provides weather protection
    whilst providing daylight to the interior.

4   Dirt deposits on an almost flat glass roof

3   4

5.1 OVERVIEW

"... and this is a Benefit which you owe the Continuance of, not to the Wall, nor to Area, nor any of these; but principally to the outward Shell of the Roof; ..."

Leon Battista Alberti [5.1/1]

The glass roof provides protection from the weather to large and deep usable floor areas whilst supplying them with natural light ____Fig. 3. The hidden risks associated with glass architecture can be avoided only by careful planning and consideration of climatic conditions and user requirements. Different functional requirements apply for thermal, visual and acoustic comfort, which may vary according to the building brief ____Fig. 1. The main needs for protection from overheating in the summer, heat losses in the winter, glare and acoustic discomfort from hall effects must be taken into account early in the planning process. This also applies to the cleaning of roof surfaces ____Fig. 4. [5.1/2, 5.1/3]

Comfort needs should be met by an appropriate building management technology which also respects the needs of our environment. Building with glass can potentially allow the main protective functions to be combined with saving and generating of energy, whilst maintaining a reasonably even energy balance throughout the year. [5.1/4]

Level of demand	D [%]	E_N [lux]	AF [%]
Low	2	100	4
Medium	4	200	8
High	10	500	20
Very high	15	750	30

Natural light	Nominal illuminance [lux]
Overcast winter's afternoon	3000
Cloudy winter's day	5000
Cloudless winter's day	10000
Slightly cloudy summer's day	20000
Cloudless summer's day	100000
Twilight	<5000

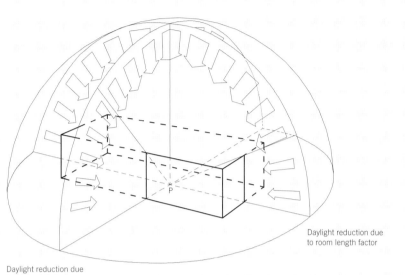

Daylight reduction due to room length factor

Daylight reduction due to room width factor

5 Double-skin, sculpturally projecting skylights accentuate the interior space, academic bookshop in Helsinki, 1969, Arch.: A. Aalto

6 Double-skin luminous ceiling for even illumination of the interior, Saxony regional library, Dresden, 2002 Arch.: Ortner + Ortner Baukunst

7 Total area of light openings AF, recommended average daylight factor D and desirable illuminance E_N, depending on light demand

8 The daylight factor D measured at point P inside the building depends on the proportions of the enclosing walls.

9 Levels of daylight and illuminance E_A inside buildings

___WEATHER PROTECTION

An adequate slope or curvature of roof surfaces is essential to ensure controlled and free drainage of precipitation water. A minimum slope of about 3 percent allows rainfall to effectively drain off a roof. At slopes of less than 2 percent glazing rebates do not dry out completely and moisture may attack the edge seal of the insulating glass unit. Normally roof slopes of less than 10 percent (about 6 degrees) should be avoided otherwise algae may grow on the beads of sealant and the glass will lose its self-cleaning effect. For safety reasons, equipment for clearing lying snow should be specified for flat roofs in areas of heavy snowfall.

___NATURAL LIGHT

The primary function of a glass roof is to supply deep spaces with natural light. The view of the open sky, the changing moods of light created from direct and diffused natural light, the superimposition of different weather conditions such as mist, fog or rain stimulate our perceptive senses, promote motivation to work and improve productivity. [5.1/5]

Skylights are particularly beneficial as the (cloudy) sky at its zenith is three times brighter at any time of year than the areas of sky near the horizon. Brightness is measured as *illuminance* $E = F/A$, which is the result of a *luminous flux* F [lumen] falling on a surface area A. The unit of measurement of illuminance is lumen per m² [lm/m²] or lux [lx]. Natural light has an illuminance which depends on the position of the sun and cloud conditions and therefore on the geographical latitude of the building, the season, time of day and the weather ___Fig. 9.

For a given external illuminance, the illumination of a top lit space depends mainly on its proportions: The more slender the space, the less direct light reaches the floor. The so-called *daylight factor* D comprises the fraction of the external illuminance that falls on a point on the interior usable floor area ___Fig. 8. In general D is calculated for

External		rigid / adjustable	reflective	Large metal louvres
			semi-transparent	Glass louvres
			absorbent	Glass louvres with PV

Integrated		rigid / adjustable	reflective	Microlouvres in glazing cavity Solar control coating
			semi-transparent	Screen print Prismatic glass
			absorbent	PV modules

| Internal | | rigid / adjustable | reflective | Microlouvres
Slatted blinds |
| | | | absorbent | Metal fabric
Screening fabrics |

10

10   Overview of solar control measures for glass roofs

11   Relative energy gain of PV modules for
     various orientations and slopes of roofs

Angle	0°	30°	60°	90°
Orientation				
East	93%	90%	78%	<60%
South-east	93%	96%	88%	66%
South	93%	100%	91%	68%
South-west	93%	93%	88%	66%
West	93%	93%	78%	<60%

11

areas of interest inside the building. D is mainly determined by the geometry of the room and the size of the openings, by the reflectance of the walls and furnishings and by the transparency of the glazing material. It is detrimentally affected by shade from any nearby buildings or trees. A dirty glass roof may mean that artificial light is required during the day.

The required daylight factor depends on the use of the area. Activities that have high demands for natural light, such as reading or office work may require over 750 lux, which corresponds to a D of about 15 percent ___Fig. 7. The strong shadows cast by direct light can provide better stereoscopic visual acuity. High quality working space must be illuminated as homogenously as possible with diffused and indirect light with a low contrast ratio ___Fig. 6, provided, for example, by north-oriented roof surfaces and shed-type roof structures. [5.1/6, 5.1/7]

___ENERGY GENERATION

Solar gain is directly linked to the transmission of natural light and hence there is often conflict between the desire for energy generation and the measures to obtain effective shading of solar radiation in order to prevent overheating of the building interior (see Section 3.1). An ideal solution is to make the detrimental proportion of solar radiation useful in terms of energy generation.

Active systems of solar energy have additional technical components and devices for the extraction, transport and storage of energy, such as ventilation units with heat recovery, solar collectors or photovoltaic modules (PV). In summer the steep angle of incident light falling on horizontal roofs ensures that these surfaces receive almost twice as much solar radiation as south-oriented facades, whilst in the winter months the effect is reversed. In central Europe a roof which faces approximately 30 degrees south enjoys optimum total average daily and annual solar radiation. Flat or inclined roof surfaces offer

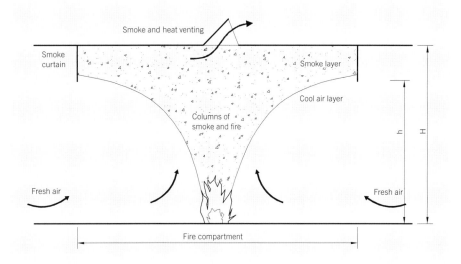

12 Fire and smoke development in a hall with a smoke
    and heat venting system: Funnel-shaped columns of
    smoke and fire rise from the fire source. The fumes
    are conducted to the outside through roof openings
    and inlets allow fresh air to flow into the building so
    that a smoke-filled layer and a cool air layer form
    under the roof and at floor level respectively.

13 Sensor-controlled ventilation openings at the rim of
    a shallow-sloped domed roof, National Botanical
    Garden of Wales, 1999, Arch.: Foster and Partners

scope for the integration of active systems such as PV ____ Fig. 11. [**5.1/8**]
Passive use of solar energy can be considered as the storage of solar
heat in the thermal mass of building components in order to use it for
heating living areas during the transition months and heating season.

____ SOLAR SHADING AND ANTI-GLARE MEASURES
Glass roofs require effective precautions against overheating to be in
place all year round.

Solar control and anti-glare measures and blinds can be differentiated into external, integral and internal systems. They may be rigid or
adjustable ____ Fig. 10. External shading devices are advantageous as
they keep the absorbed solar energy separate from the internal space.
An ideal solution is to have louvres that semi- or fully automatically
track the daily and annual path of the sun and can be adjusted to direct light in specific ways. External solar protection can also be combined with integrated measures such as solar control glazing. Exposed

to the weather, external shading devices are complex and require regular maintenance. [**5.1/9**]

Internal solar shading is significantly less effective. Heat may build
up between the internal solar control devices and the glazing, which
leads to increased surface temperatures and additional radiated heat
if there are no ventilation openings. Therefore internal shading should
only be used for inclined roofs facing east or west. However internal
devices such as roller blinds can perform as anti-glare and room
acoustic attenuating elements ____ Fig. 15. [**5.1/10**]

____ VENTILATION
Natural ventilation uses pressure differences caused by wind and temperature between the inside/outside or top/bottom of a building. *Thermal layering* and the accumulation of hot layers of air under the roof
surface play an important role in the dimensioning and positioning of
ventilation openings. Wind suction forces prevail over the full area of

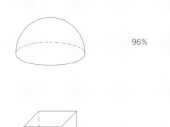

96%

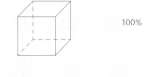

100%

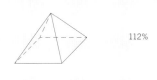

112%

14

15

16

14 Heat requirement of various roof shapes based on
their ratios of surface area to enclosed volume

15 Integration of textile blinds into the roof construction as
anti-glare and room acoustic improvement measures

16 Roof construction of the atrium: The path of sound is
blocked by the internal structure of steel main beams
and glass secondary beams. Stadtsparkasse Cologne,
2001, Arch.: Ingenhoven, Overdiek, Kahlen and Partners

free-standing roofs inclined at less than 25 degrees, which supports
natural extraction of hot air from the building. Large glazed spaces
should have air inlet and outlet openings with an area equal to at least
5 percent of floor area to ensure an adequate number of air changes
in summer. To prevent overheating air flows of at least 0.2 m/s may be
required, which room occupants may experience as draughts at air
temperatures of less than 20 °C. HVAC systems are described as *mechanical ventilation*.

Sensor-controlled roof vents with opening actuators can be designed as natural *smoke and heat venting systems* ___Fig.12. By extract-
ing the thermal load smoke vents extend the fire resistance period of
load-bearing components and play an integral role for fire-fighting and
securing escape routes. [**5.1/11, 5.1/12**]

___THERMAL INSULATION

Thermal insulation depends above all on the area and shape of the
building skin as even the best thermal insulating glazing cannot achieve
the U-values of conventional insulated components. If the ratio of surface area to enclosed volume (A/V ratio) is reduced, so are the thermal
losses ___Fig. 14.

___ACOUSTIC COMFORT

Airborne sound waves in the middle and upper frequency ranges are
strongly reflected at hard and planar glass surfaces, which may lead to
longer reverberation times inside the building. This effect is even more
pronounced with horizontal glass surfaces such as luminous ceilings
and mineral floor coverings, as the sound is thrown back- and for-
wards between the two (*flutter echo*). This hallway effect can easily be
detrimental to acoustic comfort.

19 The roof glazing integrates functions such as
thermal insulation, light deflection and power
generation. Inclined glazing on a house at the
IGA Stuttgart, 1993, Arch.: HHS Planer

20 Glazed roof surfaces over the reception and
office areas, Glasbau Seele Gersthofen, 1992,
Arch.: Kauffmann Theilig + Partner

17 Weather-protected traffic area, inclined roof
at Stuttgart Airport, 1997, Arch.: Arat Siegel
und Partner, Eng.: Ludwig und Weiler

18 Weather-protected platform, main station
Helsinki, 2001, Arch.: E. Piironen

MAINTENANCE AND CLEANING

Every roof surface must be accessible from inside and outside using suitable height access technology for cleaning, installation, maintenance, replacement or snow-clearing. Cleaning intervals may be between 3 and 12 months depending on location, climate and local conditions. There are different general types of access system: mobile, temporary, semi-fixed and fixed. The choice of the most suitable height access system depends on the cleaning interval and the size and use of the roof surface. [5.1/13]

Mobile equipment such as working platforms and scaffolding do not detrimentally affect the building's appearance, unlike fixed equipment such as gantries and maintenance bridges. Semi-fixed systems comprise permanently installed components such as rail-mounted cradles and demountable parts like working platforms. Cleaning robots with outputs of up to 200 m²/h can be used on large glass roofs. [5.1/14]

USER DEMAND PROFILES

Relative humidity and temperature of the air are the main influences on indoor climate. Comfort level depends on the activity being undertaken and the subjective perception of the user. There are three principal user demand profiles. If outdoor conditions prevail under the glass roof then this is called a *macroclimate*. In a *microclimate* the air temperature is adjusted to the activity of the user. A *meso-* or *intermediate climate* is a moderated outdoor climate zone with an extended comfort range —— Fig. 22.

THE WEATHER SKIN – THE MACROCLIMATE

In a freely ventilated glass hall serving only to provide users with short-term protection from the weather, the conditions will be largely governed by the outdoor macroclimate. Shelters over waiting and circulation areas such as railway station halls are typical examples of weather skins. If there are no enclosing facades, the requirements for weather

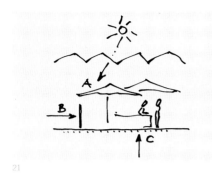

21

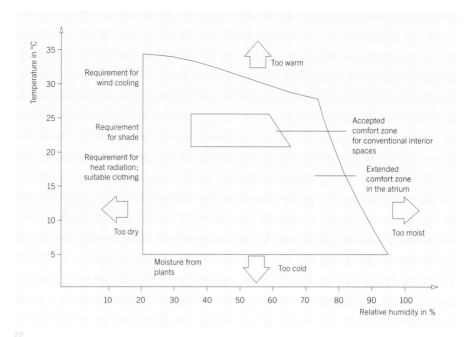

22

21 Sketch of "comfort islands" under a glass
    roof after Bauerschmidt and Hodulak
    A Shield against light
    B Shield against draughts
    C Cool air source in summer, underfloor
       heating in winter

22 Perception of comfort shown in relation to room
    temperature and relative humidity of the air after Olgyay

23 Summary of important room conditioning
    requirements for glass halls with macro,
    meso- or microclimates

	Macroclimate	Mesoclimate	Microclimate
Room temperature	Extreme fluctuations [from approx. -20°C bis +35°C]	Moderate fluctuations [from approx. -10°C bis +25°C]	Constant [depending on use]
Use	Short	Temporary	Prolonged
Circulation [+10°C to 14°C]	+/-	+	+
Assembly [+18°C]	-	+	+
Exhibition [+20°C]	-	+/-	+
PC work [+20°C]	-	-	+
Pool [up to +32°C]	-	-	+
Weather protection			
Rain protection	+	+	+
Wind protection	+/-	+	+
Sound insulation	+/-	+	+
Solar control	+/- (fixed)	+ (fixed/variable)	+ (variable)
Thermal insulation	-	+/-	+
Ventilation	Free	Natural	Natural / mechanical / artificial
Conditioning			
Temperature	-	-	+
Humidity	-	-	+/-

23

protection can be considered fulfilled if the width is at least twice the average clear height. Measures to provide shade can improve the attractiveness of these spaces during the summer period. [**5.1/15**]

____THE ACTIVE CLIMATE SKIN – THE MICROCLIMATE
A microclimate describes an artificial climate within a glazed space. With the conditioning of certain parameters (temperature, relative humidity, light levels etc.) a microclimate can allow these spaces to be used permanently despite changes in daily and seasonal outdoor climate. Microclimatised halls create "living space" for people, either as places to work or to enjoy free time and relaxation. This category also includes greenhouses and animal enclosures.

Comfort temperature is between 12 °C to 18 °C for spaces with a high level of physical activity such as sports or entrance halls. For passive and seated activities the figure is 19 °C to 20 °C. In indoor swimming or leisure pools temperatures up to 32 °C may be required. In addition to heating, other essential measures for controlling microclimate include thermal insulation and effective solar shading; air moisture content management places further demands on building technology. Light control and anti-glare measures are especially required for office spaces with workstations. [**5.1/16**]

Maintaining the microclimate in large glass-covered spaces irrespective of outdoor conditions is difficult. The climatisation of for example indoor leisure oases at 25 °C air temperature throughout the whole year is very expensive and in terms of building services technology and energy ecologically very questionable. [**5.1/17**]

____THE PASSIVE CLIMATE SKIN – THE MESOCLIMATE
Mike Davies compares the climate of large enclosed unheated glass halls with standing under a canopy of trees: "... *walking in the open across the valley to the forest one is buffeted by the chill wind and touch of rain. On entering the forest the rain stops, absorbed by the*

24 Micro- and mesoclimatic conditions under
double-skinned glass roof, thermal baths Bad
Elster, 1999, Arch.: Behnisch und Partner

*foliage canopy, the wind dies away becoming just a rustle in the tree
tops. One is 'Outside' but somehow more 'inside'. The forest is a sort of
outdoor enclosure – a world of his own – a mezzo-environment – mid
way between truly outside and truly inside."* [5.1/18] The pleasant atmosphere under a foliage canopy on a hot summer's day is due to the
major part of solar radiation being blocked by the canopy some 20 to
40 metres high and heat radiating from them being absorbed by the
layers of leaves lower down the trees. Even on days with very little
wind, the height of this "natural enclosure" creates thermal air movements to provide a cooling draught. In large covered spaces such as
arcades, railway station halls and roofed sports stadia similar effects
can be used to provide a pleasant atmosphere without artificial climatisation. This type of moderated intermediate climate tends to follow
the fluctuations in the outdoor temperature but attenuates the ex-
tremes.

The solar gain of unheated but well insulated halls at an air temperature of up to 14 °C allows them to be perfectly suitable for circulation
zones and places to sit or stand for more than a short while. In the
summer months natural air circulation, adjustable solar control and
active thermal storage masses can bring down the indoor temperature
several degrees below the outdoor temperature. People can stay for
even longer periods in comfort zones (e.g. with underfloor heating or
cooling) inside the mesoclimate, allowing different functions to over-
lap.

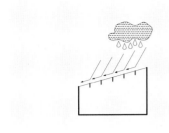

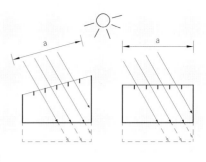

1　Inclined roofs allow rainwater to drain directly.

2　Roof glazing at the Mont-Cenis further education
　college has a six degree slope to drain rainwater,
　1998, Arch.: Jourda Architects with HHS Planer

3　Horizontal glass roofs are at risk of ponding water.

4　A flat roof will allow more natural light to reach the floor
　than an inclined roof of the same glazed area. Daylight
　factors reduce with the height of the enclosing surfaces.

5　Daylight conditions in an atrium under a low morning
　sun, glass-roofed internal courtyard Ateneum
　Helsinki, 2002, Arch.: Laiho, Pulkkinen, Raunio

5.2
SPECIFIC REQUIREMENTS FOR BUILDING SKIN GEOMETRIES

THE GLASS COURTYARD – THE FLAT OR INCLINED ROOF

These roofs have very little slope and therefore particular attention needs to be paid to measures for weather protection and solar control, winter maintenance (snow cover) and cleaning.

WEATHER PROTECTION

The deflection of horizontal glazing under its own weight makes it liable to collect standing water and ponding, which in turn can lead to dirt deposits, increased loads and wind-induced vibrations (Fig. 3). Clamping bars for supporting the panes should always be aligned in the direction of flow and have a minimum fall of 15 degrees; if there is additional internal drainage the minimum fall is 7.5 degrees. Glazing with very little fall should be made watertight with permanently elastic sealed joints.

ENERGY GENERATION

Large quantities of solar energy enter the interior of the building through horizontal glazing with the daylight, especially in the summer months ___ Fig. 4. Photovoltaic cells are able to combine the necessary solar control with active energy generation ___ Figs 8, 9. The solid parts of the building which normally surround the glass courtyard can be used in passive energy concepts to store the energy gained from solar radiation and release it during night time into the interior space.

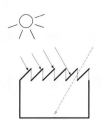

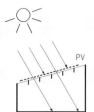

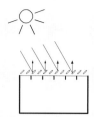

6   Inclined north-facing roofs can direct diffused
    and low energy light into the internal space.

7   Manufacturing floor illuminated by north-
    facing shed roofs, KWO factory, Berlin

8   South-facing inclined glazing with PV
    for active energy generation

9   External glass louvres with PV modules and HOE
    elements for shade and active energy gain, wintergarden
    house at the IGA Stuttgart, 1993, Arch.: HHS Planer

10   Large rigid or swivelling louvres are suitable for
     external solar control on horizontal glazing.

11   Shade provided by external glass louvres,
     Sparkasse Düsseldorf, 2001, Arch.: Ingenhoven,
     Overdiek, Kahlen and Partners

___ SOLAR SHADING AND ANTI-GLARE MEASURES

Offices facing glass courtyards also require anti-glare measures such as blinds. The choice of measures should be tailored to suit the alignment and orientation of the glazed areas. Most light enters flat glazed roofs during the middle of the day and early afternoon. Profiled external shutters are most effective, for example large louvre blades made from reflective metal ___ Figs 10, 11. Louvres made from semi-transparent materials like printed or coated glass louvres or screening fabrics may not cut out all the glare inside the room. Facade systems such as external roller or slatted blinds can also be used for the shading of steep roof slopes.

The advantages of both types of solar control can be combined in a double-skinned roof construction. The outer glass skin is usually constructed as fixed insulating glass with a high performance coating or ceramic frit. The inner skin can be constructed as movable monolithic glazing (e.g. as a louvred ceiling) or as a membrane with special light-transmission characteristics. The ventilated cavity acts as a buffer in winter, whilst in summer it can take away some of the excess solar gain ___ Figs 12, 13. [5.2/1]

___ ACOUSTIC COMFORT

With longer reverberation times, the sound is perceived to be louder and becomes more indistinct. When several communicating groups form at events with large public attendances in foyers or exhibition halls, the sound sources become superimposed upon one another to create a "cocktail party" effect. Therefore single-skinned glass roofs are hardly suitable for venues where demanding speech or music events are held. Double-skinned construction with an inner layer of microperforated textile panels can reduce reverberation times. [5.2/2, 5.2/3]

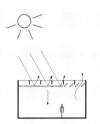

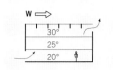

12

14

16

17

13

15

18

14 Air temperature increases with height under sloping roofs.

12 Large louvres or fabric blinds are used for internal solar control on low-slope roofs instead of slatted shutters.

13 Internal solar control blinds stretched below the glazed surface, Museum Meteorit Essen, 1998, Arch.: Propeller Z

15 Air inlets and outlets on the south facade of the Mont-Cenis further education college in Herne, in addition to the air outlets towards the top of the hall there are also ventilation spoilers attached to the central part of the roof, 1998, Arch.: Jourda Architects with HHS Planer

16 Properly designed and equipped horizontal glazing can support restricted foot traffic for maintenance work.

17 Installation of horizontal glazing

18 Access system for internal surface cleaning

MAINTENANCE AND CLEANING

The limited self-cleaning effect and heavy build-up of dirt on flat or low-sloped roofs lead to very short cleaning intervals and increased operating costs. Roofs with slopes greater than 20 degrees generally require precautions to stop or catch anyone falling. Roofs sloping at more than 45 degrees must generally be fitted with personnel safety systems.

THE GLASS BAND – THE CURVED OR FOLDED ROOF

Weather protection

With gabled and vaulted roofs the rainwater drains from the ridge or the apex to the eaves in a controlled manner. Prefabricated elements should be considered in order to ensure a watertight seal at the ridge. For suspended roofs the water from a heavy downpour may be drained over a longitudinal edge, thus preventing ponding. In areas of heavy snowfall the glazing bars and pressure plates should be parallel to the eaves so that snow slips are prevented.

ENERGY GENERATION

The cross-section of cylindrical shells or barrel vaulted roofs with their longitudinal axes running north-south, approaches that of the sun's path and results in a lower proportion of reflected light. If fitted with photovoltaic modules, the output of the cells will increase the closer the alignment of the cylinder approaches south or north ____ Figs 19, 20.

Arched and portal frame structures can be more economic in terms of member sizes than flat roofs resisting loads in bending and therefore do not contribute as much to solar shading. [5.2/4]

SOLAR SHADING AND PROTECTION FROM OVERHEATING

The least complex solution is offered by glass with solar control coatings and screen printed frits, which often can be combined with internal features such as textile banners. An external structural frame reduces the amount of incident light. In the Leipzig Neue Messe this reduction was about 30 percent ____ Fig. 23. [5.2/5]

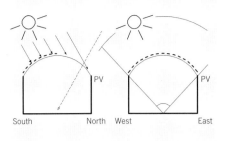

South   North   West   East

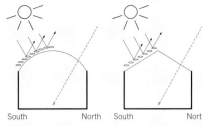

South   North   South   North

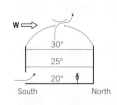

South   North

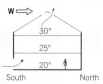

South   North

19

20

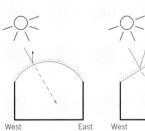

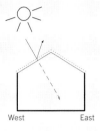

West   East   West   East

22

25

23

21 There are a number of possible installation positions for external solar control measures on curved roof glazing.

19 The amount of light admitted depends on the orientation of the curved roof surface.

20 Solar modules near the apex of a barrel roof tend to accumulate dirt and hence are less effective. Lehrter Bahnhof Berlin, 2002, Arch.: gmp

22 Solar control or screen-printed coatings are easily integrated into curved roofs.

23 Solar control on this barrel roof is provided by a combination of screen-printed areas and an external frame. Neue Messe Leipzig, 1998, Arch.: gmp

24 High wind suction pressures and strong thermals dominate at the apex of a curved roof.

25 Arrangement of smoke and heat vents in the ridge area of a barrel roof, World Trade Center Dresden, 1996, Arch.: Nirtz Pratsch Sigl

___ VENTILATION

Highly curved roofs enhance thermal buoyancy. The large wind suction forces occurring at the flat ridges of pitched and barrel vaulted roofs help to draw the air from the hall ___ Fig. 24. "Spoilers" attached to the roof improve natural ventilation at low wind speeds. Mechanical ventilation must be used when there is no wind. Depending on the wind direction and the geometry of the surroundings, curved roofs can set up complex patterns of positive and negative wind pressures, which may require wind tunnel tests.

___ ACOUSTIC COMFORT

The typical "shopping arcade acoustics" experienced under curved or folded roofs often include the focussing of sound within the cross-section of the hall, prolonged reverberation times and greater loudness ___ Fig. 26. This effect is particularly noticeable with structural elements that are flush with the reflective glass surface. Reflectors or absorbers

below the glass surface reduce reverberation times and promote better reproduction of speech ___ Fig. 27.

___ MAINTENANCE AND CLEANING

A flatter slope or curvature of the roof means the glass has a less effective self-cleaning effect. The build-up of dirt increases towards the apex on curved roof structures. Cleaning the outside of the roof is normally done by automatic cleaning and access equipment running on rails at the eaves and ridge. The inside of smaller roof surfaces can be cleaned with wheeled access scaffolding; larger roofs may require access systems such as gantries. The most efficient way of cleaning wide span barrel vaulted roof structures is by using cleaning robots ___ Fig. 31.

26   Curved roof glazing focuses sound propagation.

27   Sound reflectors to reduce echo, Quartier 203 Berlin, Arch.: gmp

28   Construction elements below the glass roof reduce reverberation times.

29   Fixed or temporary auxiliary structures are necessary to clean and maintain curved roof glazing.

30   Maintenance bridge, Design Center Linz

31   External cleaning of Neue Messe Leipzig using cleaning robots developed by the Fraunhofer Institut Magdeburg

32   Rainwater draining from roofs with opposing curves follows high and low points

33, 34   Cable net supported atrium glazing, Bürohaus Gniebel: The slope of the cable net plane prevents water from accumulating; internal fabric blinds provide solar control.

THE GLASS CORE – THE DOUBLE-CURVED ROOF

___NATURAL LIGHT

The characteristic pattern of reflections from the outside surfaces of a facetted, multi-curved glazed roof changes with the position of the observer. Inside the building as well, light entering from all sides creates reflections that contribute to a strongly three-dimensional appearance, which is further reinforced when artificial lighting is switched on.

___WEATHER PROTECTION

The quantity and speed of flow of rainwater draining from domed roofs increase towards the edges. The direction of flow of rainwater on roofs curving in opposing directions must be determined using shape-finding investigations ___Fig. 32. Tensioned cable structures with shallow concave shapes are very prone to deformation. To ensure that they remain watertight the joints must be able to accommodate the move-

ments of the structure. There is the risk of water build-up during heavy rainfall ___Figs 33, 34. [5.2/6]

___ENERGY GENERATION

The cross-sections of double-curved glass roofs can be optimised to suit the path of the sun. This can eliminate low angles of light incidence and produce greater solar gain. The designers of the spherically curved "curvilinear" greenhouses of the 19th century sought to use this effect to increase plant growth. In addition, heat losses are correspondingly lower for domed halls as their ratio of enclosed volume to surface area is smaller than that of other buildings shapes ___Fig. 37. [5.2/7]

___SOLAR SHADING AND ANTI-GLARE MEASURES

Natural light enters a spherical dome structure from all sides, which can lead to unpleasant glare when the sun is low in the sky. External

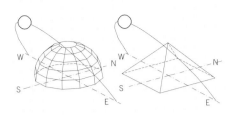

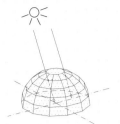

35

36

37

39

41

35   Different levels of energy admitted through different
      sectors of double curved or folded roofs

36   Glass pyramid partially covered by PV modules, Bewag
      Gelände Berlin, 1999, Arch.: A. Liepe and H. Siegelmann

37   Light and energy enters the dome from all sides, National
      Botanic Garden Wales, 1999, Arch.: Foster and Partners

38   Integrated solar control in multi-curved glazing
      composed of flat panes does not require
      additional components for shading.

39   Triangular panes with solar control coating, internal
      courtyard at the British Museum in London, 2000,
      Arch.: Foster and Partners

40   Adjustable solar shading on different sectors
      using additional internal or external measures

41   Rotating metal screen for internal solar control,
      Reichstag dome, Berlin

solar control devices in the form of fins or louvres can often shield the interior from the sun at its zenith and from sunlight entering the southern and western sectors of the dome. The most effective anti-glare protection is provided by moving screens that track the path of the sun ——Figs 40, 41.

Integrated shaped solar control devices (e.g. microlouvres) are generally not practical as the light strikes the curved glass surface at different angles. Internal devices in the form of textile banners without the complexity of external solar control measures can effectively reduce glare but not energy gain. Overheating can be prevented by exhausting the hot air through an effective ventilation system.

___VENTILATION

Whatever the wind direction, suction forces will remove air through vents in the apex of the dome ——Fig. 42. The pronounced thermal layering of air in wide span, domed halls supports natural ventilation and

smoke venting. Small surface curvatures generally produce greater wind suction forces; the air extraction openings can be distributed over the whole surface of shallow domes.

___ACOUSTIC COMFORT

The internally concave surface of a domed hall acts as a converging lens for sound thus creating considerable hall effects with long reverberation times, which can be very distracting at events ——Fig. 45. Sound attenuating absorbers, such as microperforated films, acrylic glass panels or sound deflecting reflectors on the room sides, can improve acoustics ——Fig. 46. [**5.2/8, 5.2/9**]

___CLEANING

The apex area may become particularly dirty due to the low speed of flow of water draining from the roof. External cleaning of short span roofs can be done with rotating cleaning bridges or gantries. Larger

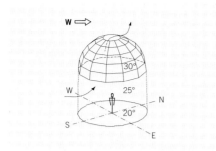

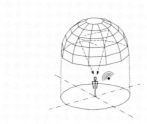

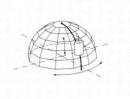

42

45

47

43

44

46

42 Natural air extraction supported by thermals and wind suction pressures.

43 Ventilation opening, Reichstag dome, Berlin, 1998, Arch.: Foster and Partners

44 External view of dome, Reichstag, Berlin

45 Multiple two-dimensionally curved domes focus sound and increase reverberation times.

46 Stretched microperforated acoustic film below a domed roof attenuates sound and reduces hall effects, Schlüterhof in Deutsches Historisches Museum, Berlin, 2002, Arch.: I.M. Pei

47 Cleaning of a domed roof with climbing or travelling platforms

glazed surfaces such as the 3000 m² dome of Berlin's Reichstag are cleaned using elevating platforms, which are driven along a revolving steel rib. These prestige buildings require cleaning intervals of about three months ____Fig. 47. [**5.2/10**]

If regular cleaning of difficult-to-access and complex roof surfaces is not possible using mobile or fixed height access equipment then roped access may be the only practical option, despite its high cost and time implications.

6

GLASS
STRUCTURES

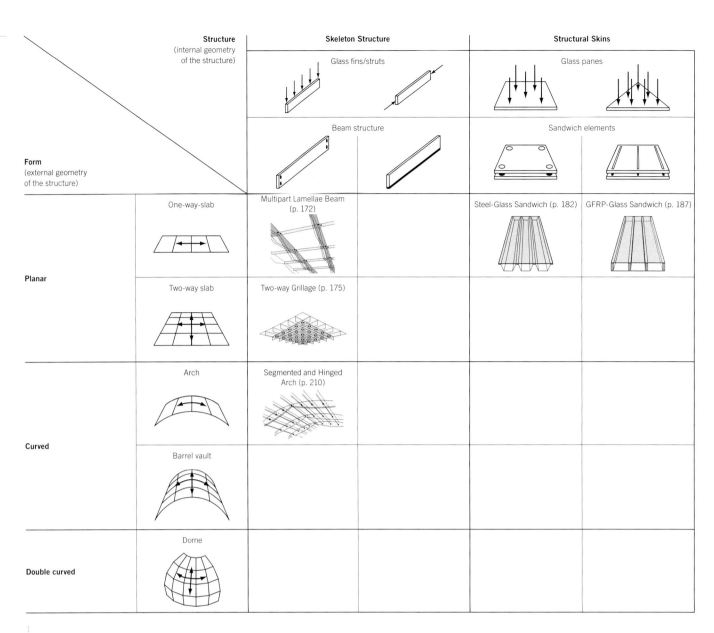

Structure (internal geometry of the structure)	Skeleton Structure		Structural Skins	
	Glass fins/struts		Glass panes	
	Beam structure		Sandwich elements	
Form (external geometry of the structure)				
Planar — One-way-slab	Multipart Lamellae Beam (p. 172)		Steel-Glass Sandwich (p. 182)	GFRP-Glass Sandwich (p. 187)
Two-way slab	Two-way Grillage (p. 175)			
Curved — Arch	Segmented and Hinged Arch (p. 210)			
Barrel vault				
Double curved — Dome				

1 Load-bearing structural forms of flat glass:
   Schematic overview of the state of technology
   (cf. the projects in Chapter 7)

6.1
FORMS OF LOAD-BEARING STRUCTURES IN FLAT GLASS

Glass skin structures combine the functional and the constructional form into one entity: Because of the outstanding characteristics of flat glass as a facade and construction material the enclosing glass skin is also the load-bearing structure. [6.1/1]

Form-finding for these structures must focus on the specific properties of the material: its planarity, limitations in panel sizes, brittleness and compressive strength of a sheet of flat glass. In a similar way to the constructional language of steel skeleton or membrane struc-

tures the construction of glass skin structures is also formulated according to a set of appropriate rules.

Such design and construction principles can be brought together in a typology in which the basic *structural forms* of flat glass are systematically described and classified in an overview. This chapter introduces one such typology for structural glass skins and describes the specific design parameters and visual implications in detail in the following sections.

The importance of the connection detail in dealing with this brittle sheet material makes it necessary to refer to the make-up of a structure and the arrangement of structural members, its *internal* geometry, as well as its overall form or *external* geometry as the primary means of differentiation. Most attention is directed towards structures which are primarily designed to resist compressive loads. The structural forms are differentiated according to the same geometric categories which have been adopted for describing the internal space. Planar,

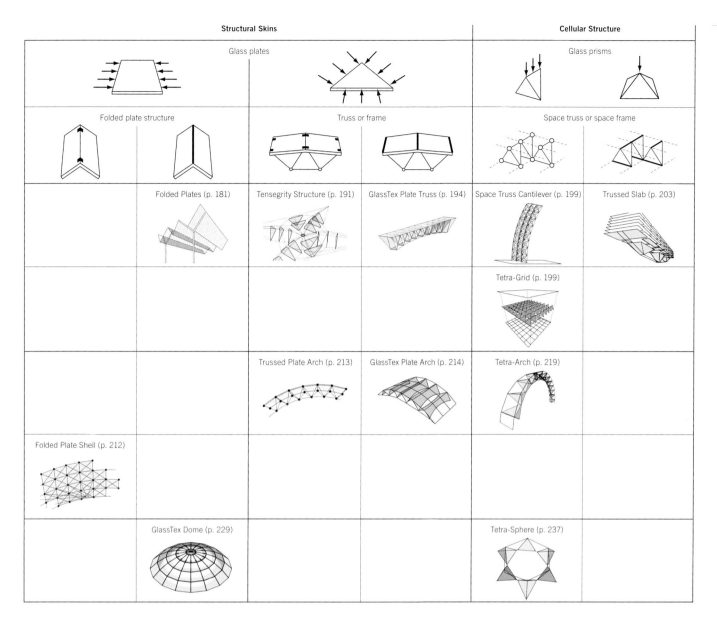

Structural Skins				Cellular Structure	
Glass plates				Glass prisms	
Folded plate structure		Truss or frame		Space truss or space frame	
	Folded Plates (p. 181)	Tensegrity Structure (p. 191)	GlassTex Plate Truss (p. 194)	Space Truss Cantilever (p. 199)	Trussed Slab (p. 203)
				Tetra-Grid (p. 199)	
		Trussed Plate Arch (p. 213)	GlassTex Plate Arch (p. 214)	Tetra-Arch (p. 219)	
Folded Plate Shell (p. 212)					
	GlassTex Dome (p. 229)			Tetra-Sphere (p. 237)	

curved and double curved systems are suitable to varying degrees to make use of glass as a compression-loaded construction element. Concave or structural geometries curving in more than one opposing direction result in tensile loads in the load-bearing elements and are therefore disregarded in this context. Flat and curved structures are divided into linear systems such as trusses and arches and planar or shell structures. The various types are presented within the categories with reference to *Dimension* D of the external geometry of the roof (downwards) and to the load-bearing elements (to the right).

The structure is classified according to the geometry of the load-bearing elements and their arrangement. Beams and frames, which are made up of linear glass elements, are also included in order to represent the current state of the technology. But at the heart of the typology is flat glass as a two-dimensional load-bearing element and the skin structures formed from them in which the load bearing structure is integral to the building envelope.

Sandwich structures can be produced by layering the materials, with outer skins resisting compressive or tensile stresses. Folding of the roof surface creates *folded plate structures*, in which bending and axial forces occur. A triangular arrangement of members in a *truss or frame structure* leads to axially loaded members only (i.e. no bending moments). In addition to structures composed of linear and planar members there is also a class called *cellular structures*, which at the moment have still to find widespread application. The connection of individual glass plates to form three-dimensional glass bodies allows the material to be used very efficiently by creating large span space frames made of identical or similar modules.

Another important difference between structure types is the way the loads are transferred between the load-bearing elements, which may be as point loads or linearly. This is relevant to considering the problem of stress concentrations in such a brittle material.

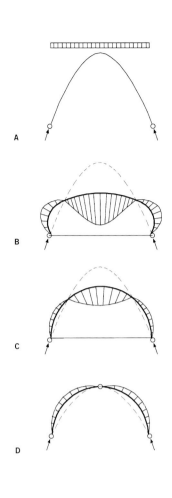

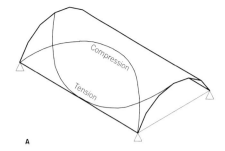

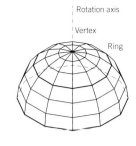

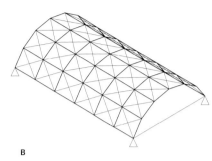

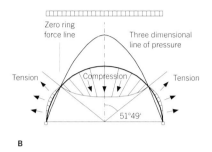

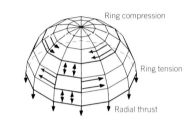

2   Bending moment diagrams for arches of
     different geometries under full load
     A   A parabolic arch follows the line of
         pressure and is moment-free.
     B   A flat elliptical arch deviates
         considerably from the line of pressure.
     C   A circular arch is closer to the line of pressure.
     D   The additional pinned hinge "swings" the line
         of pressure towards shape of the structure.

3   A   The load-bearing behaviour of a long barrel
         vaulted roof is similar to that of a profiled
         beam: The apex is predominantly in
         compression, the bottom edges are in tension.
     B   Long barrel roof as a grid shell
     C   The load-bearing behaviour of a short
         barrel vaulted roof is like that of an arch.

4   Load-bearing behaviour of a hemispherical shell
A   The hemisphere has rotational symmetry, the
     spherical surface is divided into flat surfaces by
     rings and meridians.
B, C The zero ring force line (intersection between three
     dimensional lines of pressure and dome surface)
     marks the line for a uniformly loaded dome where
     compressive ring forces in the upper part of the
     dome give way to tensile ring forces in the lower
     part of the dome.

6.2
DESIGN AND CONSTRUCTION PARAMETERS

THE EXTERNAL GEOMETRY OR FORM OF LOAD-BEARING GLASS
STRUCTURES

The flow of force within the structure and therefore the loads carried
by the structural elements depend mainly on the external geometry of
the structure ____Figs 2–4. The special suitability of glass for resisting
compressive loads is crucial to form-finding. Suspended constructions, minimum surface area and membrane structures are concave
or saddle-shaped and therefore these geometries are subject to tensile
stresses. In steelwork this can result in efficient, wide span structures

but in respect to the brittle material glass they are unsuitable. The
danger of brittle failure through stress concentrations and especially
the introduction of tensile stresses into the glass generate many unresolved problems. Freely formed structural geometries, which do not
keep their natural flow of forces within a totally compressive system,
are a completely different genre to structural glass skins. In contrast,
convex structures such as arches, barrels and shell structures, which
are primarily loaded in compression, present a great deal of potential
for the use of glass.

The classification suggested here imposes limits on form-finding
in the design of glass structures but it also opens *"a wide scope for
variations for the architect and engineer through the interplay of the
characteristics of structure and form whilst taking into account the defined rules".* [**6.2/1**] This applies especially to flat structures subject to
bending forces. The "splitting" of a bending moment acting on a section into compression and tension forces, for example in a truss, or the

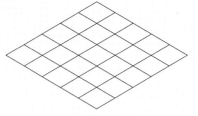

Square grid (uniform grid)

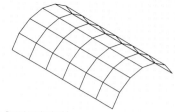

Barrel-vaulted grid

5

8

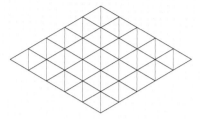

Triangular grid

Domed grid

6

9

10

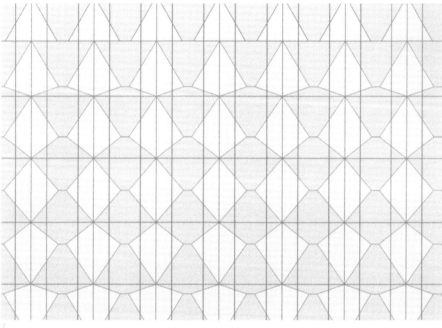

7

5, 6   Plane grids
  5   two-way uniform square grid
  6   three-way triangular grid

  7   Projection in plan of a glass barrel shell composed
     of tetrahedral modules: Superposition of triangular
     and rectangular grids for two-layer structures

  8   Single-curved grid (barrel-vault grid) with square mesh

  9   Double-curved grid with synclastic curvatures
     (dome grid)

 10   Regular grid disrupted by penetration of two barrel
     shells, Museum für Hamburgische Geschichte, 1989,
     Arch.: gmp, Eng.: Schlaich Bergermann und Partner

minimisation of tensile bending stresses in glass allows the material to be used for structural elements loaded predominantly in compression.

GRID GEOMETRY

The limitations imposed by the available manufactured sizes of flat glass products require structures to be elementalised, which results in a grid-like pattern of the building skin. In the context of the forms of construction discussed here the pattern may be classified as a *plane, curved* or *dome grid*. An important point of view when considering glass structures – in respect of their economy too – is the optimisation of the grid geometry in terms of mesh size and geometry.

In normal circumstances the designer endeavours to select the largest mesh size possible, taking into account the available manufactured sizes of heat-treated and laminated glass, the cost of transport and installation and the structural engineering requirements, with the aim of minimising the number of joints and connections. A mesh size of about 1.5 m x 1.5 m or 1.5 m x 2 m produces a rational division of the manufacturers' jumbo sheets of 6 m x 3.21 m. Even with larger glass thicknesses, the self-weight of these formats is less than 500 kilogrammes, which ensures the panes can be handled safely in production and during installation. It may be sensible to adopt a size of approximately 1 m x 1 m for panes that are subject to high bending or direct stresses and require large glass thicknesses or those which must be installed without the unrestricted use of lifting equipment.

As many of the panes as possible should have rectangular corners to keep production costs low. The glass industry applies a cost premium of between 30 and 50 percent for cutting triangular panes on top of the price for cutting rectangular sheets. This premium is necessary to cover the greater waste and longer cutting times involved. The premium for insulating glass may be as high as 100 percent. In comparison with the use of curved or double-curved glass, the cost of

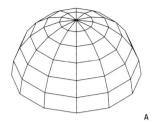

A

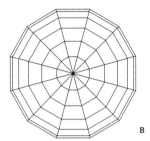

B

C

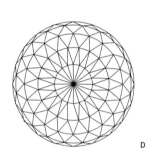

D

12

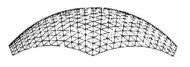

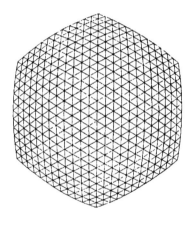

11　Geometry of ring grid domes
　　A, B Isometric and plan of a two-way ring grid dome
　　C, D Isometric and plan of a three-way ring grid dome

12　Zone grid dome with ribs, the division of top
　　ring changes from a three-way to a two-way
　　grid, school at Bornheim, 2000, Arch.: Heuer
　　und Faust, Eng.: Führer, Kosch, Jürges

13　Elevation and plan of a uniform grid dome

11

13

which may be over ten times that of flat rectangular glass, the design of a facetted building shell with flat triangular panes may offer considerable cost savings. [6.2/2]

In addition, the number of different pane types should be kept as small as possible. A uniform pattern that divides the structural surface into a regular grid is usually preferable.

Planar and single-curved surfaces such as cylindrical shells can be developed geometrically and made up of flat elements. Buildings with non-rectangular plan shapes will require additional glass formats.

The double-curved surface of domed shells cannot be built up using a regular grid pattern. A building skin can be panelized using *ring, uniform, geodetic* or *square grids*.

____RING GRID DOME

In a double curved ring grid dome the spherical surface is divided into a radial, concentric grid of rings and meridians. The rings run parallel to the central axis of the dome; the meridians run from the apex to the dome edge and are evenly spaced ____Fig. 11.

The dome surface can be developed with trapezoidal panes with the number of different formats being equal to the number of rings. The concentric geometry leads to small acute-angled formats near the apex and large heavy panes near the base. The increasingly heterogeneous appearance and non-uniform load-bearing behaviour which occur with increasing spans can be reduced by halving the number of divisions at the crown to form a zoned or trimmed grid dome.

A more even appearance is created with a triangular (diamatic) ring grid dome in which the meridians are replaced by diagonal ribs. This is made up of isosceles triangles instead of trapeziums. [6.2/3]

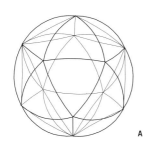

A

B

15

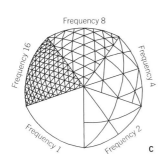

Frequency 8

Frequency 16

Frequency 4

Frequency 1

Frequency 2

C

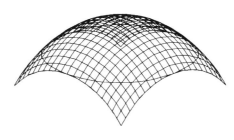

16

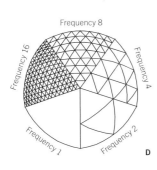

Frequency 8

Frequency 16

Frequency 4

Frequency 1

Frequency 2

D

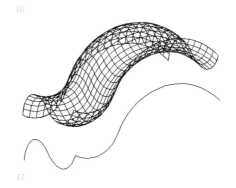

17

14   Geodetic dome division
   A   projection of an icosahedron onto a spherical
       surface
   B   Hemisphere with geodetic panelization shown
       as a wire frame model
   C   Subdivision using the "alternate method"
   D   Subdivision using the "triacon method"

15   Square grid dome at the western entrance
     to the Messe Hanover, Arch.: K. Ackermann,
     Eng.: sbp, 1999

16, 17   Form-finding of shell structures with plane mesh
         using "directrix" and "generatrix" (translation surface)

14

___ UNIFORM GRID DOME

In a uniform grid dome each node connects to the same number of panes. The grid division is created by projecting a uniform grid, which may consist of equilateral triangles, quadrilaterals or polygons, on to a spherical surface ___Fig. 13. The overall effect is one of harmony, but it is largely created without the use of symmetry and therefore requires a correspondingly large number of different pane formats. Uniform grid domes are most suitable for flatter domed surfaces. [**6.2/4**]

___ GEODETIC DOME

The surface pattern of a geodetic dome presents a very uniform overall appearance. It is the projection of a uniform grid on to a spherical surface. The basic shape is a regular polyhedron, normally a twenty-sided icosahedron. The triangular areas projected on to the spherical surface may be subdivided into smaller triangles by parallels to the outside edges (*alternate method*) or by parallels to the central perpen-

diculars (*triacon method*) of each triangular area. The number of subdivisions is described as the *frequency* ___Fig. 14. [**6.2/5**]

___ SQUARE GRID DOME

The construction principle of the square grid dome is based on a grid of square elements with the mesh deformed to fit almost any double curved shape. The lengths of the sides of the meshes are unchanged but different sizes of rhomboid are created by adjusting the angle to the curvature. Due to mesh warping, a surface can be developed using flat glass only if the curvature is slight, otherwise spherically curved glass must be used, which can lead to considerable costs.

Jörg Schlaich and Hans Schober have developed a method which allows curved surfaces to be formed with a flat polygonal mesh: "*Translating or sweeping any three-dimensional curve, called the generatrix, across another three-dimensional curve, called a directrix, creates a three-dimensional surface solely out of flat polygonal meshes*".

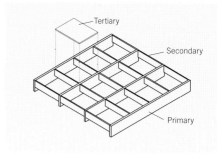

Tertiary
Secondary
Primary

20

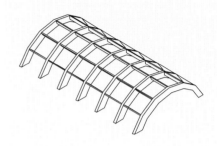

21

18 Hierarchical plane roof structure: Multi-part
glass beams form the primary structure, two-
part glass beams form the secondary. The roof
panels spanning between the main and secondary
components form the tertiary members.
Glass roof over the internal courtyard of the
IHK Munich, 2003, Arch.: W. und J. Betsch

19 Hierarchical curved glass roof: the arch-
shaped main beams span 9 m, the secondary
beams (steel tube) span 2.50 m; again the
roof panels form the tertiary members.
Glass roof over the internal courtyard of
the Lindener Volksbank in Hanover, 1996,
Arch.: Bertram Bünemann Partner

20, 21 Sketches of plane and curved hierarchical structures

[6.2/6] If the curves are a constant distance apart the grid is composed of uniform meshes. Even complex and irregular shapes can be created with planar flat elements using these *translation surfaces*. It should be borne in mind that having differently sized rhomboid panes leads to higher manufacturing costs. [6.2/7]

REDUNDANCY: SAFETY IN NON-HIERARCHICAL STRUCTURES
The geometric grid forms the basis of the structural grid, that is to say the arrangement of the structural elements on the building skin. Rectangular grids span in two directions, triangular grids in three directions. If the load is transmitted uniformly in these directions of span, i.e. all structural elements in the system axes fulfil the same function, this is called a non-directional, *non-hierarchical* structure.

On the other hand if the directions of span fulfil different structural tasks the members form a directional or *hierarchical* structure.

Hierarchical structures are divided by structural engineers into categories, which up to now have also been applied to glass structures. [6.2/8] The first category includes *primary structural members*, which *"are called upon to transmit all the forces acting on a building, including self-weight"* and the failure of these members can lead to failure of the whole structure. In the second category are *secondary structural members*, which transmit their loads to the main structural members and their failure does not endanger the stability of the whole structure. The third category of *tertiary structural members* includes members which transmit their loads to the main and secondary structural members and damage to them would not have any significant consequences. This category includes building cladding such as glazing panels.

Examples of hierarchically constructed systems include beams and arches, in which a principal glass member bridges the full span, secondary glass beams span between the main structural member axes and the glazed roof panes form the enclosure ____Figs 18–21.

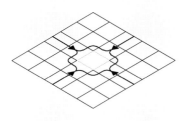

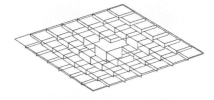

22

24

27

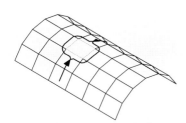

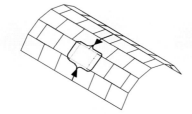

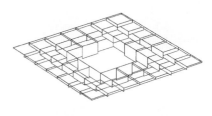

23

25

28

22–25 Redistribution of direct forces in the plane
of the glass after the failure of one glass
mesh element for various geometries
22 Plane grid
23 Barrel-vaulted grid
24 Dome grid
25 Barrel-vaulted grid with offset joints
26 View of the underside of a glass barrel shell
roof. If a plate breaks the forces must be carried
by the nodes into the adjoining panes.

27, 28 Direct stress diagram of a breakage scenario for
a bottom chord plane of a horizontal space frame
shell: As more ribs break the loads increase
on the remaining structural members.

26

This hierarchical organisation of the structural elements is similar to the logic of skeleton construction and the separation of load-bearing and filling members. "Well-behaved", tough construction materials such as steel, wood or reinforced concrete can be used for primary structural members with an almost one hundred percent assurance against failure.

As a brittle material like glass cannot provide absolute safety against failure due to its fracture behaviour, wide variations in strength and sensitivity to impact, it cannot be incorporated into a hierarchical system without complications.

In non-hierarchical systems the applied loads do not act on only a few structural elements, but on a large number of identical structural elements interconnected in a grid. This is only possible with structural systems that span in two or more axes. Each structural element is lightly loaded and has sufficient reserve capacity available that in the event of failure of one element the adjacent element can assume its load-bearing function to avoid a progressive failure of the whole building. This characteristic is called *redundancy*.

In a statically determinate system the fracture of a plate, which for the structural geometry means the effective loss of one grid mesh, leads to a change in the flow of force and to a corresponding increase in the load on the adjacent elements ⎯ Figs 27, 28. Non-hierarchical systems are more compatible with the material behaviour of glass and are therefore more suitable for glass structures. *"The disadvantage associated with the increased complexity of such systems can only be addressed by standardisation and prefabrication of individual elements and the development of a modular construction system compatible with the material."* [6.2/9]

Examples of non-hierarchical structural systems include biaxially spanning slabs and grillages, barrel-vaulted and domed grid shells. These structures are highly statically indeterminate so that in the event of failure of an individual element the load can be distributed locally

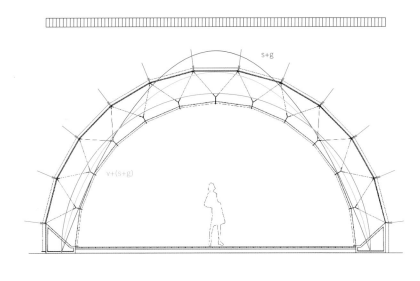

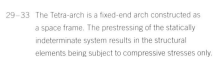

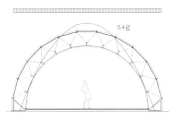

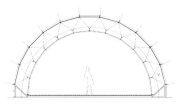

29–33   The Tetra-arch is a fixed-end arch constructed as
            a space frame. The prestressing of the statically
            indeterminate system results in the structural
            elements being subject to compressive stresses only.
29   By superimposing the load cases of dead-load g,
        snow s and prestress v (v + s + g) the line of
        pressure runs within the shape of the structure:
        The tensile forces are "compressed".
30   Load case dead load g plus snow s (s + g):
        The system geometry does not correspond with the
        parabolic line of pressure: Tensile and compressive
        stresses occur in the system.
31   Load case prestress v: The line of pressure of the
        induced stress corresponds exactly with the
        system geometry.
32   Arch with prestressing cables
33   Tensioning the cable with a torque spanner

without significant detrimental effect on the overall stability of the structure.

THE SAFE DESIGN OF GLASS STRUCTURES LOADED IN COMPRESSION

The characteristic triangular patterns in truss structures create favourable normal stresses and avoid unfavourable bending stresses. In trusses, glass can be used for the structural members loaded in compression in a way compatible with its characteristics, whilst steel can be used for the structural elements loaded in tension.

As applied loads such as dead load and wind can act in different directions and cause oppositely signed stresses in the system, the one-sided compressive stress design approach must incorporate suitable measures to avoid any stress reversal in the structural members.

Normally the structural engineer seeks to counteract the load cases which may cause undesirable tensile stresses in glass, for example, by increasing dead load or by external prestressing or pretensioning. The prestress introduces an additional permanent load into the system which mitigates the effects of alternating loads ____ Figs 29–31. Normally, prestressing forces only lead to the desirable effects in statically indeterminate systems as statically determinate systems "accommodate" the load by deforming.

The temperature load case resembles the prestressing load case: The expansion of the load-bearing elements causes additional internal forces and imposed strains, which must be accommodated by the structure.

The mechanical advantages derived from its suitability as a compressive structural element are linked with the disadvantageous risk of buckling of a glass plate: As an extraordinarily slender element it has the tendency to deform laterally under large compressive forces acting in the plane of the plate. It is therefore worthwhile to provide stiffening to the edges of the panel from adjoining structural elements or to form

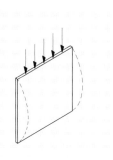 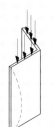 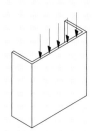 

34

36

35

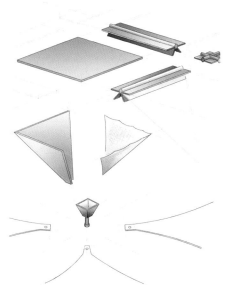

37

34   Glass plates are prone to plate buckling.
     Edge connections between adjacent
     panels increase their stiffness.

36   Section through the Tetra-glass arch:
     The plates forming the tetrahedrons are supported
     on three sides, but the buckling-prone top chord
     plate is only supported on two.

35, 37, 38   Hybrid glass constructions
     35   Radial textile sheets induce prestress into the
          dome surface and thus stabilise the structure.
     37   Concept for connecting the glass plates
          and textile sheets into a three-dimensional
          structural module (H. Bosbach, M. König)
     38   Stabilising a facade element by means of a
          pretensioned film skin (P. R. Menken)

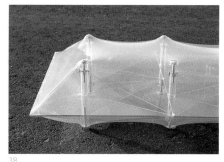

38

structural modules which have a three-dimensional stiffness ___ Fig. 34. These plates are often supported on two, three, four or more sides.

All-glass structures designed as systems under pure compression are only feasible in monolithic constructions with great self-weight – like Gothic stone vaults. Long span, lightweight structures must have tensile members for introducing pretensioning forces or for carrying tensile section forces in composite construction. This creates a requirement for glass to be combined with tension-resistant materials. Linear components such as steel cables or even planar materials such as fabrics and textiles can structurally interact with the glass to form skin structures. A structure which relies on the interaction of different materials for its load-bearing capacity is called a *hybrid*. This term is also used in the context of structures that are loaded in bending as well as direct stresses.

The combination of different materials having different thermal coefficients of expansion can lead to imposed strains, which have to be taken into account in the design of load bearing elements. In addition to the constructional possibilities, the combination of glass with other flat materials offers further interesting options in performance and appearance ___ Figs 35, 37, 38.

39

40

43

41

42

39–42   Schematic construction of a Tetra-
        glass barrel (concept: T. Unterberg)
39, 42 Individual plates are connected to form a
        three-dimensional structural module.
   40   Linking together a series of modules
        creates a component arch.
   42   Linking together a series of component
        arches creates the whole barrel.

   43   Construction of the Tetra-glass arch showing
        the elementalised arch components

MODULES AND PLANES OF CONNECTION

Cellular systems with prefabricated structural glass modules and a standardized set of details ease the task of coping with the high requirements that must be specified to ensure a uniform transfer of load into the brittle material glass. Construction systems which use identical or similar modules have a reduced requirement for load and component testing, thus simplifying approval by building authority. Various planes of connection and levels of subdivision may be required depending on the size and complexity of the structure. Structural elements can be connected in the fabrication shop to form stiff modules. These modules can in turn be formed into load-bearing subsystems, which can be finally combined into the whole structure on site —— Figs 39–42. [**6.2/10**]

Each butt joint between pairs of structural elements leads to inaccuracies due to tolerances, which must be accommodated during assembly. Therefore in glass construction in particular it is important to pay attention to accurate prefabrication at the factory, provide precise supports to the individual panes and plates and exact overall geometry in order to prevent dimensional deviations giving rise to imposed strains to the detriment of the load-bearing capacity.

It is important to avoid stress peaks in structural glass elements to ensure efficient use of the material. By prefabricating the structural modules in the factory the panes can be exactly aligned and joined linearly along their edges. Mechanical fixings along the edges or structurally bonded joints between the elements produce a uniform stress distribution across the span and ensure effective use of the load-bearing capacity of the glass. Although node connections can lead to local stress concentrations, they are often preferred by the contractors on-site as they accommodate tolerances more easily and allow the geometry of the structure to be controlled.

44

44 Structure geometry, internal composition, grid pattern
    and elementalisation interact in the form-finding for
    glass structures – shown here: the Tetra-glass arch

Dim.	Geometry		Glass element		Structure	
0		Point/node				
1		Line/edge		Beam/fin		Skeleton structure
2		Surface		Plate		Plate structure
3		Body		Glass prism/ polyhedron		Cellular structure

1–3 Examples of various geometries of load-bearing glass elements during load-testing
1 Glass beam (1D)
2 Glass pane (2D)
3 Glass body (3D)

4 Categorisation of flat glass load-bearing elements and structures

5,6 Skeleton structure with glass tubes (at glasstec 2000)

___ 6.3

LOAD-BEARING GLASS STRUCTURES

The internal geometry of the glass structure, the detailed make-up, is strongly influenced by the geometric and mechanical characteristics of the construction material.

The structure can be described in terms of three principal features: The geometry of the structural elements and their arrangement and the geometry of the connections between these elements. The structural aspects are described in relation to the characteristics of the material in the following sections.

___GEOMETRY OF THE STRUCTURAL ELEMENTS

Structural elements made from flat glass can be categorised according to their dimensions and form as *linear*, *planar* or *spatial* structural elements ___Fig. 4.

A strip of flat glass, with a length more than five times its width, is usually described as a rod-shaped, one-dimensional structural element. Connecting these members together at their ends creates *trusses* or *frames* – in a similar way to skeleton steel construction. In addition to glass beams, glass fins and strips other rod-shaped structural elements include U-profiled architectural glass and glass tubes. [6.3/1]

A glass pane or plate is described as a flat, two-dimensional structural element. Its surface is bounded by three, four or more edges. Glass panes and plates are structurally connected at their edges or corners to make plate structures or *structural glass skins*.

Joining the glass panels and faces along their edges creates a

7

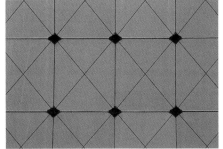

8

9

Structural element	Connection	Example	Structure
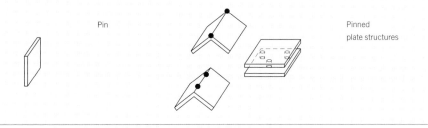	Pin		Pinned frames
	Pin		Pinned plate structures
	Pin		Pinned cellular structures
	Hinge	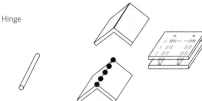	Hinged plate structure
			Simulated hinged plate structure
	Hinge	 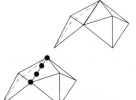	Hinged cellular structure
			Simulated hinged cellular structure

7–9   Examples of various connection geometries
  7   Pinned rod structure
  8   Pinned plate structure
  9   Pinned cellular structure

10   Overview of connection geometries

10

three-dimensional cellular structural module which can be described geometrically as a polyhedron and combined into *cellular structures*. The connections between the cells can be punctiform at the corners or linear along the edges.

GEOMETRY OF CONNECTORS – LOAD TRANSFER

The glass structure is built up of an arrangement of glass beams, plates or three-dimensional glass cells. The compression-resistant character of structural glass components lends itself to the use of fittings and connectors made of tough materials like steel.

The geometry of the connectors is essential for the description of glass structures. *Point* connections lead to load concentrations and challenge the brittleness of glass building components. Beams, plates and cells are connected to one another at nodes on their corners, edges or surfaces or to the ends of other linear structural elements such as cables and struts. Depending on the above configuration, the structures are described as pinned frames, pinned skin structures or pinned cellular structures. Closely spaced series of point connections along their edges can function structurally to simulate linear load transfer ____Fig. 10.

Linear connections along glass edges are suitable for introducing forces evenly into the component. Glass plates and cells are connected to one another at their edges or to the edges of other planar structural elements. They may be called (edge) hinged plate structures or (edge) hinged cellular structures.

As a structure is often made up of both pinned and hinged connections, for the purposes of assignment into types, the characterising joints are those between the primary structural elements or modules.

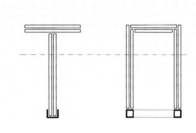

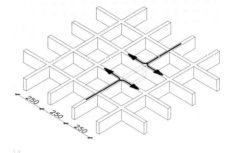

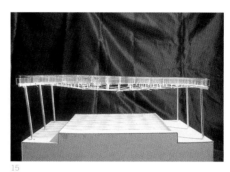

11   Multi-part glass beam, underground station
      Tokyo International Forum, 1996, Eng.:
      Dewhurst Macfarlane and Partners

12   Beam cross-section stiffened by steel
      profiles in the tension zone

13, 17   Concept grillage: D. Seiberts, S. Spengler

14   Load redistribution in a grillage

15, 16   Concept of a grillage with additional parabolic
          cable net to suit the bending moment distribution,
          Design: M. Schmidt, S. Schrennen

BEAMS AND TRUSSES

One-piece glass beams are the state of the art and a commonly used building product. There is now a widespread acceptance by the industry that glass beams can be integrated without complication into hierarchical skeleton steel structures. A span beyond the available maximum sheet size can be achieved by combining segments into multipart beams, frames, arches, grillages and ribbed shells. [6.3/2]

MULTIPART BEAM CROSS-SECTIONS

Glass beams can be combined together into multipart beams to create moment connected lap or butt joints in the longitudinal direction or to create stiffer cross-sections ___Fig. 11. For example a cross-section similar to a rolled stell profile can stiffen the tension zone and increase the shear stiffness as was done in 1951 in the exhibition pavilion for the company Glasbau Hahn. In addition tough and tension-resistant materials can be integrated into the load path of multipart glass cross-

sections to improve the structural performance and residual load-bearing capacity ___Fig. 12. [6.3/3]

GRILLAGE

Grillages composed of intersecting glass beams transfer loads along two axes, which allows the structural depth to be reduced compared with a uni-axial system. For a grillage to behave in an *isotropic* manner in response to load, the stiffnesses must be the same in both directions. At every member intersection the glass beams must be connected to one another by bolts or friction grip connections capable of transmitting bending moments ___Fig. 18.

A grillage is a non-hierarchical, statically indeterminate structure. If a glass beam fractures, its portion of the load is transferred to the adjacent beams providing they have the necessary reserve capacity ___Fig. 14.

By doubling up the cross-sections the grillage can be prefabricat-

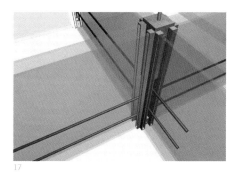

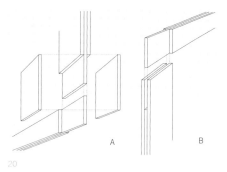

A   B

17 Multi-part beam cross-section with prestressed
    steel cables in the tension zone

18 Grillage used for roof and facade construction,
    reading room at the Arab Urban Development
    Institute (AUDI) in Riyadh, 1998, Arch.: Nabil
    Fanous Architects, Eng.: Dewhurst Macfarlane
    and Partners, Glass: Zamil Glass Industries

19 Multi-segment glass arch with a 12 m span,
    Design: N. Roufosse, A. Hübner

20 Detailed solutions for frame corners, as a
    fish joint (A) and as a lap-joint (B)

21 Corner connection at the Glass Pavilion RWTH
    Aachen, Lehrstuhl für Tragkonstruktionen, 1996

ed as a series of square modules. Four beams and the covering glass plate are structurally bonded along their edges to form an all-glass cassette assembly. The top edges of the glass beams are in compression. Each beam is relieved of some of its load and stabilised by the effective load-bearing width of the roof plate. The modules can be connected to one another on site to form a continuous grillage. The tensile bending stresses at the bottom of the system are mitigated by a cable net pretensioned between the beams ____Figs 13, 17.

____MULTI-SEGMENT BEAM STRUCTURES: ARCHES AND PORTAL FRAMES

Glass beams can be joined together to form portal frames or arch structures. Several structural elements can be joined together to form a statically determinate three-pinned arch or frame. This arrangement has advantages during erection, in the accommodation of tolerances and in its deformation behaviour. Three-pinned systems do not inher-

ently fail-safe in the event of damage. Spans of up to 12 metres can be achieved using two-segment three-pinned arches or frames ____Fig. 19.

By using moment connections multi-member arches and frames can be made from three or more elements. Normally fixed supports are preferable to moment connections in the span. Panels of triple laminated safety glass are often connected like timber construction by overlapping leaves of the multipart cross-section (lap joint). The middle leaf between the two outer leaves is set back or extended over the full depth of the section, so that the load-bearing elements can slide into one another until all the joint surfaces are in full contact with each other ____Figs 20, 21. Additional bolts can allow permanent bending moments to be transmitted. [6.3/4]

____RIBBED GRID SHELLS

The addition of linear glass beams or struts to long-span barrel and shell structures appears questionable due to their slender cross-sec-

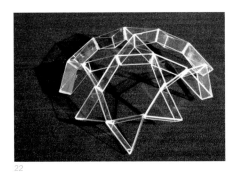

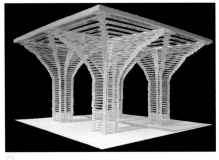

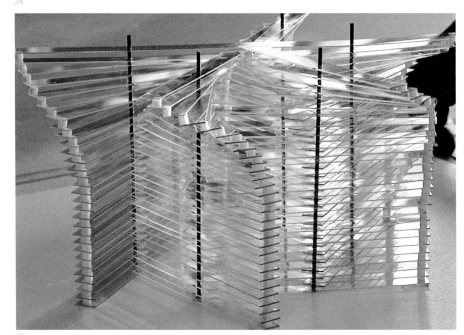

22 Structure model for a ribbed grill shell structure,
Design: A. Kruse, S. Dahlmanns, N. Fischer, N. Stoff

24 Concept for a barrel-vaulted roof using the Zollinger
construction technique, Design: E. Svarna, P. Vavra

23, 25 Concept for a trade fair pavilion based on a
stacked grillage:
23 Stacked grillage, square in plan: The structure is
stabilised by ties in the "stem" of the corners,
which are interconnected by a compression ring,
Design: S. Greuel, F. Kammann
25 Stacked grillage, hexagonal in plan: The skewing
of the layers creates a full enclosure,
Design: T. Hopp, J. Hansen

tions, which are prone to buckling, and concentrated loads at the node points ___Fig. 22. Stabilising the cross-section is possible by installing shear-resistant connections between beams and the roof plates, which allows the triangular mesh to be dispensed with in favour of rectangular mesh. Non-hierarchic lamella structures with rhomboid mesh, for example the Zollinger construction technique, might warrant further structural development ___Fig. 24.

___STACKED GRILLAGES

Three-dimensional structures can be formed by stacking linear glass elements. Enclosing sculptural structures are created by intersecting glass strips, each one slightly at a different angle in plan with respect to the one below. The span of the strips is considerably limited by their low stiffness and hence considerable deflection in bending. Advantages in terms of a high degree of prefabrication can be obtained from the similarity of the elements, despite the large amount of material used. A simple connection of elements by contact pressure and applied load can be designed in conjunction with additional stabilisation measures ___Figs 23, 25. [6.3/5]

PLATE STRUCTURES

___SANDWICH CONSTRUCTION

Panes of flat glass have been traditionally used as tertiary members to form a building enclosure. The size of these panels is generally less than the manufacturers' standard stock sizes as the span is generally limited by the small structurally effective depth and the associated bending deflection (see Chapter 4).

The panels can be stiffened to increase the span up to jumbo size mainly by layering flat components to form a sandwich, similar to the layers in laminated safety glass. A sandwich is usually made up of at least three layers, the two outer skins being called the *cover layers or skins* and the inner layer the *core layer* ___Figs 27, 28. By forming a shear

Number of layers	3	4
Cross-section profile	constant	variable
Arrangement with respect to neutral plane	symmetric	asymmetric
Material composition	homogenous	hybrid

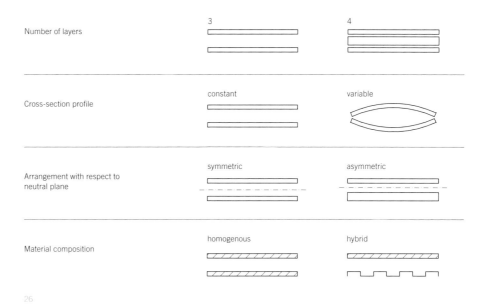

26

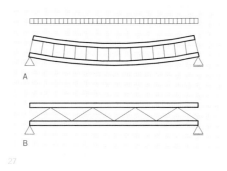

A

B

27

29

26 Categorisation of sandwich construction

27 Deformation behaviour without (A) and with (B) bond between the layers

28 Stress cross-sectional diagram for no (A), partial (B) and full composite action (C)
    1 Cover layer, skin
    2 Core layer

29, 30 Deformation of a single cover layer under self-weight and of the complete sandwich construction under a loading of 5 kN

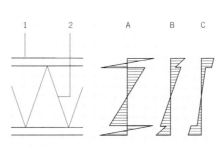

1   2   A   B   C

28

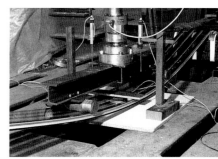

30

connection between the individual layers a system with an overall stiffness much greater than the sum of the individual layer stiffnesses is created. Stresses and deformation of the components are greatly reduced ___Figs 29, 30. The *sandwich effect* is based on distributing the shear stresses between the different layers. The bending moment is split into a force couple so that a positive moment creates compression in the top skin and tension in the bottom skin. With some non-symmetrical and hybrid sandwich components the glass plates can be positioned in the compressive stress zone. The core layer or web elements are subject to the shear forces and the associated shear stresses. The load-bearing capacity of a sandwich element is directly related to the shear stiffness of the core. Depending on its deformation behaviour the connection may be described as an *elastic* (partial) or a *rigid* (full) bond ___Fig. 28.

Stiffness and composite action are not only dependent on the material of the core or any adhesive interlayers but also on the type and duration of the load effects. An almost full bond can be assumed for short-term impact loads like gusts of wind, whilst for permanent load effects like self-weight, a viscoelastic interlayer may start to flow over time and lead to loss of composite action. Higher temperatures contribute to the flow of the interlayer. Elastic deformation behaviour is always desirable in glass structures to enable reduction of the imposed stresses arising from the differential deformation of the layers. This may be caused by differential temperatures and expansion, but more so by the use of different materials with unequal coefficients of thermal expansion. [6.3/6, 6.3/7]

In 1998 the Lehrstuhl für Tragkonstruktionen at RWTH Aachen developed systems for 3 m x 3 m insulating glazing units spanning in two axes for use as sandwich facade elements. In one prototype, the 6 millimetres thick cover layer was bonded at points by 40 mm x 40 mm

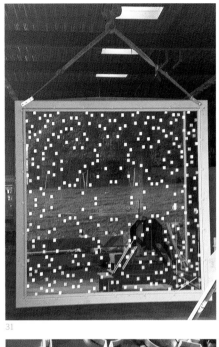

31

33

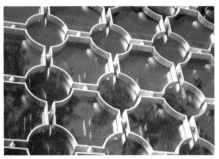

32

34

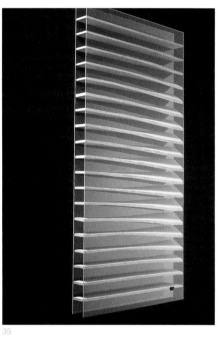

35

31, 33   Sandwich facade element: Aluminium hollow sections
         provide the shear connection between the 3 m x 3 m
         panes of an insulating glazing unit, Lehrstuhl für
         Tragkonstruktionen, RWTH Aachen, 1998

32   Glass sandwich with decorative core

34, 35   Concept models for two interactive sandwich
         constructions Design: K. Bandekow, R. Semeonova;
         right: J. Vossebürger, S. Riesenkampff

aluminium hollow sections and transparent, double-sided, self-adhesive, high performance tape (VHB) manufactured by 3M. The increasing density in the arrangement of the connecting elements towards the edges reflected the distribution of shear force ___Figs 31, 33. In this context it becomes clear that the layering of a hybrid sandwich is both a structural and functional principle in enhancing the performance of a panel.

The acceptance of sandwich construction to glass architecture depends on how much can be achieved with automated manufacturing processes in terms of economy and quality standards.

Varying the build-up of these sandwiches, selection of materials and the geometry of the layers opens a wide scope of possibilities for manufacture, function and design. It would be perfectly feasible to have translucent insulating foam in the insulating glazing cavity and stiff interactive interlayers ___Figs 34, 35.

___FOLDED PLATE STRUCTURES

Folded plate structures behave as pure structural skins. They are composed of planar, bending- and shear-resistant shell elements and present an ideal situation for the constructional use of glass. The *ridge-and-furrow* principle developed by the English greenhouse pioneer J. C. Loudon and used to great success by J. Paxton with his Crystal Palace in 1851 is an early example of folded glass roof construction. The panes were inclined in opposite directions to one another with the result that they were able to provide mutual support.

Flat folded plate structures are generally comprised of *long elements* or accordion-shaped *folded plates*, which are supported and stiffened transversely to the folds ___Figs 36–39. The glass members may be considered as inclined beams, sloping in opposite directions to one another, and can be used to form a complete enclosure. The folded shell construction effectively combines the slab (pane) and plate behaviour of the glass panels. The slab effect induces in plane

α: 90°–120°

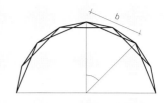

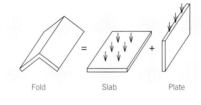

Fold   =   Slab   +   Plate

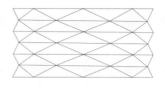

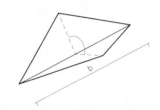

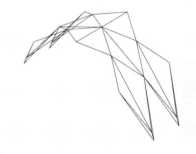

36   Ridge-and-furrow: The "folded" plates are connected
by point fixings (bolted connections). Suburban
rail station, Bretten, 1992, Arch.: J. Braun

37   Load test of folded plates, simulation of the snow
load case

38, 39   Folded plates with elongated elements:
The load-bearing behaviour of the folding
structure combines plate and slab effect.

40–43   Folded structure with short tapered elements
40, 41   Elevation and plan of a regular folded plate barrel shell
42   Fold from isosceles triangles
43   Isometric of a folded plate barrel shell with unequal
element sizes, Design: N. Leiendecker, P. Schmitz

bending moments into the glass, the plate effect out of plane compressive forces. [6.3/8, 6.3/9]

The angle between the elements should not exceed 120 degrees, otherwise the forces cannot be controlled. The skin acts transversely to the supporting ridge and furrow as an inclined 'slab', whilst acting as an inclined plate in the direction of the folds. For this load-bearing mechanism to work the folded shell edges must be able to transfer the compressive, tensile and shear forces. The main challenge in the design of folded shell structures is to achieve as linear a hinged connection between the plates as possible.

The residual load-bearing capacity of folded beam plates is just as critical as it is with conventional glass beam structures, and high safety factors must be considered. As with all glass beam structures, the achievable span is limited by the production lengths of flat glass to between 6.0 and 7.5 metres. A single-piece glass structure is not possible if the span exceeds the maximum production length. [6.3/10]

Folded plate structures based on curved and double-curved load-bearing surfaces are formed with *short tapered elements*. In form-finding for *multi-faceted plate barrel* structures, a number of geometric and manufacturing restraints and conditions must be observed ——Figs 40–43.

If two-way grids are fitted with flat rectangular panes there is the danger with multiple pinned connections that these pseudo-folded structures will lose stiffness. On the other hand three-way grids generate additional folding of the load-bearing surface in the longitudinal and transverse directions. The offset arrangement of triangular panels and the *ridge-and-furrow* give rise to a grid of stiff ribs and fold lines which in comparison to the rest of the surface have greater stiffness and hence are primarily responsible for determining the load path ——Fig. 44. As with folded plates the angle between the panes must avoid being too flat, especially in structures with spans that substantially exceed the element length. The number of hinged joints should

44

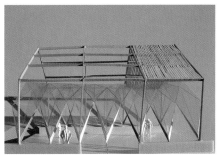

45

46

44–53   Concepts for an exhibition hall as an extension of
the Neue Aachener Kunstverein (NAK), 2003

44, 46   Regular cylindrical folded plate with a span of
12 m constructed of triangular panels. The force
connection at the joint between fold edges leads to a
partially fixed support. Design: R. Ada, M. Ayonghi

45, 47   Folded plate barrel shell structure with different
triangular shapes; the edges of the folded
structure are supported by V-shaped columns.
Design: N. Leiendecker, P. Schmitz

47

be kept to a minimum in order to achieve the greatest possible system stiffness and (in terms of manufacturing size constraints) the largest possible panel format ____Fig. 47. Elongated isosceles triangles are therefore to be preferred to equilateral triangles. As load transfer between the plates can only take place at the edges, it is advisable for practical reasons to truncate the corners of the triangles. In general cut panels are required along the supporting edge. Point fixings are to be avoided for the main supports to the structure. Restraint of the support edges increases the stiffness of the system ____Fig. 44.

In order to simplify installation some degree of elementalisation of the structure is essential. One option is to have factory prefabricated unitised modules consisting of several folded plates embedded in a perimeter steel frame. This should ensure that the modules can be transported safely and allow for any construction tolerances during installation on site.

Multifaceted folded domes have a higher stiffness than folded barrel structures due to their double curvature and are very suitable for larger spans ____Figs 50–53.

Folded plate structures have many advantages over beam and slab construction and have great potential for further development. The edge connection between the folded surfaces requires a high degree of precise prefabrication thus a standardised geometry is beneficial for larger area structures.

____TRUSSED PLATE STRUCTURES

Conventional plane trusses and frames consist of linear load-bearing elements such as struts normally connected by hinged joints. The load-bearing elements of trusses all lie in a single plane, while the load-bearing elements of space frames lie in more than one plane. In the course of their studies into the geometry of space frames B. Fuller Z. S. Makowski and J. Borrego showed how linear and planar mem-

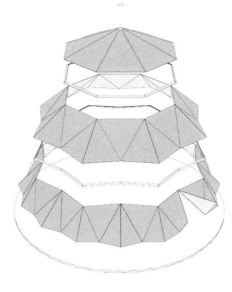

48, 49   Internal view of a folded plate barrel structure
with different optical coatings applied to the
folded surfaces, Design: Chr. Mayer, A.
von Storp, B. Czempiel, D. Erbar

50–53   Concept of a folded plate dome structure with
a span of 20 m, Design: H. Kosel, U. Ernst

50   Isometric of the structure

51   Computer-simulation

52, 53   Views of model

bers can be combined. In the following passages the term "truss" is also applied to structures with planar load-bearing elements such as flat glass pates. [**6.3/11, 6.3/12**]

Peter von Seidlein at Stuttgart University and Mick Eekhout at TU Delft produced proposals in 1988 and 1989 respectively on how flat glass could be integrated in truss structures. [**6.3/13**] The design for the atrium roof of a bank in The Hague has a fish-belly beam with a compressive top chord and a tensile bottom chord made from flat glass elements, which are both connected to steel struts by point fittings ____Fig. 57. [**6.3/14**]

Trussed plate structures offer a great deal of potential for the structural use of glass. The characteristic triangular frames of the structure leads to bending moments being dissolved into axially loaded members so that it is possible to use glass as a compression element. All components can be connected to one another by hinged joints. In addition the dimensions of the components in trusses gener-

ally come within the limits imposed by the manufacturers' stock sizes for flat glass. By adopting shorter elements, the buckling or plate buckling requirements of the structural elements can be addressed ____Figs 55, 56. [**6.3/15**]

The distribution of normal forces in a truss depends on non-variable factors such as beam shape, support conditions and geometry of the truss members and the variable load pattern. During form-finding thorough comparative structural analyses are necessary to ensure that the distribution of compressive and tensile stresses is consistent for all load cases and combinations. These dependencies were understood in the trusses of the 19th century and their combinations of compression-resistant cast iron with tension-resistant wrought iron.

The normal forces in the struts depend on the loads, span and effective structural depth. In a single span beam subject to a uniformly distributed load the positive moments increase towards mid-span ____Fig. 54. Consequently this is where the largest compression and ten-

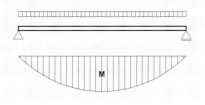

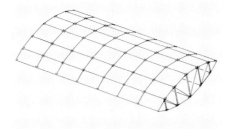

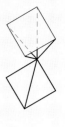

54

57

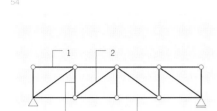

55

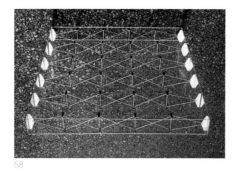

58

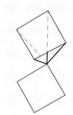

59

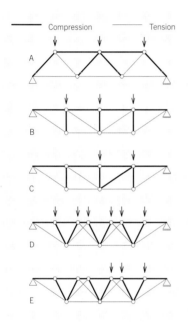

Compression   Tension

A

B

C

D

E

56

54   Bending moment diagram for an equivalent single
span beam

55   Description of truss elements
1   Top chord
2   Diagonal member
3   Vertical member
4   Bottom chord

56   Distribution of axial forces in various truss structures
A   Truss with parallel chord: For a uniform
load across the full span the diagonals are
alternately in compression or tension.
B, C   Truss with parabolic bottom chord: For
a uniform load across the full span the
diagonals are in tension and the verticals
in compression; for an asymmetric load
some diagonals are in compression.
D, E   Statically indeterminate structure: By
prestressing the tensile diagonals the
axial forces can be stabilised.

57   Isometric of the trussed plate structure for the AMRO
Bank in The Hague: Glass plates form the top and
bottom chords, steel struts and cables the diagonal and
vertical members. Arch.: M. Grasveld, Eng.: M. Eekhout

58   Model of a parallel chorded truss with top and bottom
chords of glass, Design: U. Knaack

59   Examples for the integration possibilities of plate
elements in space frame structures

sion occurs in the top and bottom chords respectively. Diagonal or vertical members transmit the shear forces, which increase towards the supports, and these shear forces may be compressive or tensile depending on the type of beam and arrangement of members ___Fig. 56. The force in the top chord will generally always be compressive if the wind suction forces do not exceed the self-weight of the structure. For single span beams, the roof glazing can thus be designed as a compression chord, combining the structural with the enclosing skin. If there are more members in the truss than are required for stability then this creates internal static indeterminacy. These members can be used to provide alternative load paths or apply prestress to the system in order to stabilise the distribution of axial forces under alternating loads. [6.3/16] Point connections to the glass elements can be avoided if the diagonals are made of flat materials and therefore can be attached in the hinged joints of the top chord.

CELLULAR STRUCTURES

___THE GLASS PRISM AS A STRUCTURAL MODULE

The combination of several flat panels to form a three-dimensional cell or body is described as *folding*. Folding can be simulated by the use of adhesives or solder to form material connections of the panels. A fold consists of two planar components with a common edge. Regular polyhedra are created by *pyramidal* and *prismatic* folds. Unlike pyramidal folding the edges of a prismatic folded structure are parallel to one another. The *tetrahedron*, *hexahedron (cube)*, *octahedron*, *dodecahedron* and *icosahedron* are regular polyhedra composed of equilateral polygons (the five Platonic Bodies). Tetrahedra, octahedra and icosahedra consist of equilateral triangles, the hexahedron of regular quadruples and the dodecahedron of regular pentagons ___Fig. 70.

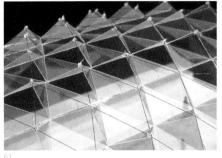

60–66 Concepts for cellular structures
60, 61 Barrel-vaulted shell with diagrid cable
net composed of tetrahedron modules,
Design: Chr. Schlaich, J. Wong
62 Faceted trussed frame construction: Glass plates
form the compression-loaded diagonals, steel plates
the tensile elements. Design: N. Bogatzki, R. Herkrath
63, 64 Elliptic barrel-vaulted plate structure,
Design: N. Reuters, T. Glitsch
65, 66 Barrel shell with stabilizing cable ties reflecting
the bending moment envelope, Design:
S. Dreyer, T. Gilich, L. Heimann

6.3

SPACE FRAME STRUCTURES

The tetrahedron and the half-octahedron on a square base are stable non-sway bodies which, because of their regularity, are suitable for use as structural modules for systematically assembled cellular structures. These bodies can be combined and sequenced as elemental building blocks in space frame structures. Linear or radial arrangements create trussed beams or arches. Biaxial arrangement on plane, arched or domed grids creates highly statically indeterminate systems of trussed and multi-faceted slabs, grillages, barrels or domes.

As an example the biaxially spanning slab is described in more detail below: On a plane and continuously interlocked with one another, the edges of the cells, alternating tetrahedra and the semi-octahedra, form the grid pattern of the space frame. The surfaces of the top and bottom chords each form a square grid, with the top and bottom grids being displaced a half-mesh with respect to one another in each direction ____Fig. 67.

The implementation of the geometric model in a cellular structure is done by having two types of polyhedron; one forming the load-bearing modules and the other the intermediate voids. A *tetra-grid* consists of solid tetrahedra, an *octa-grid* of half-octahedra. In both cases the structure must be supplemented by linear members at least in the area of the tension-loaded bottom chord plane, the top chord plane being formed, for example, of glass plates. The remaining edges of the cell form the three-dimensional diagonals, which are loaded in compression or tension and interconnect the top and bottom planes.

The structural use of glass can be extended to the diagonal members in compression, the plate buckling is prevented by the stiffening effect of the adjacent planar elements of each tetrahedron or half-octahedron. Membrane stress may occur in the glass elements, which produces low, uniform stress levels.

Extending the work done by Makowski and Fuller, experimental cellular structures were constructed using materials in sheet form,

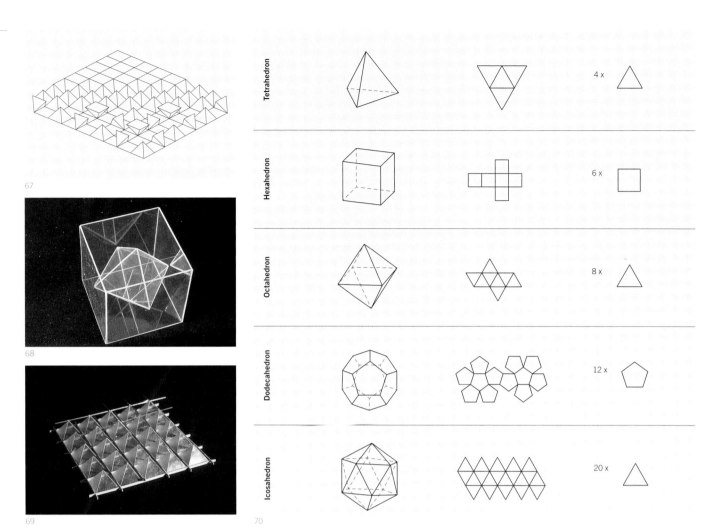

67

68

69

70

Tetrahedron			4 x
Hexahedron			6 x
Octahedron			8 x
Dodecahedron			12 x
Icosahedron			20 x

67   Tetrahedra and half-octahedra can be packed
together into a dense, planar spatial arrangement.

68   Geometric relationship between hexahedra
and octahedra

69   Model of an *octa-grid*, a cellular structure composed
of half-octahedra

70   Overview of the five Platonic bodies (solids)

such as aluminium and plywood. For reasons of economy this approach did not gain acceptance for use in preference to traditional
trusses with rod members and hinged joints. Although Borrego wrote
that cellular structures allowed the use of materials that were *"unsuitable for conventional structures because of their brittleness"* until now
the use of glass for three-dimensional cellular structures had not been
thoroughly investigated. U. Knaack discusses octa-grid structures in
his PhD thesis and book of the same name *Konstruktiver Glasbau*
(Structural Glass) but does not clearly differentiate between glass
compression members and steel tension members. [**6.3/17, 6.3/18**]

    The main reason why glass cellular structures have not entered
into consideration up to now is without doubt that adhesive technology,
an important preliminary for the production of prismatic or pyramidal
structural modules, has not been adequately researched.

7

PROJECTS

9–11   The load-bearing structure consists of steel beams
with trapezoidal cross-sections, which are additionally
supported by articulated steel tubes between the
hull and the walls of the original dry dock and by
glass beams that run parallel to the ship's axis. The
roof is composed of 4.35 m x 1.5 m laminated glass
panes consisting of 2 x 10 mm heat-treated glass.

12   The glass beams consisting of 3 x 10 mm
heat-treated glass are connected to the
main steel beams by shoe brackets.

nents were laminated for redundancy and post-fracture integrity. The
plates which support the water are laminated from two layers of 10 millimetres heat-strengthened glass. The beams were laminated from
three layers of 10 millimetres heat-strengthened glass. The glass
beams run fore and aft, parallel to the axis of the ship, and their ends
were supported on fabricated steel beams of trapezoidal cross-section, pin-jointed to plates bolted to the dock wall and propped by steel
struts from pads on the dock floor. The in-plane shear stiffness of the
1.5 m x 4.35 m glass plates stabilises the steel beams and their props.
The ends of the steel beams adjacent to the hull are connected by a
series of trimmer beams and carry the flexible joint that seals the plate
to the hull.

The glass panels were bonded to the top edges of the steel beams
using structural silicone between stainless steel strips factory-bonded
to the panels and the steel beams. Structural silicone also bonded the
long edges of the panels to small stainless steel sections which had

been factory-bonded to the tops of the glass beams. The bond also
provided attachment to generate membrane forces in the panels to
assist in maintaining their integrity in the event of significant damage.

The ship was known to expand, contract and bend sideways in
response to shifts in temperature. Therefore the junction between the
waterline plate and the ship had to accommodate these movements
while containing the reflecting pool. A number of structural adhesives
were studied and tested for compatibility with the existing paintwork
on the hull, and eventually a stainless steel T-section was bonded to
the hull, after extensive in-situ tests and ultrasonic examination of the
entire length of the bonded joint to identify weak areas in the hull. A
Hypalon membrane was then bonded and fastened to the new section
to form a flexible collar to the new waterline plate. The flexible joint was
continued along the fore and aft axis of the ship, separating the waterline plate into two halves to allow for the movement of the dock walls.
[7.2/2]

13

14

15

17

13 Cantilevers composed of glass and acryl glass
fins span a width of 10.6 m; glass canopy at the
underground station of the Tokyo International
Forum, 1996, Arch.: Rafael Vinoly,
Eng.: Dewhurst Macfarlane and Partners

14–16 Glass roof above interior courtyard at the IHK
in Munich: each beam axis spans roughly
14 m and is composed of thirteen glass fins with
interlocking glass leaves, each 4.5 m long.

17 Installation of the 2.7 m x 2.3 m
insulating glass panes

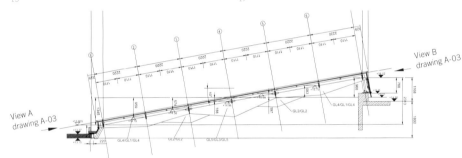

16

GLASS ROOF FOR INTERNATIONAL CHAMBER OF COMMERCE (IHK) MUNICH, 2003

___ ARCHITECTS: BETSCH ARCHITEKTEN, MUNICH

___ ENGINEERS: LUDWIG UND WEILER GMBH, AUGSBURG

___ SPECIALIST CONTRACTOR: ANDREAS OSWALD GMBH, MUNICH

The built-up beam technique, originating from timber construction, in which smaller component cross-sections are combined into a larger, stiffer beam through lapping and nailing, was applied to glass construction for the first time by Dewhurst Macfarlane and Partners in the glass canopy above an entrance of a subway station in Tokyo, realised in 1996 ___ Fig. 13.

The project for a roof above the interior courtyard at the International Chamber of Commerce (IHK) in Munich, broadens the scope of the principle by applying it to a multipart simply supported single span across a width of approximately 14 metres. Five main beams, each composed of thirteen individual glass fins and weighing approximately 3.5 tonnes, form the primary load-bearing structure of the lean-to roof with an incline of 10°. The centre-to-centre distance of the main beams is 2.7 metres, with similarly constructed secondary glass beams adding to the structure between the beam axes at intervals of roughly 2.2 m ___ Figs 14–16.

The interlocking individual glass fins, each 4.5 metres long, are staggered by half a fin length; at the centre of the span they form a five-part cross-section and at the support end they form a three-part cross-section. The outer glass fins are composed of 2 x 12 mm heat-strengthened glass; the inner fins consist of a three-layer laminate with a 19 millimetres fully tempered glass pane sandwiched between two 10 millimetres panes.

The bending moment, which increases towards the middle, translates into the increasing structural depth of the segments. Consistent

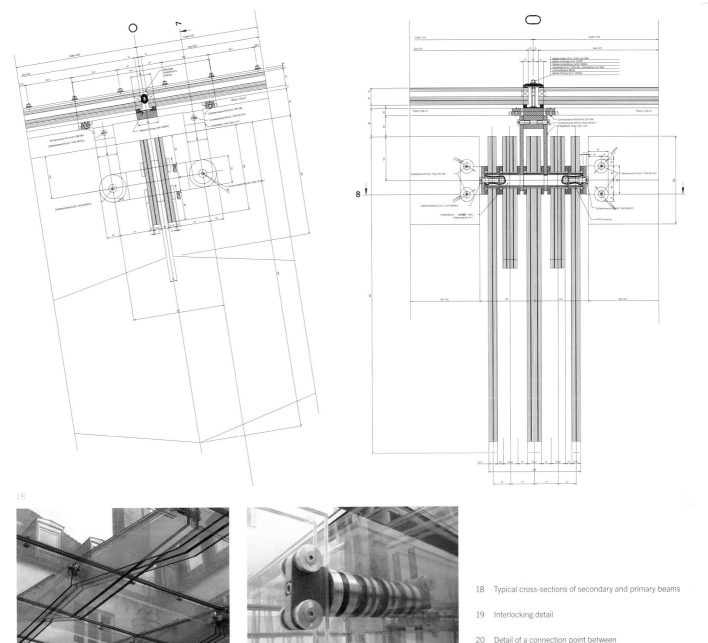

18   Typical cross-sections of secondary and primary beams

19   Interlocking detail

20   Detail of a connection point between
primary and secondary beam

flexural strength is ensured by made-to-fit bearing bolt connections at the end and centre points of the fins. The contact connection between bolt and glass bearing is ensured with *Hilti Hit HY-50* injection mortar, for which injection openings are provided in the fittings. The main beams are stabilised by the binding piece connection of the secondary beams consisting of 2 x 10 mm heat strengthened glass, linked to the beam ends with a pair of M10 bolts.

The roof glazing panels are framed on four sides by a structurally bonded steel section, connected to the principal and the secondary load-bearing structure by profiles that sit on the top of the beams.

The roof construction requires an extremely high degree of precision in the manufacture of the beams, the bolt connections (0.1 mm accuracy of fit) and in the assembly.

The almost square plan would also have been suitable for a biaxially spanning load-bearing structure, although this could not have been realised with the built-up beam principle. [**7.2/3, 7.2/4**]

21

23

22

21 Support detail of load-bearing glass beam (four- layer
    laminated beam) and connection elements for fastening
    the lateral panes and the glass floor. The vertical loads
    consisting of dead load and live loads are transfered by
    setting blocks along the bottom edge of the glass beam.

22 Bottom view:
    Structural steel members and connection elements are
    positioned only in direction of the main span. At the top
    the solid building walls on roof panels are crossed; the
    open joints require intensive and regular cleaning.

23 All glass elements are fashioned from low-
    iron glass; the top layer of the glass floor has
    an anti-slip screen-printed surface.

GLASS BRIDGE, SCHWÄBISCH HALL, 2005

___ARCHITECTS: KRAFT + KRAFT ARCHITEKTEN, SCHWÄBISCH HALL
___ENGINEERS: LUDWIG UND WEILER GMBH, AUGSBURG
___SPECIALIST CONTRACTOR: ANDREAS OSWALD GMBH, MUNICH
    GLAS TRÖSCH HOLDING AG, BÜTZBERG

The glass bridge provides a weather-protected link between two Sparkasse buildings on the Hafenmarkt; it crosses over a set of steps below
that lead to St Ulrich's church. The two lateral glass beams of laminated
glass (four layers, 2 x 12 mm tempered glass at the centre, and one
12 millimetres heat-strengthened glass on either flank) run across the
entire length of 6.2 metres and also function as a balustrade and a
protection barrier from falling. Along the sides, the edges of the beams
are held over their full height of approximately 1.1 metre in a U-shaped
steel channel, which provides both a restraining effect for the beam
against lateral buckling and edge protection for the load-bearing leaves.

Steel angle brackets are connected along the bottom edge of the beam
to the inner side of the bridge floor with bearing bolt and adhesive connections; these serve as a continuous support for the floor panels of
4 x 12 mm heat-strengthened glass. To improve the residual load-
bearing capacity, the floor panels are connected to the flange of the
steel section with bolts at the ends and at the centre. The top layer has
an anti-slip ceramic frit to ensure safe foot traffic across the bridge. On
the outer sides of the bridge, the 2 x 10 mm heat-strengthened glass
side panels are connected with stainless steel cylinders and clamping
plates. The lateral panels are also fixed at the height of the safety rail,
which is "mounted" on top of the beam over its full length. The roof
panels are structurally bonded to the top of the lateral panels. [7.2/5]
The reduction in terms of design and construction achieved through
the use of large-format panels and structural silicone is compromised
by steel cables running below the roof plane to provide a mechanical
safety measure in the event of damaged roof panels.

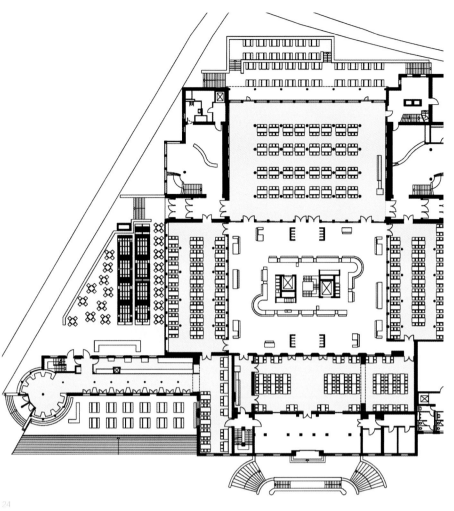

26

24

25

24 Ground plan of the "Alte Mensa" after the conversion:
the former courtyard, now converted into a cafeteria
at the centre of four dining halls lies above the student
residence on Mommsenstraße.

25 Concept of courtyard enclosure: the glass roof surrounds
the solid central "table" like a ring. The roof structure
is composed of ladder-shaped load-bearing modules
composed of primary and secondary beams.

26 Joint between glass roof and longitudinal side of
the "table"

GLASS ROOF FOR REFECTORY AT THE TU DRESDEN, 2006

__ DESIGN: MAEDEBACH, REDELEIT & PARTNER
ARCHITEKTEN BDA, BERLIN/DRESDEN
__ STRUCTURAL DESIGN: LEONHARDT, ANDRÄ UND PARTNER,
BERATENDE INGENIEURE VBI, GMBH, DRESDEN
__ CONSULTING LOAD- AND RESIDUAL LOAD-
BEARING CAPACITY TESTS: PROF. BERNHARD WELLER, THOMAS
SCHADOW, INSTITUT FÜR BAUKONSTRUKTION, TU DRESDEN
__ SPECIALIST CONTRACTOR: HUNSRÜCKER GLASVEREDELUNG
WAGENER GMBH & CO KG, KIRCHBERG

The student residence on Mommsenstraße, designed by the Dresden
city architect Paul Wolf and inaugurated in 1925, is the centrepiece of
the "Alte Mensa" (old refectory) at the Technical University of Dresden. Following several additions and expansions between 1930 and
1960, it now also encompasses the Vice-Chancellor's offices of the

university. Within the context of a complete refurbishment of the building complex located south of the main campus, the interior courtyard
was covered by a glass roof and converted into the central food court
for the four adjacent dining halls __ Fig. 24.

__ LOAD-BEARING STRUCTURE

The cooking, grilling and deep-fry facilities required for the food serv-
eries are installed in a massive "table" at the centre of the roughly
24 m x 30 m interior courtyard. The new glass roof stretches between
the outline of this table and the former exterior walls of the courtyard
in the shape of a shallow curved cushion __ Fig. 25.

Given the historic context of the "Alte Mensa", the formal and
structural design process for the glass roof was focussed on developing a neutral, open and "self-contained" load-bearing structure that
would stand out from the heterogeneous existing building.
The load-bearing structure is composed of principal and secondary

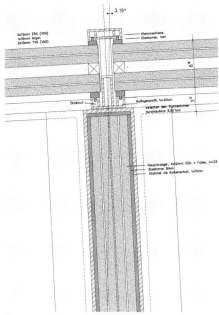

27

29

28

27　Detail of cruciform node connection: showing no
structural hierarchy.

28　The beam hierarchy is evident in the context: the
principal beams span between the former courtyard
facade and the edges of the "table"; the secondary
beams cover only a 1.45 m span between the
principal beams.

29　Design drawing of node connection: vertical section
of principal beam

glass beams, which form a ceiling grid of identical squares for supporting the weather skin of insulating glass panels (1.45 m x 1.45 m).
Visually speaking the load-bearing structure is a grillage. The cruciform junctions and the identical beam depths suggest a beam splice
joint in both span directions ——Figs 27, 28. In terms of construction,
however, this is a hierarchical load-bearing structure of continuous
principal beams and secondary beams in between. The principal
beams span a maximum distance of 5.75 metres between table edge
and courtyard enclosure. The junctions with the secondary beams are
spaced at a centre-to-centre distance of roughly 1.45 metre.

At the corners of the courtyard ——Fig. 38 the hierarchy had to be
reversed: in these areas, the principal beams are subjected to higher
loads than all other beams. One side of the principal beam is subjected at this position to the loads from three secondary beams, the other
side to loads from two secondary beams and an additional orthogonal
principal beam, which carries the bulk of the roof load at the corner.

The beam depth of 350 millimetres necessary at these points and the
beam build-up were then applied to the entire load-bearing structure
to achieve the desired uniformity in appearance. Tests had to be undertaken to ascertain the load-bearing and residual load-bearing capacity at the corners.

—— CONSTRUCTION AND DETAILS

Generally speaking every second principal beam is connected in shear
with the three adjoining secondary beams by a pair of bearing bolt
connections (M12 bolts), resulting in a ladder-like load-bearing module. The node connectors are fabricated from steel plates; EPDM gasket strips prevent contact between the steel and glass surfaces
——Fig. 29.

The principal and secondary beams consist of four 12 millimetre
fully tempered and heat soaked glass leaves with interlayers of 1.5 millimetre PVB. The outer leaves serve as protective and sacrificial layers

30–34   Installation of roof structure
    30   Installation of secondary beams
    31   Preparation for installing the roof panels: placing
         the sealant strips and sealing the connection joints
32–34   Installation of principal beams

for the load-bearing inner plates.

The four-leaf laminated construction means that the main beams have "only" a slenderness of roughly 1:7 in relation to the entire span width. The shear and compression connections provides additional stiffening for the principal beam and prevents failure as a result of lateral torsional buckling. The ends of the principal beams are held in place on the support edges by shoe brackets ____ Figs 35, 36.

In addition to the linear support of the insulating glazing for snow- and dead load, the aluminium sections, which are structurally bonded to the upper edge of the beams, also provide a second line of defence and cavity drainage. Clamping bars are installed in the fall direction along the length of the principal beams to carry wind suction forces. The minimum incline of six degrees ensures controlled water runoff. The exterior joints transverse to the fall direction are sealed with silicon to create a smooth roof skin.

The bottom pane of the insulated glazing consists of 2 x 12 mm heat-strengthened glass. The 16 millimetre cavity is filled with argon for better heat insulation. Since the glass roof must be accessible to foot traffic for maintenance and cleaning, the upper pane also consists of laminated glass.

____ LOAD- AND RESIDUAL LOAD-BEARING CAPACITY

For the individual approval by building authority necessary in Germany (ZiE or Zustimmung im Einzelfall), proof of stability was demonstrated by tests on original building components. Three tests each were carried out for the load-bearing capacity and the residual load-bearing capacity of the glass beam subjected to the highest stresses in the corner area of the roof. The number of tests and the test regime were stipulated by the state authorities for building technology.

The test protocol for the building component tests encompassed the glass beam subjected to the highest stresses as well as three secondary glass beams and one additional principal glass beam ____ Fig. 35.

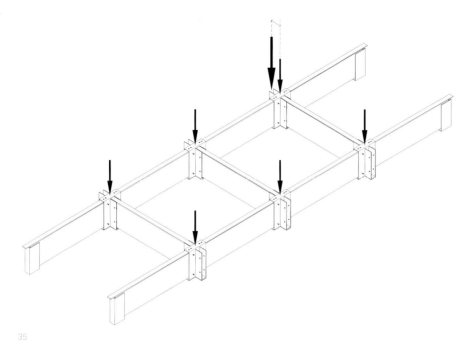

37

35   Position of loads for load-bearing capacity
     and residual load-bearing capacity tests
     of the glass beams roof structure

36, 37 Load-and residual load-bearing capacity
     test of the glass structure in the test hall
     at the Institut für Baukonstruktion at the
     Technical University in Dresden

The stress was applied exclusively at the joints of the construction and was roughly P = 10 kN per joint during the test for load-bearing capacity and approximately A = 60 kN at the joint subject to high stress at an eccentricity of roughly 120 millimetres ____Fig. 37. During the test for the residual load-bearing capacity, the regime allowed for this load to be reduced to roughly one quarter. The load was applied to the specimen both directly and with the aid of a three-dimensional loading frame of steel sections.

To pass the test for load-bearing capacity successfully, the roof structure of glass beams had to be capable of carrying at least three times the rated load without incurring any damage. In this case, the sag in the beam was 24 mm. Passing the test for residual load-bearing capacity meant that that the dead load and half of the snow loads had to be shown to be carried for at least twelve hours and without further increases in deformation following a partial destruction of the glass beams ____Fig. 36. Once the six tests were carried out successfully, the

breaking load – here roughly 4.5 times the rated load – was established with the help of the specimen.

____FUNCTION AND FORM

The need for additional exterior and interior shading was obviated thanks to the use of a selective solar control coating with a g-value of 0.36 (and a τ of 0.63) in combination with the mechanical ventilation system. Glare protection measures were not required. Smoke and heat extraction is effected via louvres integrated in the massive coping of the "table" with the result that the glass construction did not have to fulfil these functions.

The glass roof acts as a new connecting element in the heterogeneous context of the "Alte Mensa" and has played a considerable role in improving the quality of the complex, as is evident since the completion of the construction in the use of the spaces for official events. With its neutral structure, the ring-shaped glass roof is distinct from the

38

38   Corner section of the load-bearing
     structure composed of glass beams

historic buildings, which have been placed under a conservation or-der, while at the same time creating an identity-forming centre for the surrounding building fabric. The covered interior courtyard with the food stations is experienced as a "market square" – and thus a direct continuation of traditional glass courtyard models. [7.2/6, 7.2/7]

____CONCLUSION

The design of the glass construction does more than follow construc-tional perspectives in the sense of an "honest" or material-efficient building method. Visually, the load-bearing structure of primary and secondary beams has the appearance of a grillage, but biaxial load transfer only occurs at the corners. The uniform beam height and thickness means the majority of the glass cross-sections are not load-ed to their full capacity. The high degree of redundancy is countered by the low number of required components and thus the rational and cost-efficient assembly, which is achieved through the minimised

number of connections.

The project exemplifies a new approach to structural glass design, in which the construction is subordinate to the architectonic concept. Achieving the desired spatial effect is given precedence over an em-phasis on the flow of forces.

39, 40 Protective roof over a brick ruin on the experimental site of the Lehrstuhl für Tragkonstruktionen at the RWTH Aachen (demolished): the roof covering constitutes the compression member of the trussed system.

41–43 Inclined facade of Koop library: the facade plane constitutes the middle member subject to compression forces in a three chord truss construction.
   41 Interior
   42 Exterior
   43 Detail of construction

GLASS FACADE, KOOP LIBRARY RWTH AACHEN, 1996

___ DESIGN: ULRICH KNAACK WITH VALERIE SPALDING, MARIO RUNKEL AND STUDENTS

___ ENGINEERS: WILFRIED FÜHRER, LEHRSTUHL FÜR TRAGKONSTRUKTIONEN

A steel-and-glass skeleton frame system – which had previously been successfully tested in the form of a roof above a masonry ruin on the experimental site of the faculty ___ Figs 39, 40 – was further developed for the 20 m x 6 m large inclined glazing on the north facade of the Koop Library at the RWTH Aachen.

In the library glazing, an array of parallel, vertical three-cord trussed girders spaced at intervals of 2 metres, supports the glass skin spanning across the 6 metres high opening ___ Figs 41, 42. The middle compression chord is formed by the short edges of the 0.8 m x 2 m insulating glass units of the inclined glazing, each composed of two 6 mm tempered glass panes. The steel cables running parallel to the joints internally and externally of the facade function as top and bottom chords respectively. V-shaped galvanised steel struts and diagonal cable bracings, attached half way up the panes with clamping plates, complete the skeleton frame structure ___ Fig. 43. The forces are channelled along the short panel edges as a result of the local support brackets between the steel members and the glass plates. The spreading action of the compression strut prevents lateral displacement of the top and bottom chord. The prestressing forces of 20kN load the glass plate as a compressive force and is 'short-circuited' by the guying so that the inner chord and the outer chord also participate in the load transfer by decreasing the tensile forces – for inner chords in the case of wind suction and for outer chords in the case of positive wind pressures. [7.2/8]

The trussed girder is a closed system with no force deriving from the pretensioning being transferred into the foot or head connection.

44

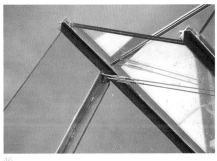

46

45

44–46 Canopy construction to the Freie Evangelische
Gemeinde, Aachen: The folded plates
along the sides are supported by V-shaped
props. Steel cables are strung between the
props beneath the fold in the centre to provide
mechanical safety in case of breakage.

CANOPY FOR A COMMUNITY CENTRE, AACHEN, 1999

___ DESIGN: ULRICH KNAACK IN COLLABORATION WITH
THOMAS LINK AND STUDENTS

___ ENGINEER: WILFRIED FÜHRER, LEHRSTUHL FÜR
TRAGKONSTRUKTIONEN

___ EXECUTION: STUDENTS PARTICIPATING IN THE "KONSTRUKTIVER
GLASBAU" SEMINAR

The canopy for a community centre was designed as a folded plate
structure above an area that is roughly 3 m x 5 m in plan. The folded
roof is composed of six laminated glass panels consisting of 2 x 10 mm
float glass, which alternate to form the ridges and valleys. The largest
plate measures 5.70 m x 1.32 m. The outer folds rest on V-shaped
steel supports that are rigidly fixed to the heads of tubular steel columns. The middle fold spans the 5 metres without column support,
although it is secured by steel cables. Load tests were carried out to
determine the load-bearing and residual load-bearing capacity (see
also Chapter 4.1 ___ Fig. 40). A linear hinge connection between the
glass edges is achieved with steel sections, structurally bonded to the
glass at the factory and bolted together on site. The steel profiles absorb some of the compression and tensile forces at the edge of the
glass. The geometry of the fold must be precise for the linear joint to
work properly. The laminated glass plates could be manufactured with
low production tolerances because they were fashioned from annealed
float glass. The tolerances present in the steel construction were accommodated by using a viscoelastic, high-performance structural silicone. [7.2/9]

47 Bottom view of a roof structure with the steel-
glass composite system across 15 m span; model
project study "New Roofing for St. Pius X"

48 Prototype with a span of 5 m during load test

SELF-SUPPORTING, SEMI-TRANSPARENT ROOF MODULE
PROTOTYPE FOR A MODULAR SYSTEM, 2001

____ DESIGN AND CONSTRUCTION: ANDREA HÜBINGER, SILKE FÖRST

____ PROJECT DIRECTOR: JAN WURM

____ TECHNICAL SUPPORT: MATTHIAS MEISSNER, SAINT-GOBAIN
GLAS DEUTSCHLAND, AACHEN

The point of departure for this project was the hitherto unused potential
of steel trapezoidal profiles with acoustic perforations. Trapezoidal profiled steel sheets are chiefly employed as roofing elements for medium
spans in industrial buildings; perforations in part or all of the web and
top flange improve the acoustics – although their light transmittance is
not utilised in these cases. Combining steel trapezoidal profiles with a
transparent roof covering not only opens up new visual and functional
possibilities, it also creates new constructional options when shear
connections are used.

____ LOAD-BEARING SYSTEM

The module consists of a steel trapezoidal profile with acoustic perforations joined by a shear connection to a glass roof covering in order
to be able to use the entire composite depth structurally as a sandwich. The glass has a restraining effect on the top chord of the system
and reduces the risk of buckling of the steel profile. Given the positive
moments in the single-span slab, compression forces can be assigned
to the glass and tensile forces to the bottom flanges and webs of the
steel profile in accordance with the specific material properties.

Due to the stock lengths of the rolled steel profiles, the bottom
chord of the system can be continuous. The width of the members is
determined by the component width of the sections. The dimensions
of the sheets making up the upper chord take into account the manufactured stock sizes of the glass. Compression forces are easily transmitted between the glass sheets through contact butt joints.

Installing the slab-shaped building elements side by side creates a

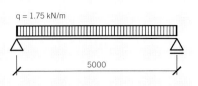

q = 1.75 kN/m

5000

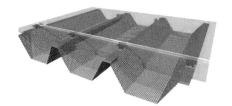

49

52

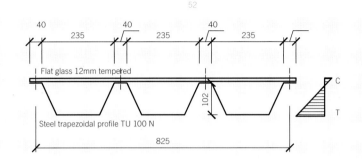

40   235   40   235   40   235

Flat glass 12mm tempered

102

C

T

Steel trapezoidal profile TU 100 N

825

50

49 System sketch of steel-glass composite
    system across a 5 m span

50 Schematic cross-section of sandwich: in the
    compression zone, the glass strengthens the
    top chord of the steel trapezoidal profiles.

51 Plan and elevation of prototype with STP
    TU 100 N across a 5 m span

52 Sandwich build up (detail)

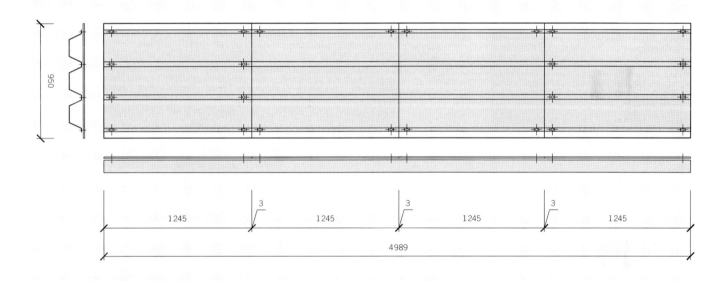

950

1245   3   1245   3   1245   3   1245

4989

51

continuous, structural roof skin. The system can also be employed for curved or double-curved roof geometries by using curved trapezoidal profiles. Domed roofs would require an additional, gradual narrowing of the profiles.

___CONSTRUCTION

With an envisioned span of 15 metres, the modular system was tested as a prototype across a span of 5 metres. The steel trapezoidal profile type TU 100 N *(ThyssenKrupp Stahl)* was used for the test series. The element is 825 millimetres wide and 1.25 millimetres thick, while the perforation profile is a standard pattern with roughly 28 percent of total perforated surface (5 mm hole diameter, 9 mm centre-to-centre distance). Given the stiffening of the profile cross-section provided by the shear connection with the glass plane, the steel profile can be installed upside down, that is with the narrow flanges at the top, in contrast to the usual practice. These upper flanges, which are roughly 40 millime-

tres wide, serve as supports for the glass; like a small portion of the web, they are not perforated. The glazing is composed of four equal panes of 12 millimetres tempered glass measuring 950 mm x 1245 mm. Although used as overhead glazing, laminated glass is not necessary in this case because the glass fragments fall into the trapezoidal profile, posing no risk to pedestrians passing underneath. Multipane insulating glass units are also an option for the roofing material.

___DETAILS

The glazing is connected to the steel profile by undercut anchors *(Fischer-Zykon-Panelanchor für Glas (FZP-G))*, which had just been introduced to the market at the time this project was developed. These anchors are distributed by Saint-Gobain Germany, for example, under the name *Point-XS*. The 8 millimetres diameter steel bolts are connected to the glass by undercut holes and to the steel plate by friction grip connections. At the fixing points, the coating is stripped off the

53

55

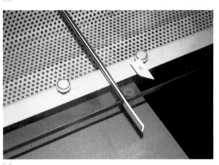

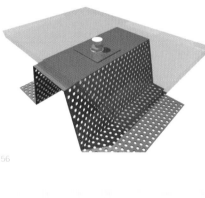

54

56

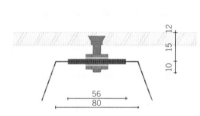

53   Built prototype

54, 55   Packing of joints and installation of plate elements

56–58   Connection detail of undercut bolts

57

58

steel and the upper flange of the trapezoidal plate is reinforced with additional steel sheeting. The number of point fixings reflects the distribution of shear forces, which diminish from the support ends to the centre of the member. Thus the middle glass plates are connected by two bolts at the transverse panel edges to the steel profile; the outer plates are connected by four bolts. The joints between the plates are packed with dry fibre gaskets of 3 millimetres hard-elastic *Klingersil* ____ Figs 54, 55.

A non-perforated strip is provided at the profile ends to enable the bottom chords to be mechanically connected to a substructure by means of bolts and brackets ____ Figs 53, 58.

____ LOAD-BEARING CAPACITY

The steel cross-sections have been designed to have the necessary load-bearing capacity without taking the shear connection to the glazing into account, albeit without satisfying the deflection serviceability criterion, which is only achieved with composite action. This greatly facilitates the process of being granted building authority approval.

In addition to the shear forces, imposed strains must also be taken into consideration at the bolted connections due to the differing deformation behaviour of steel and glass.

Load-bearing capacity studies demonstrate that the total stiffness of the composite member is twice that of an identical structure without composite construction. Accordingly, the few point fixings achieve a 50 percent effective shear connection. The composite effect can be further improved by increasing the number of point fixings, which will also reduce deformations and stresses in the glass.

The test results can be used to deduce corresponding values for other span widths and profile cross-sections ____ Fig. 61.

____ FUNCTION AND DESIGN

A distinguishing feature of this modular system is that essential build-

59

60

	TU 100/275	T 83/280	T 126/326
Span l	500 cm	500 cm	700 cm
Glass thickness t	1.2 cm tempered	1.2 cm tempered	1.2 cm tempered
structural depth h_{TOTAL}	12.5 cm	10.8 cm	15.1 cm
req. moment of inertia I	200 cm⁴	183 cm⁴	502 cm⁴
act. I_{STP}	191cm⁴	123 cm⁴	306 cm⁴
act. I_{GLASS}	14.4 cm⁴	14.4 cm⁴	14.4 cm⁴
calc. $I_{100\% COMPOSITE}$	822 cm⁴	503 cm⁴	1078 cm⁴
act. I_{TEST}	approx. 400 cm⁴	approx. 250 cm⁴ (estimated)	approx. 540 cm⁴ (estimated)
act. τ_{STP}	6.6 kN/cm²	9.1 kN/cm²	11.6 kN/cm²
act. τ_{GLASS}	1.8 kN/cm²	2.1 kN/cm²	2.7 kN/cm²
Anchors at support	4	6	6

59, 60   Load-bearing capacity tests on the
prototype: the deflections in the centre of the
member were measured for various loads
with and without composite action.

61   Determining geometrical and structural parameters
for sandwich elements with a 5 m or 7 m span

61

I_{TOTAL}

7.2

ing physical requirements are integrated by simple means. On the one hand, the perforation of the steel plate provides sound absorption (in keeping with its original use), which is important for the acoustics in large halls; on the other hand, the plate serves as sun and glare protection that is integrated into the construction. Incident sunlight is deflected at the perforated screen and the interior is illuminated with soft, glare-free light. The lighting scenario can be specifically adapted to individual preferences through the perforation geometry (hole pattern and ratio of holes to solid surface), the profile cross-section and the finish of the steel surface. Despite a hole-to-solid surface ratio of only 28 percent, the prototype has a high degree of transparency because the sky, which is much brighter than the interior, is visually perceived as a composition of individual "pixels".

Since the plate functions as internal sun protection, any resultant heat gain has to be evacuated along the troughs in the trapezoidal profile sheet. Light transmission can be additionally manipulated through screen printing a dot-matrix on the glass surfaces. Attractive moiré effects are generated by the interference of the different patterns of the perforated sheet metal and the fritted glass.

CONCLUSION AND OUTLOOK

Thanks to its composition, the building component is transparent, self-supporting and multifunctional. The composite steel-and-glass system consists of industrial semifinished products and is thus easy to fabricate and to install. Despite its characteristics as a system, the choices of steel profile, perforation pattern and glass surface treatment open up a broad spectrum of visual possibilities. The span width and the degree of transparency of the modules can be designed on a project-by-project basis. [7.2/10] Further studies with regard to structural performance and the passage of light are necessary for other application scenarios before this module can be developed into a standardised building system.

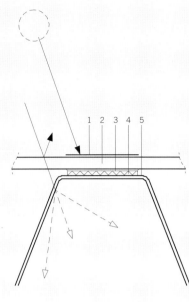

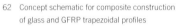

62

62   Concept schematic for composite construction
       of glass and GFRP trapezoidal profiles
       1   Screen print
       2   Glass pane
       3   Primer
       4   PUR adhesive
       5   GFRP trapezoidal profile

63   Atmospheric quality in the interior created
       by the semi-transparency of the composite
       steel-glass system (model simulation)

63

The load-bearing characteristics can be improved by using translucent trapezoidal profiles of glass fibre reinforced plastic (GFRP) instead of steel profiles ⎯Fig. 62. Due to similar thermal expansion coefficients, shear connections of both materials through rigid linear adhesion are possible, without having to tolerate stress concentrations resulting from imposed strains. However, the replacement of damaged
glass elements would be a difficult challenge.

64   Insulating glass composite unit with integrated sun
      protection louvres, prototype with 3 m span

65   Daylight simulation on model

MULTIFUNCTIONAL GLAZING
PROTOTYPE FOR COMPOSITE INSULATING GLASS UNIT WITH
INTEGRATED SOLAR SHADING, 2002–2003

____ CONCEPT AND DESIGN: CHRISTOF HELMUS, MARC MEVISSEN
____ PROJECT DIRECTOR: JAN WURM
____ BUILDING COMPONENT TESTS: LEHRSTUHL FÜR STAHLBAU,
      RWTH AACHEN
____ TECHNICAL SUPPORT: FRANK WELLERSHOFF, RWTH AACHEN

The trend in building skins is towards using multifunctional glass units. Innovative multipane insulating glass units with integrated light deflection and solar shading systems in the cavity highlight this evolution. In the case of adjustable micro-louvres, deformations must be kept to a minimum in order to avoid compromising serviceability. This project demonstrates that fixed louvres can be used to reinforce the elements,

thus reducing the pane thickness and dead load, and ultimately the cost, of such insulating glass units.

____ LOAD-BEARING SYSTEM

The two panes of an insulating glass unit are structurally bonded to a core layer of glass fibre reinforced plastic pultrusions (GFRP), which are arranged in parallel in the glazing cavity. The result is a uniaxial, composite slab component. The effective stiffness of the sandwich element is the result of the cross-section and the relevant modulus of elasticity of both materials. At 7000 kN/cm², the modulus of elasticity of glass is twice as high as that of GFRP (modulus of elasticity of GFRP or E_{GFRP} = 3000 kN/cm²).

Tensile forces are generated on the bottom skin of the sandwich panel and compressive forces on the top skin. The flanges of the profiles are reinforced by an effective load-bearing plate width in the top and bottom chord. The shear forces are transmitted by the structurally bonded joints.

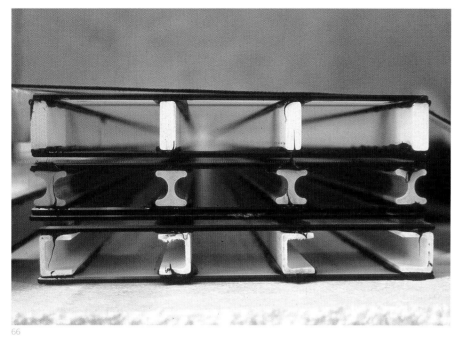

66

68

	C-profile 25/20/3	I-profile 22/20/4		Solid profile 30/10	
Prototypes	P1	P2	P3	P4	P5
Width profile w_P	20 mm	20 mm	20 mm	10 mm	10 mm
Height profile h_P	25 mm	22 mm	22 mm	30 mm	30 mm
eff. depth sandwich h_s	36 mm	33 mm	33 mm	41 mm	41 mm
Moment of inertia glass pane I_G	0.45 cm⁴	0.45 cm⁴	0.45 cm⁴	0.45 cm⁴	0.45 cm⁴
Moment of inertia profile I_P	1.6 cm⁴	1.6 cm⁴	1.6 cm⁴	2.25 cm⁴	2.25 cm⁴
Moment of inertia $I_{eff, no\ composite\ action}$ *	3.0 cm⁴	3.0 cm⁴	3.0 cm⁴	4.1 cm⁴	4.1 cm⁴
Moment of inertia $I_{eff, monolithic}$ *	68 cm⁴	68 cm⁴	68 cm⁴	72 cm⁴	72 cm⁴
Failure load $F_{U,K}$ (2P)	4.5 kN	5.3 kN	5.5 kN	6.3 kN	5.4 kN
Failure moment $M_{u,k}$	2.25 kNm	2.7 kNm	2.75 kNm	3.15 kNm	2.7 kNm
Failure stress $\sigma_{u,k}$	6.9 kN/cm²	8.7 kN/cm²	7.8 kN/cm²	8.4k N/cm²	7.3k N/cm²
Failure deformation $\delta_{u,k}$	8.9 cm	9.8 cm	12.3 cm	14 cm	13.1 cm
Service load q_{Rd} **	1.5 kN/m²	2.0 kN/m²	2.0 kN/m²	2.5 kN/m²	2.0 kN/cm²
Deformation δ_{Rd}, q_{Rd} = 2.5 kN/m²	3.4 cm	3.4 cm	4.1 cm	3.8 cm	3.9 cm
Moment of inertia I_{Rd}	36 cm⁴	36 cm⁴	30 cm⁴	33 cm⁴	32 cm⁴
Eff. composite connection	53%	53%	44%	46%	44%

*E_{eff} = E_G = 7 000 kN/cm²; **taking into account the partial safety factor γ_M = 2.4 and γ_F = 1.4

67

66 Tests were carried out on prototypes with differing profile geometries

67 Geometric and structural parameters for the prototypes P1 to P5

68 Cross-sections of prototypes P1, P2 and P4

The structural performance of the composite elements is largely dependent on the stiffness of the pultrusions and the adhesive, the layer thickness of the adhesive and the distance between profiles. For a given load, reducing the profile height, the shear modulus of the adhesive, the adhesive thickness or the number of profiles leads to higher stresses in the glass and hence to a higher probability of failure.

___ CONSTRUCTION

A series of tests was carried out to determine the influence of the profile geometry on the structural performance. The design span was roughly 7 metres. Five prototypes with a length of 3.0 metres, a width of 250 millimetres and differing GFRP profiles were produced. GFRP is an ideal joining partner for glass since it has a similar expansion and deformation behaviour and has only one third of the weight of steel in combination with comparable material strength.

C-profiles were used for prototype P1, I-profiles and similar "dog-bone" profiles were used for prototypes P2 and P3, and solid box sections were used for prototypes P4 and P5 ___Figs 66, 68. With the exception of the profile cross-section, the build-up of the prototypes was identical. The glass skins consisted of 4 millimetres heat-strengthened glass. *SikaTack HM,* a high-modulus, polyurethane-based windscreen adhesive, was used on all glass-to-profile contact areas. The adhesive volume was manually applied and calibrated to result in an adhesive thickness of roughly 2 millimetres once the two surfaces were pressed together. Black-tinted primer *206 G+P* was applied to the glass surfaces prior to bonding to protect the adhesive from the disintegrating effect of UV radiation. After twenty-four hours, the prototypes were ready for transport and after one week they were fully cured and hardened.

___ LOAD-BEARING CAPACITY

The theoretical assumptions with regard to load-bearing capacity and breaking behaviour were verified by four-point bending tests. As an-

69

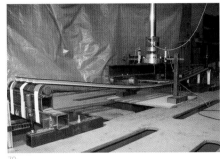

70

71

72

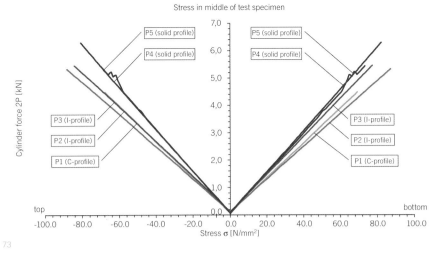

Stress in middle of test specimen

73

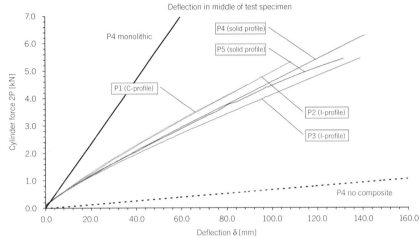

Deflection in middle of test specimen

74

69–71   Four-point bending test on one of the prototypes

72   Fracture pattern of bottom glass skin in the tensile zone

73   Tensile stress in the mid-span of the test members: prototypes P4 and P5 exhibit the greatest stresses.

74   Deflection in the centre of the test member: The deflection in the prototypes is roughly 200% by comparison to a full composite action.

ticipated, failure occurred in the area of maximum bending moment in the centre third of the bottom skin subjected to tension stress. Reaching up to 140 millimetres, the deformation prior to breaking equals roughly 1/20 of the span. There was no evidence that the bond failed. The five composite cross-sections showed a similar moment of inertia and thus comparable stiffness ____Fig. 67. In prototypes P4 and P5, the greater effective depth and the higher rigidity of the GFRP profiles are cancelled out by the lesser profile width, because the diminished bonded area also reduces the composite effect of glass and GFRP. If one includes the standard partial safety factors, the resulting working loads exceed 2.5 kN/m².

Due to the structural action of the GFRP profiles, the composite elements have a high residual load-bearing capacity. After breakage on the tension-stressed bottom skin, the system configuration is that of a composite beam-and-slab structure, capable of carrying a continually increasing load even with considerable deformations.

To reduce the climate loads, the pressure between the individual chambers of the cross-section must be equalised.

____FUNCTION AND DESIGN

The micro-louvres in the glazing cavity help to provide sun and glare protection. The arrangement, orientation and form of the profiles can be utilised to respond to specific climate conditions. Z-profiles can be employed to optimise solar shading and provide full protection when the sun is high in the sky ____Fig. 77. The shading effect was simulated for different installation scenarios and solar altitudes ____Figs 75, 76. The component structure can be varied for each project with regard to load-bearing capacity, shading and thermal insulation.

____CONCLUSION AND OUTLOOK

Since the louvres cannot be regulated according to solar altitude, the system is less effective, albeit more maintenance friendly, than adjust-

75

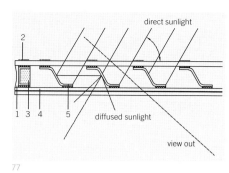

77

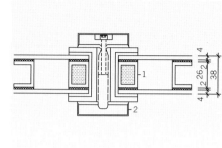

78

76

75, 76 Simulation of light effect for different
construction and daylight situations

77 Element cross-section when solar shading
effect is maximised through the use of Z-profiles
1 Edge seal
2 Screen print as UV protection
3 Edge profile
4 Laminated safety glass
5 GFRP Z-profile

78 Sketch of fixing interface between units
1 Edge connection, GFRP profile filled with
dessicant
2 Clamping bar and pressure plate

able systems. By comparison to standard insulating glazing, the weight is noticeably reduced and this results in cost reduction. The total weight for a component measuring 6 m x 2 m or 4 m x 3 m is less than 500 kilograms, and standard glass suction equipment can be used without problem during the installation.

When GFRP gratings are used as a core layer, insulating glazing can be further strengthened and simultaneously equipped with sun and glare protection. When supported continuously along the perimeter, the component height and the dead load can be reduced – a promising prospect in the context of glazing designed for foot traffic.

With regard to developing the prototype into an insulating glazing standard, the cavity must be appropriately sealed along the edges ——Fig. 78, and the impact of climate loads must be studied in detail. In a prefabrication scenario, the necessary connections for fixing to a primary structure at the roof or facade plane could also be integrated.

[7.2/11]

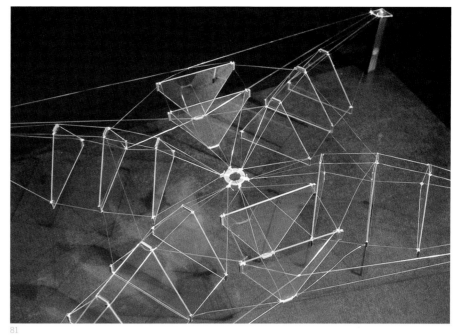

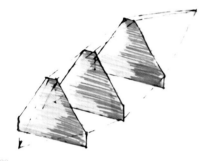

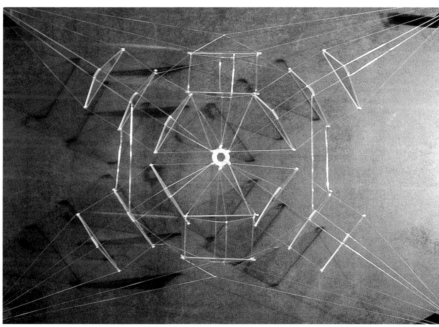

79　Preliminary design model Tiziana Monti

80　Individual cable truss, sketch by Rüdiger Schmidt

81, 82　Diagonal view and elevation of construction model

EXHIBITION ARCHITECTURE "GLÄSERNER HIMMEL" (GLASS SKY)
2001
____ CONCEPT FOR SHOWREIFF EXHIBITION: ULRICH KÖNIGS,
　　　JÖRG LEESER

____ CONCEPT AND DESIGN: RÜDIGER SCHMIDT

____ PROJECT DIRECTOR: JAN WURM, WILFRIED FÜHRER

____ TECHNICAL SUPPORT: JOCHEN DAHLHAUSEN, HANS-WILLI
　　　HEYDEN, MICHAEL SCHUBERT, MICHAEL STARK

The Lehrstuhl für Tragkonstruktionen (Department of Structures) presented its work to the public with the luminous ceiling "Gläserner Himmel" (or "Glass Sky") project, a contribution to the *showreiff* exhibition at the German Museum of Architecture in Frankfurt.

____ LOAD-BEARING SYSTEM

The geometry of the flexible, pretensioned cable structure with a span of 5.4 m x 3.6 m is governed by the structural conditions of the modular system of the exhibition box. Since the wall components – sandwich panels with a cardboard core – lack sufficient bending resistance, only the relatively stiff corners of the box are suitable as support points.

Radiating out from a central tension ring, a cable truss is strung to each corner of the box. Two additional trusses in the transverse axis of the box are also tied back to the box corners. The cable trusses consist of two pairs of parallel cables, which are forced apart by three triangular glass plates acting as rocker members and on the longitudinal sides by two triangular plates. The dead load of the glass is carried by the lower, polygonally-running, load-bearing cables. The upper pretensioning cables introduce additional, constant forces, thus stabilising the position of the glass plates. Since the cable trusses are com-

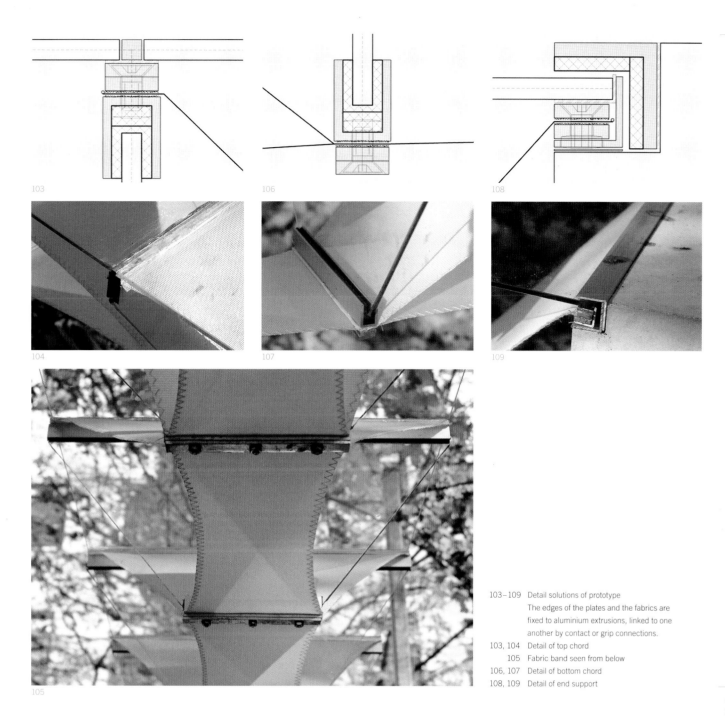

103

106

108

104

107

109

105

103–109   Detail solutions of prototype
               The edges of the plates and the fabrics are
               fixed to aluminium extrusions, linked to one
               another by contact or grip connections.
103, 104   Detail of top chord
       105   Fabric band seen from below
106, 107   Detail of bottom chord
108, 109   Detail of end support

web of this profile to frame the edges of the top chord plates. The aluminium web between the edges is used to transfer the compression forces. The diagonal fabric strips are clamped between the flanges of the profiles by stainless steel bolts. To prevent the fabric from slipping out, its edge is held in a rail. The connection between bottom chord, diagonals and strut is also realised with a lamping bar.

At the support edge, the edge profiles of the top chord are countersunk flush lengthwise in the white concrete foundation block and covered with aluminium plates. At its termination, the bottom chord course is formed in the shape of a paraboloid pocket. The prestressed cables strung within this area are guided through the foundation block on both sides, turned to the vertical through deflection sheaves and connected by turnbuckles to the steel profiles, which are anchored to the foundations.

___ FUNCTION AND FORM

According to Robert Danz the combination of compression-resistant, transparent glass plates and tension-resistant, translucent fabric bands has resulted in *"a bridge that achieves outstanding formal qualities in the sense of a minimalist design sensibility"*. [7.2/13] The arrangement of the diagonals draws the eye of the pedestrian into the depth below the bridge until he reaches the centre point. From the centre onwards, the diagonals run opposite to the direction of the gaze, with the result that the user seems to float "on clouds" above the depth. Thus the construction enhances a more intense sense of perception with regard to the process of motion ___ Figs 112, 113.

___ CONCLUSION AND OUTLOOK

The pretensioning allows the bridge to be designed as a trussed system with specific structural roles for the different materials. Flat glass panels are used as compression plates in conjunction with glass fibre

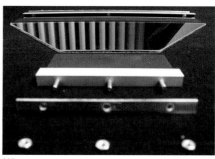

110

112

113

114

115

111

110 Elevation of fitted bottom chord band

111 Angled view of prototype

112, 113 Bird's eye views of completed prototypes
112 Head-on view of diagonals in bridge
section from centre to edge
113 View along the diagonals in bridge
section from edge to centre

114, 115 Fittings

textile bands which carry the tensile forces of the system. In doing so, the traditional principle of the frame or trussed beam is interpreted in such a manner that the cross-sectional arrangement deviates from the course of the forces acting on a simply supported single span. In combination with the necessary initial prestressing forces, this translates not only into higher material expenditure but also into the elevated design quality and legibility of the construction. [7.2/14, 7.2/15]

The structural calculations demonstrate that the system is suitable, in principle, for transposition on a scale of 1:1. Greater precamber in the top chord to achieve a combination of truss and arch effects would be worthwhile in order to reduce the forces in the struts and fabric bands. Top chord and struts would have to be constructed from laminated glass, the surface of which is treated with a slip-resistant ceramic frit. The edge profiles incorporating brackets for installing handrails at either end can be made flush with the glass floor by using stepped laminated glass.

116

117

118

116 Elevations of the glass screen on a scale of 1:3

117 View during projection

118 Photomontage of projection wall overlooking
theatre forecourt at midday

PROJECTION WALL "GLASS-SCREEN", AACHEN, 2002

____ DESIGN: RALF HERKRATH, GERALD KAMAU, JÖRG MATTHAEI,
TOBIAS MÜLLER, IBRAHIM TÜRK

____ PROJECT DIRECTOR: JAN WURM, RALF HERKRATH

____ PLANNING AND CONSTRUCTION: KERSTIN BANDEKOW, JONA
KNOKE, MALGORZATA MEDER, PETER-RENÉ MENKEN

The starting point for this project was the desire of the local theatre of
Aachen to improve its public relations with a projection screen overlooking the forecourt. The goal was to avoid limiting the presentation of
the theatre to the contents projected onto the screen but to expand it
to the overall appearance of the structure. Changeability and variety in
visual expression were seen as opportunities to stage the advertising
surface as a "play" in its own right without competing with the fabric
of the classistic theatre building. The "Glass-Screen" is a self-supporting glass sculpture characterised by formal autonomy.

____ LOAD-BEARING SYSTEM

The "Glass-Screen" is a 7.5 metres high cantilever with a fixed support
at its foot. All components subject to compression are constructed of
glass and all components subject to tension are composed of rod-
shaped steel elements.

The projection surface – describing a concave curvature from the
front – is composed of three identical cantilever beams, each of which
constitutes an independent subsystem. Each beam axis consists of
eight pyramidal glass modules composed of two different, flat plate
elements with different dimensions: a square glass plate stiffened at
its back by two and at the support by four perpendicular, equilateral
triangular plates. Stacked on top of each other at the edges, following
a circular shape, the modules combine with the guyed cables forming
a curved truss.

A steel cable running from the top of the cantilever extension
across the tips of the pyramids to the support constitutes the top chord

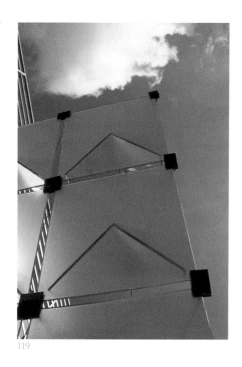

119

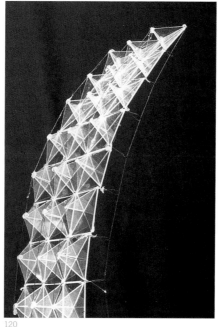

120

122

123

119 Detail of built prototype

120 Working model on a scale of 1:25 (with
prestressing cables, which were later
unnecessary when the project was executed)

121 Isometric of the construction: the projection screen
is composed of three load-bearing axes, each of
which is composed of eight glass modules and
each glass module consists of several glass plates.

122, 123 Types of glass modules
122 Glass module with V-shaped arrangement of panes
123 Special module at support with X-shaped
arrangement of plates

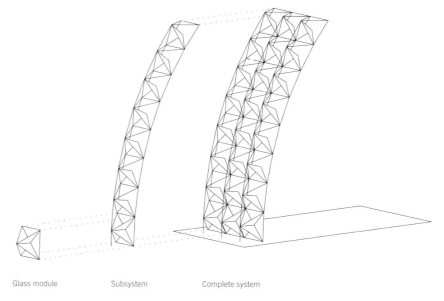

Glass module   Subsystem   Complete system

121

of the system. The square panels of the projection surface, joined with articulated fixings, create the bottom chord plane. The diagonals are formed by the edges of the triangular panels and the steel cables, which are attached to the corners of the bottom chord plates ⎯Fig. 121.

The design of this trussed system relies upon the distribution of forces along the curved girder under dead load. In this load scenario, the bottom chord is subject to continuous compression forces and the top chord to continuous tension forces. In the diagonals, compression and tension forces alternate with the exception of the module at the very bottom. The latter is subject exclusively to compression forces; accordingly, the cables are replaced in this area by additional glass elements ⎯Figs 122, 123.

The stabilisation of the load-bearing structure against wind pressure acting frontally on the projection surface is particularly important. These wind loads may lead to reversed force distributions, to com-

pression forces in the top chord cables and hence to system failure. To avoid compromising the quality of the projection, additional external prestressing elements were to be avoided. Calculations showed that – on a scale of 1:1 – the entire structure could be stabilised by increasing the joint width to reduce the area exposed to wind, increasing the dead load of the upper glass panels in particular, and reducing the radius of curvature to achieve a longer lever arm. The increased dead load should also be achieved through a stainless steel profile, which serves both as a visual and constructual completion of the load-bearing structure ⎯Fig. 125. [7.2/16]

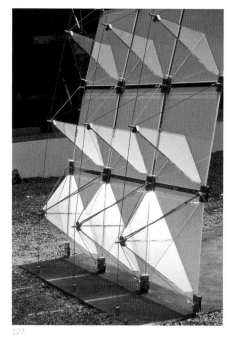

124

126

127

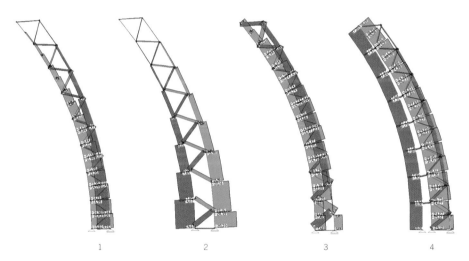

125

1   2   3   4

124   Front elevation of projection wall

125   Numerical analysis of load-bearing structure: normal
      force diagrams for differing load cases (tensile forces are
      purple and compression forces are rendered in blue)
      1   Load case dead load
      2   Load case dead load and wind
      3   Load case increased dead load and wind
      4   Load case prestressing and wind
        (structural alternative)

126   Rear elevation of projection wall

127   Detail of load-bearing structure

CONSTRUCTION AND DETAILS

The prototype on a scale of 1:3 was conceived for installation in the lobby at the headquarters of one of the principal sponsors. The basic module has an edge length of 330 millimetres. The projection screen, which is composed of 3 x 8 elements, has a height of 2.5 metres, a radius of 3.65 metres and is roughly 1 metre in width. All glass elements are composed of 6 mm float glass. The joints between the glass elements measure 18 mm. The use of laminated glass was deemed unnecessary.

All connectors between the glass plates are fashioned from aluminium semi-finished products. The panels of the projection plane are blocked apart with a wedge-shaped 15/6 solid bar with hard rubber padding and fixed in place with 2 mm cold-bent node plates. Diagonal cables (with a diameter of 1.5 mm) are attached by an eyelet bolt and cable clamps at the centre of gravity of the node fixing _____ Figs 128, 129. The attached U-profiles are joined by a gusset plate which is con-

nected to a cylinder bushing with an internal thread. The diagonal and top chord cables run through and are held in place by the bushing _____ Figs 130, 131.

The load-bearing structure is connected to the 12 millimetres ground plate with base fixings and turnbuckles. The plates of the projection plane interlock with welded steel brackets.

One key aspect is the prefabrication of the glass modules. Adjacent glass triangles are structurally-bonded along the base edge with the surface of the projection panel and along the perpendicular edge to each other. *Photobond GB 368* manufactured by *DELO* was used as an adhesive: this is a transparent acrylic adhesive, which hardens when exposed to UV light and has excellent ageing properties. Should one glass element in the central load-bearing axis break, the forces can be redistributed to the subsystems on either side. [7.2/17]

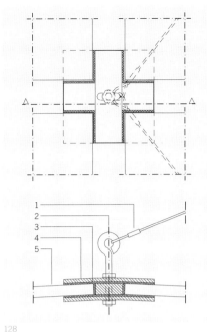

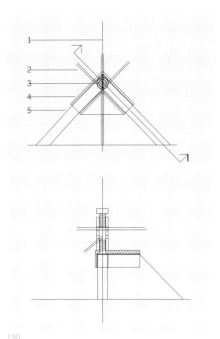

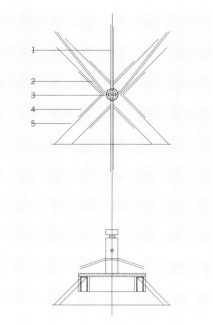

128

130

132

129

131

133

128, 129 Detail of bottom chord connection
    1: Tensile diagonal members with cable clamp
    2: M4 eyelet bolt
    3: 15/6 wedge-shaped solid bar
    4: 2 mm cold-bent node plates
    5: Compression chord, 6 mm float glass

130, 131 Detail of top chord connection (details)
    1 Tension chord, 2 mm cable
    2 Diagonal tension member, 1.5 mm cable
    3 M4 cylinder sleeve with internal thread
    4 Aluminium top plate fitting
    5 Diagonal compression member,
      6 mm float glass

132, 133 Detail of top chord connection detail (at support)
    1 Tension chord, 2 mm cable
    2 Diagonal tension member, 1.5 mm cable
    3 M4 cylinder sleeve with internal thread
    4 Aluminium top plate fitting
    5 Diagonal compression member,
      6 mm float glass

FUNCTION AND FORM

The "Glass-Screen" is a self-advertising tool for the theatre. The glass plates of the projection surface are fitted with a translucent self-adhesive film; images are projected onto the surface from the front. For a realisation on a scale of 1:1, translucent PVB interlayer embedded in laminated glass would be a more appropriate choice. The curvature of the projection surface, which is calculated in relation to the projection distance, ensures an image that is free of distortion. Moreover, the "Glass-Screen" can also be experienced as a kind of light sculpture as the changing daylight passes across the surface. The curved glass surface generates a multifaceted play of light with shadows, mirror effects and transparencies.

CONCLUSION AND OUTLOOK

The curvature of the projection wall was designed in response to the constructional, functional and aesthetic requirements. The aesthetic of the structure is first and foremost a product of the clear allocation of compression and tensile forces and the material and tectonic translation of these forces.

Since the structure is stabilised through its dead load, additional load-bearing elements were not necessary, although this aspect must be adjusted according to the prevailing wind conditions on site. A final evaluation of this load-bearing structure can only be completed once tests on the susceptibility to vibrations and on the breakage behaviour of the structurally bonded glass modules have been carried out.

134

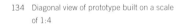

134　Diagonal view of prototype built on a scale
　　of 1:4

135, 136　Scheme for glass roof over St Pius X in Cologne
　　　　Flittard, load-bearing structure seen from
　　　　below, interior of model on a scale of 1:50

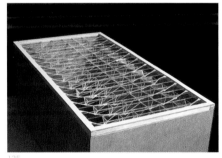

135

136

GLASS ROOF FOR THE "SOLAR BRIDGE"
PROTOTYPE FOR A ROOF ELEMENT WITH INTEGRATED
PHOTOVOLTAIC MODULES, 2001–2002

____CONCEPT, DESIGN AND CONSTRUCTION: JAN CYRANY,
　　RON HEIRINGHOFF, DALIBOR HLAVACEK, FLORIAN NITZSCHE
____TECHNICAL CONSULTATION: CHRISTOF ERBAN, SAINT-GOBAIN
　　GLAS SOLAR, AACHEN
____PROJECT DIRECTOR: JAN WURM

The "Solar Bridge" is based on a proposal for a new roof structure over an existing church. The design team envisioned that the incident daylight would be refracted at the glass ceiling, similar to the effect of light on a crystal chandelier, and then distributed evenly throughout the interior. The selection of glass as the constructional material was therefore based in the desired crystalline character of the roof structure.

One load-bearing axis of the scheme was executed by *Glass Solar* as a simple trussed beam on a scale of 1:4 and presented at the glasstec trade fair in 2002. The project was named "Solar Bridge" because of the integrated photovoltaic elements.

____LOAD-BEARING SYSTEM

The glass roof intended to span across the 12 metres nave is composed of a series of trussed beams. The glass plates forming the top chord of the truss are at the same time the weather skin of the hall. The geometry of the cable corresponds to the distribution of bending moments of the simply supported single span under a uniformly distributed load. As a result, the plate and struts can "rest" on the cable. When load distributions are asymmetrical, bending moments are generated which are then absorbed by the stiffness of the top chord. The design of the top chord as a continuous, bending-resistant glass plate emerged as the key challenge.

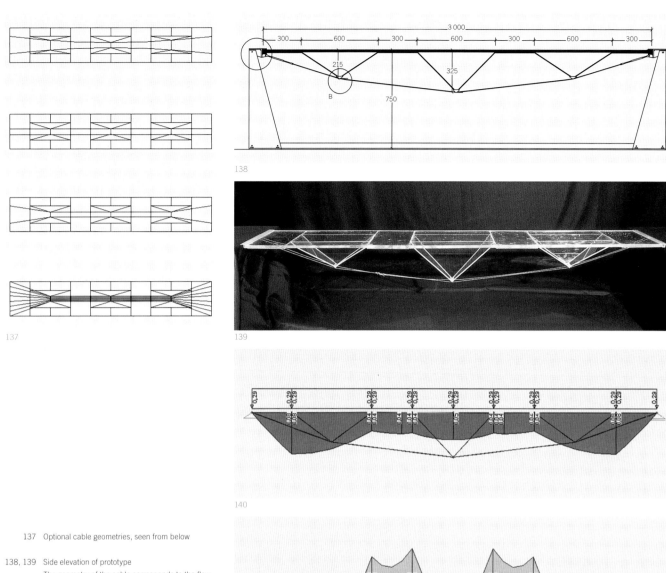

137 Optional cable geometries, seen from below

138, 139 Side elevation of prototype
The geometry of the cable corresponds to the flow
of forces of the simply supported single span under
an uniformly distributed load.

140, 141 Flow of forces in the roof plate under an evenly
distributed load with and without prestressing in
bottom chord cables (in kNm): prestressing allows
for the balance of support and span moments.

___CONSTRUCTION

Since the projected span of 12 metres exceeds the maximum stock
size of flat glass, the top chord cannot be executed as one monolithic
element – and this was to be taken into consideration in the scaled
down version of the prototype for a span width of 3 metres. The continuous bending stiffness is achieved through staggered splice joints
of a total of four glass leaves of 4 millimetres heat-strengthened glass.
The total thickness of the plate is 22 millimetres. The 500 millimetres
wide panes with differing lengths (300, 600 or 900 mm, respectively)
create a composite structure that is stiff in shear. The effective load-
bearing cross-section at any given point corresponds to half the total
beam height ___Fig. 142.

The truss is formed by two parallel Inox-stranded 3 millimetres cables; at 300 millimetres, it has an apex height of l/10. Three prismatic
"cellular" glass props are supported on the cable. They are 600 mm
long, 250 mm wide and 300 mm i.e. 195 millimetres high and are

composed of 4 millimetre trapezoidal float glass. A structurally bonded
joint along the edges prevents the planar elements from buckling.
Where the pyramidal glass cells interconnect with the top chord, the
bottom glass plane of the multi-layered build-up is discontinuous to
allow interlocking of the structural components ___Figs 143–147.

___DETAILS

The fabrication of the glass pyramids and the continuous top chord
pose special challenges with regard to adhesion technology. The individual parts of the glass pyramids are bonded along the edges with
Araldite 2020, a low-viscosity, water-clear adhesive with an epoxy
resin base. The bond increases the stiffness of the modules and also
ensures that the enclosed volumes are sealed. Should the bond fail,
the cable trusses below secure the position of the panes.

The individual panes of the top chord area are surface-bonded by
2 millimetres interlayers of cast-in-place resin. The working method of

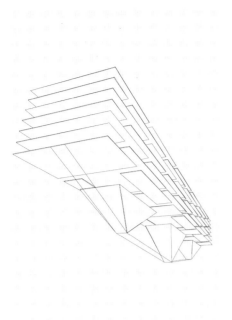

142

143

144

146

142 Concept sketch for layering the load-bearing
    elements (the layering sequence does not
    correspond to that in the built prototype)

143 Bird's eye view of semi-transparent
    prototype with photovoltaic cells

144, 145 Connection between glass plate and glass prop
    1 Multipart glass plate, 4 mm laminated glass
       and 2 mm interlayers of cast-in-place resin
    2 Glass plate, 4 mm float glass body

146, 147 Connection between trussed beam and glass prop
    3 3 mm Inox cable
    4 3 mm steel sheeting connecting element
    5 Injection mortar

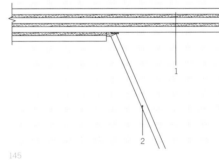

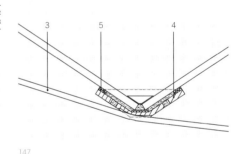

145

147

applying the adhesive to the individual panes is similar to that used in the production of photovoltaic modules.

Due to the lamination technology, the shear forces can be evenly transferred across the surface area of the multipart cross-section of the plate when the stress levels in the resin are kept low. The resin is UV-stable, although it does lose rigidity with high temperatures due to its rheologic characteristics.

On the sides, the plate rests on a 40/35/5 U-profile to which the cables of the trussed beam are also attached with turnbuckles. To transfer the compression forces in the top chord, the cavity between plate and steel profile is filled with *Hilti Hit-HY 50* to form a uniform contact connection ——— Fig. 148.

___LOAD-BEARING CAPACITY
For the calculation, the system was idealised as a space frame. The calculated frame member forces were converted for a load-bearing plate width to estimate of the stresses in the glass. Under full load, the placement of the props leads to support moments in the glass which correspond roughly to the span moments in the top chord, which are generated due to the asymmetrical load component under a one-sided snow load. To optimise the flow of forces, the system was prestressed by means of bottom chord cables. The bending moments require an effective structural depth of 10 millimetres at each point of the top chord. The tensile forces of 1 kN each that are used for the calculation of the cables are based on a full load scenario (dead load and snow). The bending resistance of the top chord was determined through load-bearing capacity tests. By comparison to a monolithic plate, the composite plate delivers a better residual load-bearing capacity due to the composition of smaller glass elements. Each joint represents an artificial phase boundary, which means that crack propagation remains limited. Should the plate lose its bending strength altogether and sag, the cables of the truss would prevent the glass element from falling.

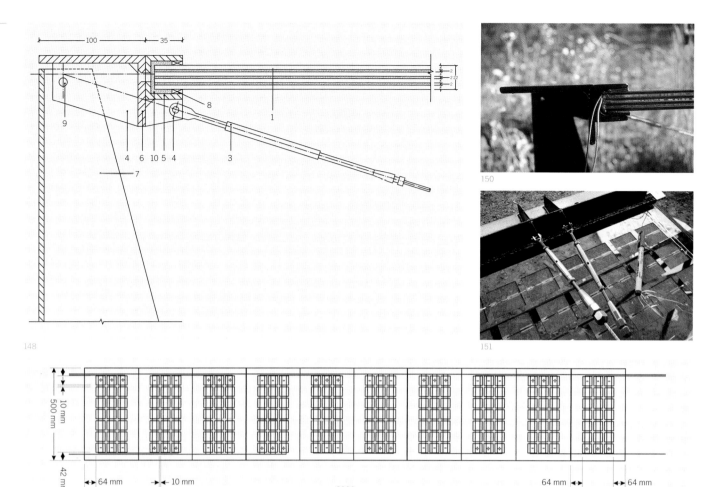

148 Connection between trussed glass plate and
   support structure
   1 Muli-layered top chord
   2 3 mm Inox cable
   3 Fork fitting with external thread and turnbuckle
   4 3 mm steel plates
   5 40/35/5 U-profile
   6 100/65/8 L-profile

7 5 mm steel plate bracket
8 Cellular rubber sealing
9 8 mm bolts
10 Injection mortar

149 Multi-layered glass plate: distribution of
    photovoltaic elements and cables

150 Glass plate on support edged with a U-profile
    with cable slots

151 Connection of trussed beam to secondary structure

___FORM AND FUNCTION

Cast-in-place resin technology allows for the integration of photovoltaic cells into the top chord, combining active energy generation and sun protection. Below the top glass layer of low-iron glass, ten photovoltaic fields of twenty-one cells each are integrated in correspondence with the grid of the glass panes ___Fig. 149. The layout of the cells can be varied to meet differing requirements. The plasticity of the prismatic glass elements is clearly perceptible. With regard to building physics, they serve as reflectors both for incident sunlight and for acoustics.

___CONCLUSION AND OUTLOOK

Full surface structural bonding of glass panes with staggered joints is a concept that allows for continuous bending stability in large glass plates. In-depth studies on the rheologic behaviour of the resin are required to prepare for application in practice and to further develop fabrication processes. [7.2/18]

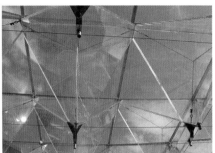

152 Preliminary design for a roof enclosure, St Pius X in
Cologne Flittard, grillage on an area of 15 m x 24 m

153, 154 Structural model of Tetra-Grid on a scale of 1:5

155 Computer simulation of the space-framed
plate structure on a 12 m x 12 m plan

TETRA-GRID

PROTOTYPE FOR A GLASS ROOF AS LUMINOUS CEILING, 2001

____ DESIGN AND CONSTRUCTION: JIRI HLAVKA,
SASCHA RULLKÖTTER, DANIEL SEIBERTS, SEBASTIAN SPENGLER,
IBRAHIM TÜRK
____ PROJECT DIRECTOR: JAN WURM

Another variation on the roofing for the nave envisions interpreting the roof structure above the 15 m x 24 m space as a daylight grid. The 3:5 ratio of longitudinal to transverse sides in plan allows for a biaxially spanning load-bearing system supported on all sides. Given the high tensile bending stresses in the glass beams, the first approach of realising the structure as a grillage was abandoned in favour of a space frame structure, which was developed for a reduced plan dimension of 12 m x 12 m. A structural model of this Tetra-Grid was realised in perspex on a scale of 1:5.

____ LOAD-BEARING SYSTEM

The load-bearing system is conceived as a square shaped two-way slab supported on four sides. The internal geometry and layout is based on the geometrical model of a space frame with hinged connections (see also Chapter 6); the equilateral tetrahedron serves as a three-dimensional structural module. In combination with a top chord and a bottom chord plane, the planar arrangement of the tetrahedra forms a three-dimensional frame. The edges of the tetrahedra represent the diagonals. The top and bottom chord plane each form a square grid; the grids being off-set a half mesh with respect to one another in each direction. Figs 155–159.

In this "space framed plate structure" the geometry is translated by means of linear and planar elements. The tetrahedra are composed of four triangular glass elements. The tetrahedron edges, formed by butt jointing the glass panes, constitute the diagonals of the system. The top chord plane, largely subject to compression

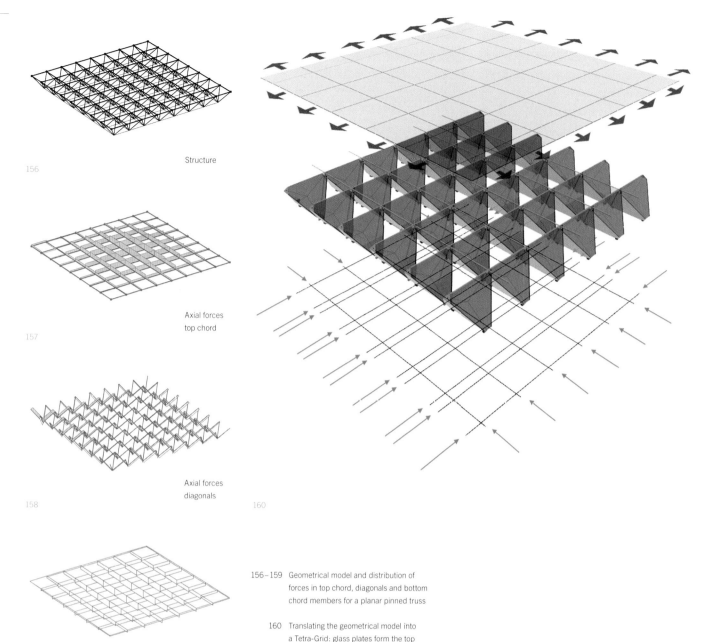

156

Structure

157

Axial forces
top chord

158

Axial forces
diagonals

160

159

Axial forces
bottom chord

156–159 Geometrical model and distribution of
forces in top chord, diagonals and bottom
chord members for a planar pinned truss

160 Translating the geometrical model into
a Tetra-Grid: glass plates form the top
chord, glass tetrahedra the diagonals and
a cable net the bottom chord plane.

stresses, is created through glass plates and the bottom chord plane is created through a flat–tensioned cable net which is point-fixed to the tetrahedra.

To reduce the tensile forces in the diagonals, the individual glass elements are prestressed with internal steel cables.

___CONSTRUCTION

The structure was transformed in a model on a scale of 1:5 in the form of a square plate with an edge length of 2.4 metres, a mesh size of 400 millimetres and a height of approximately 300 millimetres. The structural model, which allows one to experience the complex geometry of the load-bearing structure, was fabricated from 4 millimetres thick perspex sheet material.

The space frame is generated by six tetrahedra with an edge length of 400 millimetres in both load-bearing axes with the result that a total of thirty-six such glass components form the structure. The individual

plates of the tetrahedra are joined by structurally bonding the edges with a special transparent adhesive.

___LOAD-BEARING CAPACITY

Statically, the three-dimensional load-bearing structure is highly indeterminate; in other words, there is a multitude of different load paths. As a consequence, several load-bearing elements can fail without resulting in a system failure of the whole structure. Falling of damaged load-bearing elements can be prevented with the help of the cable net in the bottom chord plane.

Hypothetically, the bottom chord plane can provide the residual load-bearing capacity should all glass elements fail; this requires that the cable net can act as a membrane with appropriate anchors being provided at the supports.

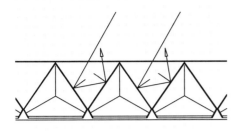

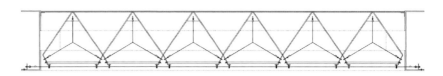

161

163

162

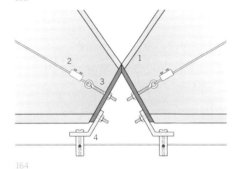

164

166

161   Schematic of multiple reflection and light
       deflection at the glass surfaces of the tetrahedra

162   Computer simulation of glass
       bodies for a 12 m span

163   Elevation on a scale of 1:5

164, 166   Bottom chord connection node
       1 4 mm acryl glass tetrahedron
       2 1 mm galvanised steel cable, connected to eye
          bolt with Simplex clips
       3 Top plate, 3 mm aluminium sheeting
       4 2 mm cable and galvanised cable cylinder
          sleeve with internal thread

165   Diagonal view of model

165

___FUNCTION AND FORM

The prismatic glass components exhibit an optical behaviour that is similar to prisms or light-deflecting glass. Given the appropriate orientation of the load-bearing structure to the incident sun, direct incident sunlight can be deflected through multiple reflections on the tetrahedron surfaces. The daylight deflection can be enhanced through special selective and/or reflective coatings applied to the glass surfaces. Internal solar shading can be provided by integrating translucent or opaque GFRP panels in the construction of the tetrahedron.

___CONCLUSION AND OUTLOOK

The modular construction system allows for a high degree of prefabrication, rational assembly and ease of adaptation to differing span widths. On the other hand, the structural module of the glass tetrahedron is very demanding with regard to manufacturing and detail finishing.

Structural simplifications are possible in the course of the necessary development of the system for implementation on a scale of 1:1. Thus the nodal joints between the tetrahedrons can be avoided if the bottom and top chord planes are executed as rigid grillages and are connected to the edges of the tetrahedron.

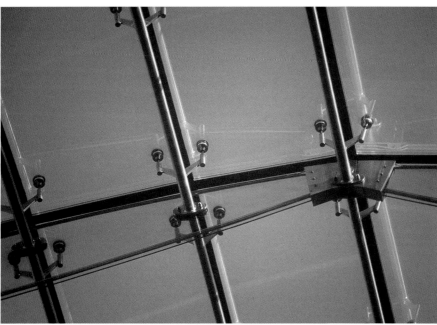

1, 2 The principal load-bearing structure of the roof consists
of three-pinned arches, each composed of two laminated
glass fins.

7.3
THE GLASS BAND – CURVED LOAD-BEARING SYSTEMS

LINDENER VOLKSBANK, HANOVER, 1996
____ARCHITECTS: BERTRAM BÜNEMANN PARTNER GMBH, HANOVER
____ENGINEERS: LUDWIG & WEILER GMBH, AUGSBURG

For the refurbishment of a bank, a fully glazed roof structure was designed and engineered to cover the 9 metres wide interior courtyard. The principal load-bearing structure is formed by five three-hinged arches at intervals of 2.5 metres. Each of the arches consists of two linear laminated glass elements with a 15 millimetres tempered glass leaf at the core and two outer 10 millimetres heat-strengthened glass leaves, which are connected by a pin joint at the ridge. To prevent lateral buckling, the linear glass elements are connected to one another with steel tubes. The tubes also serve as secondary beams for the roof panes, which are approximately 2.5 m x 0.8 m and fastened with V-shaped brackets and stainless steel point fixings. The linear glass elements are cast into stainless steel shoe brackets at the support points ____Figs 1, 2. [7.3/1]

To ensure the residual load-bearing capacity of the arch in case all three leaves of the laminated safety glass fail, a steel cable capable of carrying the full tensile bending force runs along each of the bottom edges of the fins.

The gain in transparency achieved through the glazed principal load-bearing structure is somewhat diminished by the tubular secondary beams, which have a strong visual presence.

3–5 The loggia is composed of several bent glass elements,
which are delivered to the building site preassembled.

7.3

LOGGIA, WASSERALFINGEN/AALEN, 2000

___ ARCHITECTS: FREIE PLANUNGSGRUPPE 7, STUTTGART

___ STRUCTURAL DESIGN: WEISCHEDE, HERRMANN UND PARTNER
GMBH, STUTTGART

The roof construction is composed of cold bent glass elements developed by the firm *Maier-Glas* as glass building elements for overhead and facade glazing (see Chapter 3).

The canopy is 14 metres long and 6 metres wide. Seven bent glass units rest on two lateral rows of supports. Each element is roughly 5.4 metres long and 2 metres wide and features a laminated glass panel consisting of 2 x 12 mm fully tempered glass leaves. The elements are mechanically fixed at four clamping points which are located slightly inwards from the panel corners. Opposing pairs of support points are connected by a tie rod. Fixing brackets are integrated into the tie rods to facilitate connection to the substructure. Due to the continuous support, each element exhibits the load-bearing behaviour of a short barrel shell. The rise of 300 millimetres is created by cold forming a flat glass panel under force resulting in a statically indeterminate, prestressed system. The tie rods fix the geometry of the arch. Load transfer at the clamping fixings is by 100 millimetres long milled parts, which are attached using injection mortar to allow for a mechanical interlock connection to the panel edge. The curvature stiffens the elements; the compression forces allow efficient use of material. Detailed studies on the shear strength of the PVB interlayer were required for the certification procedure. For the snow load case, the composite action effect of the interlayer was taken into consideration.

The component tests for the purpose of demonstrating the residual load-bearing capacity show that the bearing capacity of the system remains fully intact even if one of the leaves in the laminated composite structure breaks. Should both leaves break, the element sags on to the tie rods. [7.3/2, 7.3/3, 7.3/4]

6

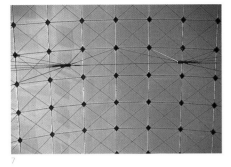

7

6–8   As a result of the diagrid tension net attached
       to the corners of the plates, the cylinder
       barrel exhibits the load-bearing behaviour of
       a folded plate barrel shell. The construction
       is stabilised by additional cable trusses.
6   The glass barrel in the urban context
7   Detail of the construction
8   Interior view of the load-bearing structure

8

MAXIMILIANMUSEUM, AUGSBURG, 2000

____ DESIGN: HOCHBAUAMT AUGSBURG

____ ENGINEERS: LUDWIG & WEILER, AUGSBURG

____ SPECIALIST CONTRACTOR: SEELE GMBH & CO. KG, GERSTHOFEN

The 13.5 metres wide and 37 metres long historic courtyard of the Maximilianmuseum in Augsburg was covered with a glazed barrel-vaulted shell with a rise of 4 metres. The circular cylinder barrel is composed of identical, nearly square panels (0.97 m x 1.17 m). The compression forces are transmitted by individual shoe connectors that are fitted to the truncated glass corners with injection mortar. Stainless steel nodes provide a mechanical interlock between the connection shoes with the result that the glass plates are fully utilised as structural elements. [7.3/5, 7.3/6, 7.3/7]

The barrel is stabilised by a diagrid net of prestressed steel cables and additional cable trusses at every fifth transverse axis. The cables are attached by the star-shaped central nodes to the glass plane; clamping plates fix the brackets in position and transfer cable differential forces. Load-bearing and residual load-bearing capacity tests on a barrel segment on a scale of 1:1 were required to get approval by building authority.

The glass plates are subjected to a maximum load of 5 t per corner. Given the extreme slenderness of the flat glass, the thickness of the laminated panels of 2 x 12 mm heat-strengthened glass were less dependent on the maximum compression stresses than on the analysis of stability failure as a result of buckling. The buckling load is increased by the restraint at the nodal point achieved with the clamping plates. The entire structure was assembled on site with the help of timber scaffolding. The construction documents the remarkable potential of glass skin structures ____ Figs 6–8.

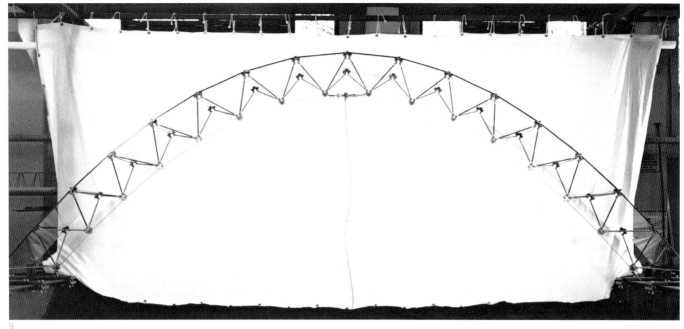

9

10

11

12

9–12   Prototype of the paraboloid trussed arch
          construction with a span of 5 m

9   Total system
10   Top chord connection
11   Bottom chord connection
12   Support connection

PROTOTYPE OF A ROOF AS NOISE BARRIER
TU HAMBURG-HARBURG, 1999

_____ DESIGN: THOMAS SCHADOW AND FRITHJOF VELLGUTH IN
         COLLABORATION WITH PROF. WOLFGANG MAIER AND
         PETRA WEILER

A three-chord arch construction with a span of 10 metres was designed as a proposal for the enclosure of a six-lane urban highway to
provide noise protection for nearby residents.

In the structure resembling a space frame, the glass covering assumes the primary load-bearing functions as a compression chord. In
order to benchmark models of the structural performance of the construction, a test mock-up was designed and built on a scale of 1:2
_____Fig. 9.

The glass arch follows the shape of the line of pressure. To stabilise the structure under asymmetric loads, the glass plates are connected by a trussed steelwork. Steel rods form the three-dimensional
diagonals. The bottom chord cable is prestressed by displacement of
the support, thus stabilising the entire construction. In the test of the
mock-up, symmetrically and asymmetrically distributed area loads
were simulated by means of weights suspended from the nodes.

Laminated plates of 2 x 5 mm tempered glass were used for the
mock-up. During the preliminary calculations, only the bottom leaves
were taken into consideration for the load path. Load redistribution
onto the upper laminated leaf was simulated by destroying the bottom
leaf. The residual load-bearing capacity outcome in case of total failure of one glass panel could not be tested in the context of this study
on a single framed arch. However, using heat-strengthened glass for
the plates seems sensible with regard to residual load-bearing capacity. [7.3/8]

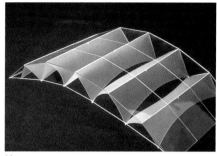

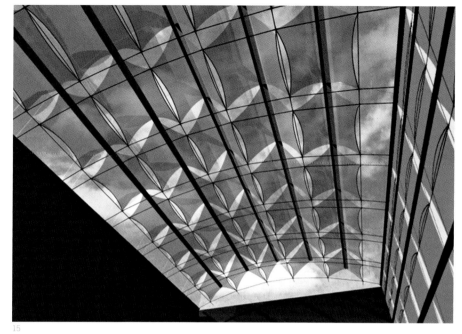

13 Preliminary design: model (author: H. Bosbach, M. König)

14 Model of a construction segment: the "GlassTex arch"

15 The total construction seen from below,
computer simulation

16 Built prototype of arch on a scale of 1:4

GLASSTEX ARCH
PROTOTYPE OF A GLASS ROOF WITH INTEGRATED SOLAR SHADING
2001
____CONCEPT AND DESIGN: HENRIKE BOSBACH, SABINE EINHÄUSER,
MICHAEL KÖNIG, AGI SOBOTTA
____PROJECT DIRECTORS: RALF HERKRATH, JAN WURM

The "GlassTex arch" is a based on a study for the refurbishment of an existing church. The design team wanted to supply glare-free, evenly distributed daylight to the interior of the church and reduce the effect of direct sunlight to prevent overheating. The goal was to allow patrons in the interior to experience the variations in natural daylight according to the time of day and the seasons.

The approach to form-finding was motivated by the desire to integrate solar shading into the construction. The prototype with a 15 metres span was presented at the glasstec fair in Düsseldorf (2002) on a scale of 1:4 and awarded the prize of the Bund deutscher Baumeister (Association of German Architects).

____LOAD-BEARING SYSTEM

The top chord of the "GlassTex arch" is formed by identical glass plates with hinged edge connections; it is therefore a folded plate arch structure. Given the arch effect, the glass elements are subject to compression forces under dead load. Due to its lack of bending stiffness, the system must be stabilised for asymmetrical load cases such as wind and snow by means of prestressing forces. These radially oriented forces are transferred evenly to the glass plates by fabric panels, in a truss-like arrangement and attached to the edge joints, and carried by the bottom chord cables and the valley tie cables of the fabric banners
____Figs 17, 18.

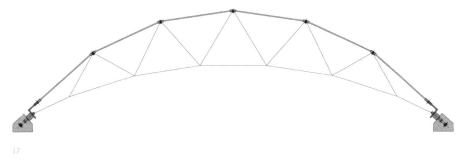

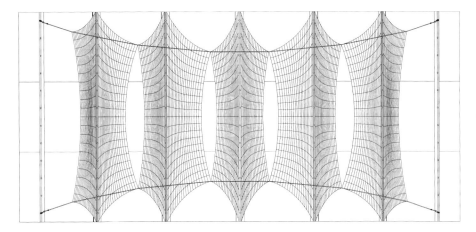

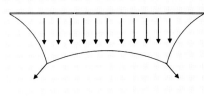

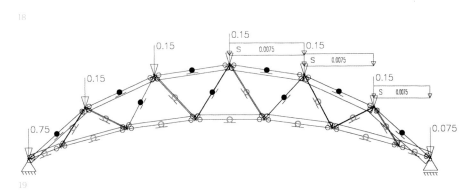

17 Side view: the fabric panels are placed
    in a truss-like arrangement.

18 View from below: the bottom chord
    prestressed cables also follow a paraboloid
    shape in plan. The fabrics are represented
    in the form of a mesh structure.

19 Normal forces with self-weight [kN] and one-
    sided snow load [kN/cm] for a 1 m span
    (without prestressing): compression forces
    are marked in black, tensile forces in blue.

20, 21 Schematic of longitudinal section: radial
        prestressing forces stabilise the arch.

___ANALYSIS

The geometry of the construction was determined using a combination of graphical and numerical methods. The radial geometry of the bottom chord is defined with a rise of l/10 in the projected elevation. The shape of the line of pressure of the glass arch based on dead load is superimposed on that of the prestressing forces. In order to define the prestressing force, the system is first analysed without prestressing as a plane frame; to this end the member forces for all load cases are ascertained ___Fig. 19. The prestressing force can then be determined on the basis of the maximum compression force in the diagonals (approx. 0.3 kN); this prestressing force needs to provide a 1.5 safety factor in achieving a pure tensile force distribution in the webs of fabric representing the diagonals. Once the prestressing force is established the geometry of the prestressing cables is defined in the vertical plane. Cables and fabric panels can then be fabricated taking the elongation of the components under tensile force into consideration. The rise of

the valley tie cables is also l/10. Based on the now known prestressing force, the bearing reactions in the valley tie cables and hence the shape of the prestressed cables in plan can be determined by a graphical method.

___CONSTRUCTION AND DETAILS

The segment of the barrel construction built on a scale of 1:4 is composed of six rows of three square glass panels, each measuring 600 mm x 600 mm. With a span of roughly 3.6 m, the rise of the prototype is 900 mm. A total of five connected fabric panels, attached to the longitudinal joints of the glass, form the ten diagonals of the trussed plate structure. A coated ethylene-tetrafluoroethylene fabric (ETFE) with a tensile strength of 1200 N / 5 centimetres was chosen for the textile material. With a transmittance of 90 percent it possesses excellent light transmission characteristics ___Figs 22, 24.

The detail design of the prototype is adapted to the scale. For cost

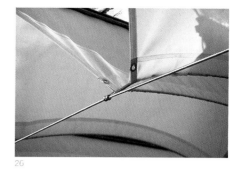

26

27

22

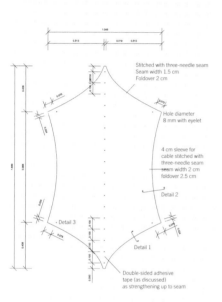

Stitched with three-needle seam
Seam width 1.5 cm
Foldover 2 cm

Hole diameter
8 mm with eyelet

4 cm sleeve for
cable stitched with
three-needle seam
seam width 2 cm
foldover 2.5 cm

Detail 2

Detail 3

Detail 1

Double-sided adhesive
tape (as discussed)
as strengthening up to seam

23

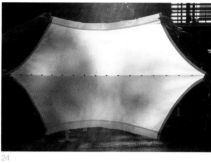

24

25

22   Detail of the construction

23   Geometry of a fabric panel

24   The ETFE fabric has a light transmissivity of 90%.

25, 26   The fabric banners are connected to the bottom
chord cable with valley tie cables and eye bolts

27   Diagonal view of prestressed bottom chord
cable with connection to fabric panels

efficiency, a decision was made not to use laminated glass for the overhead glazing; instead, 6 millimetres fully tempered glass was used. The glass plates are connected by clamping bars made of 3 millimetres cold-bent duraluminium sheets. A prismatic aluminium rod, padded with hard rubber, ensures transfer of the compressive forces along the glass edges. The fabrics are attached by clamping bars to the underside of this edge profile. Like the ridge detail with which the fabrics panels are fastened to the clamping bar, the lateral edges of the fabric elements are reinforced with mesh ribbons sown into the fabric.

The stainless steel valley tie cables are threaded like draw cords through fabric sheaths and connected to the 6 millimetres bottom chord stranded cables with eye bolts ____Figs 26, 27. On the transverse sides, these cables are joined by articulated connections to a 90/90/6 stainless steel equal-angle profile, which also serves as a support for the bottom glass plates ____Fig. 31. The flange of the profile is identical in thickness to the glass and can therefore also be attached by the

same clamping bar detail. The steel angle is fixed to the precast, fine-grained concrete support blocks with M16 bolts.

____LOAD-BEARING CAPACITY AND INSTALLATION

This is a redundant system: in other words, if one glass plate should fail, the forces are redistributed to adjacent plates through the hinged edge fittings. The I-shaped profile cross-section of the edge fitting, composed of cold bent edge plates and spacer bar, has sufficient bending stiffness for this purpose ____Fig. 30. Scaffolding is required to assemble and install the glass arch in order to place and orient the individual panes ____Fig. 32. To absorb the horizontal reactions of the arch effect, the supports are connected with steel tubes during installation.

____FUNCTION AND DESIGN

Since the fabric allows only diffuse and low-glare light to pass through,

28, 29   The truss-like construction allows for views
         of the sky and the translucent fabric panels
         disperse direct incident daylight.

30, 31   Detail connections

32   Installation with the help of scaffolding

it is also suitable as a means of providing internal sun and glare protection. The curvature of the valley tie cables creates lens-shaped openings in the fabric banners which provide views of the sky.

   The sound-absorbent fabric panels diminish sound reflection from
the hard glass surfaces, making a decisive contribution to improving
the acoustics in the interior.

   In combination with the transparent glass shell, the translucent
fabric panels create a varied and changing light effect depending on
the time of day and the season.

_____CONCLUSION AND OUTLOOK
The aesthetics of the construction are founded in the customised use
of glass, textile, steel and concrete, elevating the various specific mechanical properties of the building materials to a theme. The prototype
shows that the interplay of compression-resistant and transparent
glass surfaces and tension-resistant, translucent fabrics creates not

only a constructional, but also a functional and aesthetic unity. Further
development of such hybrid constructions is fundamentally dependent on more progress in the field of industrial fabrics. [7.3/9, 7.3/10]

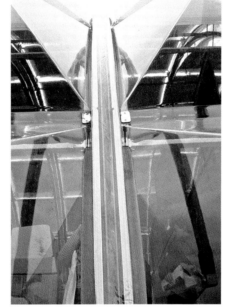

33–37   The pavilion, which is easily installed and
dismantled, was conceived for a travelling
exhibition through major cities in Europe.

33, 34, 36   Exteriors

35, 37   Details of the construction

IBM EXHIBITION PAVILION, 1984

——— ARCHITECT: RENZO PIANO BUILDING WORKSHOP, GENOA

——— STRUCTURAL DESIGN AND ENGINEERING: ARUP, LONDON

Throughout the early 1980s, the IBM travelling exhibition pavilion was sent to various European cities such as Lyon, London, Rome and Milan, to profile the products of the computer manufacturer and to advertise the concept of the "home computer".

The pavilion is designed to be a light and elegant modular construction system. In essence, it consists of the floor platform, into which the building services were integrated, and the weather skin composed of a series of identical semicircular three-hinged arches.

The arches themselves are also composed of three different elements: glulam timber ribs, cast aluminium fixings and deep drawn, transparent polycarbonate pyramids.

Each three-hinged arch forms a trussed three-chord beam, whereby the three-dimensional diagonals are formed by the pyramid edges which are connected in the top and bottom chord by glulam rods. In this manner, the pyramids also provide longitudinal stiffening for the barrel-shaped load-bearing structure. The triangular surfaces of the semi-octahedra act as weather skin and load-bearing structure simultaneously. Since the arch is split into a trussed structure, the load-bearing elements are subject to axial loads (compression or tensile forces) and hardly any bending stresses. The bearing capacity of the structure was determined by experiments on scale models. [7.3/11]

The exhibition pavilion exemplifies the design potential of transparent cellular structures. The application of such a system in glass construction requires the appropriate adhesive or welding technology for the fabrication of the three-dimensional structural modules.

38

40

41

39

38   The "Tetra arch" with a span of 8 m presented
at glasstec 2000 in Düsseldorf

39   Model of a "Tetra barrel": several arches
arranged in sequence combine into a barrel
construction with a span of 8 m.

40   Structural model of a "Tetra barrel" with a
12 m span, design: A. Bauer, T. Unterberg

41   Preliminary design for station hall in Berlin-Spandau,
design: Chr. Leffin, D. Stuttmann

TETRA GLASS ARCH

CONSTRUCTION SYSTEM FOR ARCHED ROOFS UP TO A SPAN WIDTH OF 30 M, 2000

___CONCEPT AND DESIGN: NICOLA BOGATZKI, TOBIAS GLITSCH,
RALF HERKRATH, NADINE REUTERS, DANIEL STUTTMANN,
THORSTEN WEIMAR, JAMES WONG

___PROJECT DIRECTORS: JAN WURM, WILFRIED FÜHRER

The proposals for station platform enclosures based on modular construction systems were conceived at a time when the German magnetic levitation (maglev) railway association still placed their faith in the future export success of the Transrapid train. The railway station in Berlin-Spandau (approx. 20 m x 150 m) served as a pilot project for the Hamburg-Berlin route. The principal function of the hall was to provide naturally ventilated protection from the weather.

The partly visionary preliminary concepts for arch and barrel shell constructions were amalgamated in the constructional principle of the Tetra arch. A prototype of the arch construction was presented at the glasstec fair in 2000. [7.3/12]

___LOAD-BEARING SYSTEM AND CONSTRUCTION

The semicircular arch, composed of twelve equilateral tetrahedra with an edge length of 0.9 metres, has a span of 8 metres and an apex height of 4 metres ___Figs 49, 50. The basic geometry of the arch corresponds to a symmetrical space frame composed of tetrahedra and half-octahedra. In the Tetra Arch, linear members are replaced by the edges of adjoining elements to create load-bearing modules in the form of closed tetrahedra ___Figs 46, 52.

In the longitudinal direction of the arch, the bottom edges of the tetrahedrons create a continuous polygonal member, the bottom chord of the system. The edges on the opposite side of the tetrahedrons run transverse to the bottom chord and form the supports for the roof

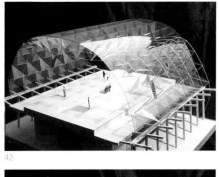

42

43

46

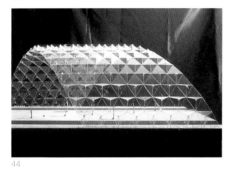

44

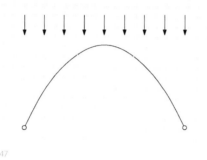

47

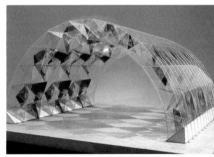

45

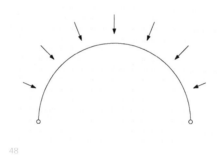

48

42–44 Preliminary designs for Transrapid station in Berlin-
Spandau: detail models of roof construction on a
scale of 1:50

42 Prestressed and trussed arch (S. Dreyer, T. Gilich,
L. Heimann)

43 Trussed elliptical arch (T. Glitsch N. Reuters)

44 Trussed folded shell (Chr. Schlaich, J. Wong)

45 Revised design for station hall: model on a scale
of 1:25 (N. Bogatzki, R. Herkrath, N. Reuters,
D. Stuttmann)

46 Detail model on a scale of 1:10

47, 48 Line of pressure for evenly distributed vertical forces
(Fig. 47) and evenly distributed radial forces (Fig. 48)

plates, which are thus exterior skin and top chord in one. The diagonals of the load-bearing structure are formed by the remaining tetrahedron edges. With the mechanical interlock connections at either end of the top and bottom chord, the system is a fixed-ended three-chord trussed arch.

To ensure that the glass is always subject to compressive stress, the shape of the load-bearing structure must conform with the line of pressure for all load cases. In the case of the Tetra Arch, this is achieved by means of introducing additional prestressing forces. Two parallel, prestressed cables run along the polygonal, semicircular top chord. A constant, radially oriented force is transferred into the system through the tetrahedron edges at each bend of the cables. The result is a semicircular line of pressure which corresponds to the shape of the load-bearing structure ___Fig. 48. The prestressing force is sufficiently great to compensate for the deviations in the lines of pressure of other load cases.

___ DETAILS

Fabricated steel frames which transfer the compression forces from the top and bottom chord into the ground serve as arch supports ___Fig. 51. The horizontal force components of the arch thrust are resisted by sets of four 12 millimetres diameter bolts. The 6 millimetres stainless steel prestressing cables are also attached to the steel frame by turnbuckles. Since the cables are guided freely through the hinged edge fixings without being clamped, additional turnbuckles are not necessary.

Due to the modular geometry of the system, all load-bearing elements have identical connections. Two details define the appearance of the Tetra Arch: the nodal connection of the tetrahedra in the bottom chord and the linear edge connection between tetrahedron and top chord pane.

All glass elements are laminated panes composed of 2 x 6 mm heat-strengthened glass and all fixings are made of anodised alumini-

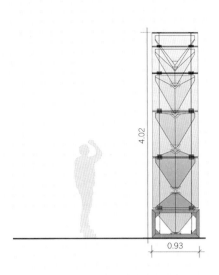

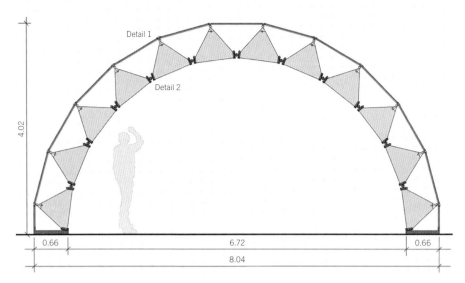

49

50

49, 50   Side views of built Tetra Arch with a span of 8 m
         (dimensions in metres)
    51   The Tetra Arch at the glasstec 2000

    52   The load-bearing module of the Tetra
         Arch: the glass tetrahedron

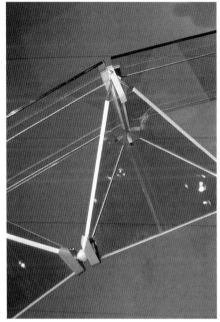

51

52

um. The joints in both the bottom and the top chord can be realised as contact joints because of the permanent compression stresses generated in the system.

A total of six plates from two adjacent tetrahedra converge in one nodal point in the joints of the bottom chord. The panels are cut at right angles to the bottom chord edge to increase the edge length available for force transfer. The edges are framed by a U-profile bolted onto a cap-like top end plate. These "caps" distribute the load to the U-profiles and must be milled due to their complex geometry. They are connected to one another by an articulated ball joint. The joint accommodates tolerances arising from fabrication and assembly, thus enabling the load transfer points to be free of imposed strains.

The tolerances of up to 3 millimetres, which may result between the edges of the laminated leaves and the flanges of the U-profiles as a result of the lamination process, are accommodated by *Hilti Hit-HY 50* injection mortar in the cavity between profile and glass. Injec-

tion and venting openings with a diameter of 6 millimetres must be provided for the mortar ___ Figs 53, 54.

The approximately 1 m x 1 m top chord panels rest on the tetrahedron edges, supported on both sides, where they are connected linearly to bent aluminium plates. This bent plate is bolted to a prismatic solid bar that is, in turn, linearly connected by injection mortar to the upper, open tetrahedron edge. The profile is screwed to the bent plates on the longitudinal sides to fix the support position and act as a body seal. The prestressed cables beneath the roof covering are guided through grooves in this profile, so that all forces resulting from dead load, snow and prestressing are transferred in linear fashion to the glass edges of the upper tetrahedron plates. The lateral brackets, which provide a mechanical safeguard to prevent pane elements from falling down should the structurally bonded joint fail, are connected to the bar ends of the solid profile with shims. Load transfer between the top chord panes is effected by two contact blocks with a length of 80 mil-

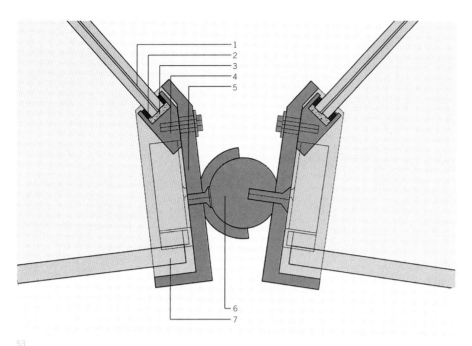

53

53, 54 Connection between node and bottom chord
(see "detail 2" in Fig. 50)
1 2 mm x 6 mm laminated glass of heat-
treated glass, SGG Contrasplit
2 3 mm cellular rubber
3 Injection mortar Hilti Hit-HY 50
4 U-profile, milled, F28 aluminium alloy, anodised
5 Aluminium cap, milled
6 Articulated joint, milled
7 GFRP edge pultrusion

55 Model of node

56 Exploded sketch of node

54

55

56

limetres. Here, too, the injection mortar assumes the task of force transfer and tolerance accommodation. In the area of the blocks, the panes are clamped to the prismatic rod with 100 millimetres x 100 millimetres clamping plates to counteract wind suction ____Figs 57–59.

The key theme in this project is the monolithic glass body of the tetrahedron composed of individual plates with homogenous characteristics in edges and faces. The closed glass cell provides aesthetic appeal and ease of installation, but its structural behaviour is its chief advantage. When the edges of adjoining surfaces are linked by mechanical interlock connections, they stabilise one another and reduce the risk of buckling – the load-bearing potential of the module can be fully utilised.

Since a direct glass-to-glass structural bonding of the mitred edges was not feasible due to the angle of roughly 70°, glass fibre reinforced plastic (GFRP) was used for the edge profiles.

The thermal expansion coefficients of glass and GFRP are nearly

identical. Imposed strains can be avoided for the most part. Profile and glass edges were structurally bonded with a two-component epoxy-resin adhesive. The adhesive is viscoelastic, stress-equalising and has good gap-filling properties.

____LOAD-BEARING CAPACITY

The calculations for the entire system as a three-dimensional truss carried out with the help of the structural analysis program *Infograph*; a finite-element model (FEM) was created to study connection points and stress distribution.

By applying a prestressing of 6 kN per cable, i.e. a radial force of 1 kN per top chord node, all possible combinations of load cases generate purely compression forces in the top and bottom chord; minimal tensile stresses remain only in the diagonals. A higher level of prestressing was not adopted so that the stresses exerted on the overall system would remain low. With the given prestressing force, the maxi-

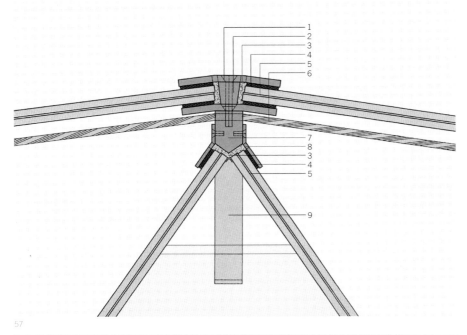

57

57–59 Connection edge fitting to top chord
(see "detail 1" in Fig. 50)
1 100 mm x 100 mm clamping plate, F28 aluminium
alloy, anodised, with 6 mm injection holes
for position 3
2 Aluminium block profile, approx. 20 mm x 20 mm
3 Injection mortar Hilti Hit-HY 50
4 3 mm hard rubber strip
5 2 x 6 mm laminated glass of heat-treated glass,
SGG Contrasplit
6 6 mm Inox cable
7 Aluminium prismatic rod
8 Aluminium edge plate
9 Clamp for securing the glass

58

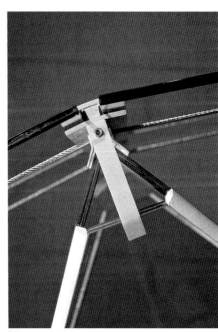

59

mum compression force is approximately 6 kN in the top chord and approximately 8 kN in the bottom chord. In the top chord this corresponds to a maximum stress of roughly 0.5 kN/cm² and in the bottom chord to roughly 0.4 kN/cm². No proof of buckling resistance was deemed necessary because of the low compression stresses. The forces determined in the truss model were verified with the FEM model —— Figs 60, 61.

Impressive proof of the stiffness of the glass module was provided through component testing. The bottom chord edge was subjected to longitudinal stress with the help of a compression cylinder —— Fig. 62. The first crack appeared longitudinally to the direction of force at a distance of approximately 120 millimetres from the edge of the tetrahedron when the compression force reached 90 kN. Stress-induced failure at the force transfer point finally occurred at 190 kN (that is, 19 tonnes). Taking the entire force transfer area into consideration, the resulting failure stress exceeds 9 kN/cm², which is roughly three times

the allowable stress level for heat-strengthened glass but lies below the compressive strength of glass. Due to the considerable plastic deformation of the aluminium components, failure is a result of transverse tensile stress in the glass. Stability failure was not observed even once breakage had occurred – the edge bond prevents folding of the broken plate elements. [7.3/13]

—— ASSEMBLY AND INSTALLATION
The modular system allows for a high level of prefabrication. A multifunctional installation scaffold, on which the individual plates of the tetrahedra are cleaned, placed and structurally bonded is essential —— Fig. 66. The fittings are put in position with the help of templates and fixed by mechanical interlock with injection mortar. The scaffold also serves as a transport and assembly frame for the tetrahedra.

A full scaffold is necessary for installation because the arch action only comes into effect once the contact connections in all load-bear-

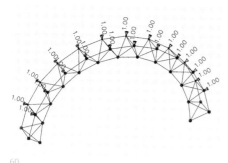

60

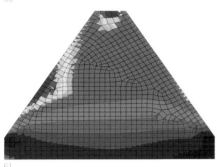

61

62

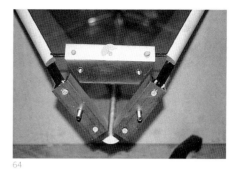

64

65

63

66

60 Illustration of truss model with radial
prestressing forces

61 FEM analysis for a glass plate element at the
support – the colours illustrate the flow of
compression forces in the glass. The largest forces
occur along the bottom chord edge (dark blue).

62 Load exerted on a tetrahedron in a component
test with a compression cylinder.

63 Model with printed glass surfaces for solar shading

64, 65 The edge fittings before and after the component test

66 Assembly of arch construction

ing elements are in place. Installation proceeds in a side-symmetrical
manner, that is, installation proceeds simultaneously on both sides of
the arch. Each tetrahedron can be put in position while being held in
a supporting frame. To ensure structural stability during the construction phase, the joints between the top chord panels are temporarily
fitted with setting blocks. Once the tetrahedra have been oriented and
placed, the prestressed cables are tensioned until contact pressure
can build up at all setting blocks. Loosening the installation supports
then encourages a natural shape to the load path. Once the injection
mortar has hardened in the contact connections, the full design prestress force can be applied to the system.

FUNCTION AND DESIGN

To provide the necessary solar shading, the faces of the tetrahedron
and the roof plates can be printed with image details which merge into
a whole at certain viewing positions, thus giving an experience of the
multilayered nature of the load-bearing structure. Depending on the
light source and the observation angle, the prismatic arrangement of
the glass plates creates light effects in which reflection and transparency converge seamlessly. The focus was not on increasing transparency but on the materialisation of light ___ Figs 67–70.

CONCLUSION AND OUTLOOK

The project demonstrates the constructional and design potential of
structurally bonded edge connections. In principle, transparent edge
bonding is possible with the help of acrylates that cure when exposed
to light. While this means that suitable adhesives are available given
the current state of the technology, suitable application procedures
have yet to be developed for mass production. Exchanging damaged
glass modules and the bridging of the flow of force that is required
during such procedures also have to be studied in detail.

Structurally bonding the individual panels into rigid glass modules

67–70 The arch at the Reiff Museum in
Aachen, seasonal aspects

simplifies the assembly and installation of the glass construction to a
great degree. With a span width of 8 metres, the edge bonding is especially relevant with regard to the residual load-bearing capacity.

The system construction opens up the possibility of applying for and
receiving a certificate of approval for the entire system (classified as a
"kit" according the European certification standards), provided the parameters are standardised, in order to allow for applications without a
need for project-specific approvals within the studied boundaries.

Studies show that spans of up to 30 metres are possible with the
same tetrahedron dimensions if the cap fixings are reinforced. [**7.3/14**]

1–4 Multi-faceted steel and glass shell;
the dome surface is divided by a
homogenous triangular net.
1 Elevation
2 Detail of domed plate structure

7.4

THE GLASS CORE – DOUBLE-CURVED LOAD-BEARING SYSTEMS

SPHERICAL HOMOGENOUS SHELL STRUCTURE
GLASSTEC 1998, DÜSSELDORF

DESIGN AND CONCEPT: LEHRSTUHL FÜR BAUKONSTRUKTION 2
STUTTGART UNIVERSITY IN COLLABORATION WITH SEELE GMBH
& CO.KG

STRUCTURAL DESIGN: LUDWIG & WEILER GMBH, AUGSBURG

SPECIALIST CONTRACTOR: SEELE GMBH & CO.KG, GERSTHOFEN

Glasbau Seele presented a self-supporting glass dome at the glasstec
1998. The geometrical dimensions of the construction correspond to
the glass dome at the Weltbild Verlag building in Augsburg, which was
also erected in 1998, albeit with insulating glass.

LOAD-BEARING SYSTEM AND CONSTRUCTION

The dome structure is a flat spherical dome resting on a circumferen-
tial steel ring supported by steel columns. The diameter of the ring is
12.3 m; the rise of the glass structure is 2.5 m.

The division is realised with a homogenous system of equilateral
triangles projected onto the spherical surface. The 282 flat triangular
facets required for the construction can be assembled into 27 different
formats.

The laminated safety glass plates composed of 2 x 10 mm heat-
strengthened glass have a maximum edge length of 1.1 m. The corners

3 Detail of node
4 Execution with insulating glass, Weltbildverlag, Augsburg

of six triangular panels are interconnected at the nodes with steel shoes.

A three-way system of steel cables runs beneath the glass plane. The steel cables transfer the constant prestressing force to the nodes with the result that the dome surface is subjected to permanent compression stress and force connections can be realised by setting blocks at the contact points. The stability of the structure even in case of uneven loads and simultaneous failure of up to six adjacent glass elements was demonstrated in component tests.

In comparison to the construction exhibited at the glasstec fair, the Weltbildverlag dome is less transparent because the spacer bars of the triangular insulating glass panes have a greater optical impact. According to data provided by *Glasbau Seele*, a similar construction can be employed for diameters up to 20 metres.

____FORM

The form is certainly convincing from a constructional point of view; visually, however, the triangulation of the load-bearing surface and the individual load transfer points give the impression of a steel skeleton structure rather than a structural skin. [7.4/1]

5

7

6

5, 6   Fully glazed dome on the experimental
site at ILEK, Stuttgart University

7   Dome segment as prototype at glasstec 2002

"STUTTGARTER GLASSCHALE" ("STUTTGART GLASS SHELL")
PROTOTYPE FOR A STRUCTURALLY BONDED SPHERE
STUTTGART, 2003

____CONCEPT AND DESIGN: PROF. WERNER SOBEK AND
LUCIO BLANDINI, INSTITUT FÜR LEICHTBAU UND KONSTRUKTION
(ILEK), STUTTGART UNIVERSITY

____LOAD-BEARING SYSTEM AND CONSTRUCTION

At glasstec 2002, a prototype for a flat dome calotte was presented, composed of four spherically curved glass panels ____Fig. 7. In the following year, a glass dome with a diameter of 8.5 metres, and a rise of 1.76 metres was erected on the department's experimental site. The spherically curved glass panels are composed of 8 millimetres annealed float glass and 2 millimetres chemically strengthened glass. The plate elements are solely connected at the butt joints by an epoxy resin bondline about 10 millimetres thick. The ratio of panel thickness to span is thus a mere 1:850. The linear transfer of force is combined here with high aesthetic quality; the design creates reliable load-bearing capacity in the shell.

The fabrication period was approximately three months. Since the adhesive could only be applied under controlled environmental conditions, a temporary protective skin had to be erected during the installation work. The replacement of damaged panes seems an unresolved challenge.

____FORM

The construction illustrates the tremendous design potential of adhesion technology. The structural bonding obviates any need for metal parts between the shell elements. Promoting a "minimal construction" it assumes several functions: in addition to load transfer and joint sealing, it also ensures that building component tolerances are accommodated during installation.

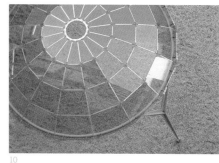

8–11 Views of the dome construction with a span of 5 m

"DELFTER GLASKUPPEL" ("DELFT GLASS DOME")
PROTOTYPE FOR A GARDEN PAVILION
DELFT, 2002–2004

——— CONCEPT AND DESIGN: EWOUT BROGT, MARJON DOESER,
GERARD ENGEL, ROY HENDRIKS, XANDER WINDSANT
——— PROJECT DIRECTOR: JAN WURM, MICK EEKHOUT
——— TECHNICAL CONSULTATION: MICK EEKHOUT, GERRI HOBBELMAN,
PETER VAN SWIETEN, FRED VEER

The dome was created at the Technical University of Delft in 2002. The research goal was to develop a construction system for self-supporting glass shells up to 25 metres in diameter.

The plan envisioned a prototype with a span of 5 metres. The principal focus was on the development of the connections. After the structural performance of the dome had been observed over the course of several months, the structure was erected on the grounds of the faculty.

——— LOAD-BEARING SYSTEM

The spherical shell structure with a diameter of 5 metres is based on the rotational-symmetrical geometry of a ring grid dome with an open apex. Four rings (or hoops) and 16 meridians divide the dome surface into 64 trapezoid, flat plate elements with four differing sizes ——— Fig. 15. The use of flat instead of double curved elements means that the dome surface deviates only slightly from the ideal shell geometry, saving the considerable additional costs required for thermal bending processes. Due to the shear-resistant hinged connection of the panes, the construction represents a folded plate structure in plan and cross-section.

Axial forces are dominant in the glass elements of the folded plate shell; small bending moments are only generated by the local force transfer between the folds. Since the dome surface with a rise of approximately 90 centimetres lies above the zero ring force line, only compression forces occur under dead load both in the direction of the

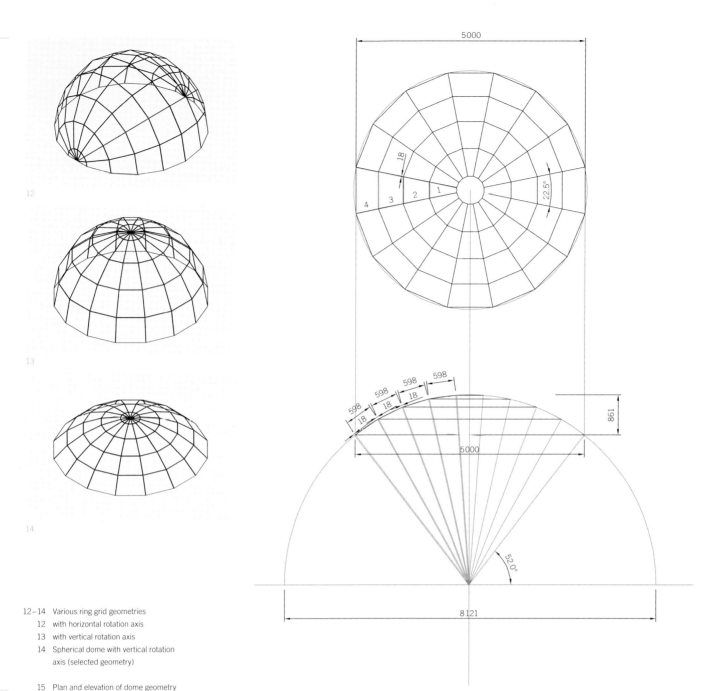

12–14   Various ring grid geometries
12   with horizontal rotation axis
13   with vertical rotation axis
14   Spherical dome with vertical rotation
        axis (selected geometry)

15   Plan and elevation of dome geometry

ring and of the meridians. Tensile stresses occur only under the action of asymmetrical loads such as wind or unevenly distributed snow. Given the low tensile and tensile bending stresses, the shell can be very thin walled. With a glass thickness of 8 millimetres, the construction exhibits a slender ratio of 1:700 in relation to the span.

___ DETAILS

The hinged edge connections between the glass plates are conceived to support the load-bearing behaviour of the skin. Point fixings were not considered since they lead to a channelling of the forces and to local stress peaks within the glass elements. Only a linear connection can ensure even distribution in the transfer of compression, tension and shear forces to the edges of adjoining pane elements.

Per connection element, a total of 6 millimetres i.e. ± 3 millimetres of fabrication and installation tolerances have to be accommodated in the transverse and longitudinal direction of the profile. The moulding

of the joints between the panels with a structural clear resin would enable stress-equalising and evenly distributed force transfer while accommodating the tolerances. Since this would however render the replacement of panels more difficult, connections that are realised purely with adhesive were rejected during the concept development stage.

The detail developed for the dome unifies the advantages of mechanical and structural bonded connections ___ Fig. 18. Stainless steel profiles with a cross-section of 6 mm x 6 mm are attached by adhesive to the edges of the trapezoidal glass elements. The viscoelastic behaviour of the adhesive can accommodate tolerances in the direction of the meridian. The stainless steel rods of adjacent plates are connected in the ring direction through friction grip connections in order to accommodate tolerances there. Contact pressure is ensured through clamping bars (steel flats) and bolts with washers at 100 millimetres intervals.

16

17

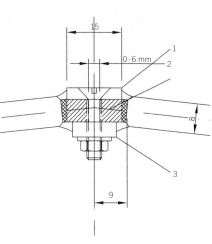

18

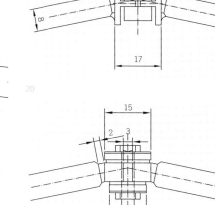

20

21

19

22

16　Joint intersection between linear connection elements

17　Stainless steel zenith ring with a diameter of 0.6 m

18　Cross-section of join connection with stainless steel
　　profiles
　　1　15/3 flat steel
　　2　6/6 square rod
　　3　12/4 flat steel

19, 22　Tubular steel ring supporting for glass shell

20, 21　Preliminary designs for connection details

In addition to the desired elastic deformation behaviour, the adhesive must also provide sufficient compression strength. Both requirements are fulfilled by the PUR adhesive employed here with a tensile strength of 4 N/mm² and an elongation at break of 300 percent.

The edge profiles are set back from the 4-way corner junctions on the one hand so as to avoid transferring forces to the delicate glass corners and on the other hand to avoid creating the impression of a continuous steel skeleton ____ Fig. 16.

The glass construction is fixed by brackets to a cold-bent tubular ring beam with a diameter of 82.5 millimetres and a wall thickness of 9 millimetres. The lower plane of each glass panel runs tangentially to flat steel elements, which are bolted to a corresponding plate welded to the flange of the brackets. Slotted holes make it possible to adjust the orientation and placement of the flat steel and thus of the glass elements. The ring is supported by pinned connections to three Y-shaped articulating columns. Towards the apex, the glass construction

terminates in a polygonal ring in the plane of the glass capable of carrying bending moments to counteract any diminution of the shell effect due to the opening at the apex ____ Fig. 17.

____ LOAD-BEARING CAPACITY

The short-term strength of the adhesive connection determined in a series of tests is far greater than the calculated required value of 1 N/mm². The shell construction demonstrates excellent load distribution behaviour when a glass element fractures. The residual load-bearing capacity of the structure was demonstrated in an experiment by removing panel elements during and after the installation. No noticeable permanent deformations were recorded through observing the structure in its exterior setting over the course of several months.

____ FUNCTION AND FORM

As a garden pavilion, the roof structure provides an open air shelter ____ Fig. 5.

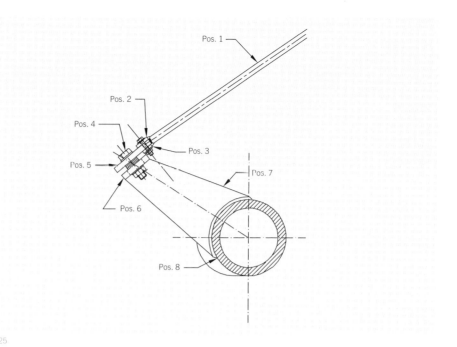

23   Connection detail between support ring and prop

24   Base of prop

25, 26   Connection detail between glass and steel ring
     Pos. 1   8 mm tempered glass pane
     Pos. 2   6/6 stainless steel edge profile
     Pos. 3   Stainless steel clamping bars
     Pos. 4   M 12 bolts with washers
     Pos. 5   6 mm flat steel
     Pos. 6   Flange, 6 mm flat steel
     Pos. 7   Bracket, 10 mm flat steel
     Pos. 8   82, 5/9 bent steel tube

Light reflected from the facets of the folded plate shell structure creates a prismatic, three-dimensional appearance that is further enhanced by the green hue of the glass. Seen from the inside, the structure is extraordinarily transparent, since all connections are integrated into the joints between the glass elements. The open joint intersection between the glass edges underscores the "floating" appearance of the edge profiles. [7.4/1]

_____CONCLUSION AND OUTLOOK

In form and division, the geometry of the dome reflects the characteristics of glass as a building material. The linear hinged connections emphasise the load-bearing capacity of the dome and the diaphragm action of the glass and are reminiscent of putty-glazed grid shell structures of 19th-century glasshouses.

An adhesive system that is suitable in the long term for such complex requirements must be developed in additional experimental studies, which could not be carried out within the context of this project. The fixing detail for the use of insulating glass panes is currently undergoing further development at the Technical University in Delft.

27, 28　Model views of GlassTex dome at night and in
daytime: prestressed fabric bands serve as sun
and glare protection during the day; at night they
are light banners that are visible from afar.

29, 30　Load-bearing variation: the prestressed bands
running in the direction of the meridian.

"GLASSTEX" DOME

DESIGN FOR AN EXHIBITION AND EVENT PAVILION, 2003

____ PROJECT DIRECTORS: JAN WURM, RALF HERKRATH

____ CONCEPT AND DESIGN: RALF HERKRATH, THORSTEN WEIMAR

____ TECHNICAL CONSULTATION: PILKINGTON DEUTSCHLAND, ESSEN;
CENO TEC, GREVEN; SIPRO, WIESBADEN

The "GlassTex" dome was developed for the LAGA – the North Rhine-Westphalia Garden Show in 2003, held in Gronau-Losser. The location for the dome at the foot of a 15 metres high observation pyramid was envisioned in close proximity to Gronau's town centre. In the form of a parasol, the dome was conceived to provide a sheltered area planned for catering. The necessary ancillary functions and services would be housed in a separate pavilion. Once the garden show had closed, the GlasTex dome was to serve as a shelter for a nearby playground.

____ LOAD-BEARING SYSTEM

The dome is a spherical shell with a diameter of 8 metres, the area of which is divided by a grid of 20 meridians and five rings into trapezoidal panels and a circular opening at the zenith ____ Fig. 33. The flat glass serves as enclosure, weather skin and load-bearing structure in one. Since the glass shell lies above the zero ring force line, the plates are subject to compression stresses under evenly distributed vertical loads in the direction of the ring and of the meridians. When asymmetrical loads such as wind load occur, a total of four prestressed fabric bands in the ring joints compensate tensile ring forces by compressing the panel edges.

____ CONSTRUCTION

Given the low stresses in the glass, laminated glass panels composed of 2 x 6 mm annealed float glass with low fabrication tolerances can be used. The flat glass elements with a fine ground edge finish are

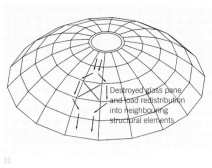

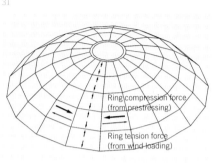

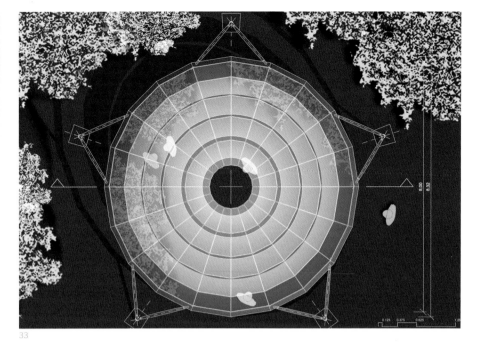

31 Re-distribution in case of failure of one
glass element

32 Distribution of compression and tensile
forces under wind load

33 Plan

34 Elevation

linked by extruded aluminium profiles serving as continuous setting blocks along the hoop. In the meridian joints, the setting blocks are integrated into the dry gaskets. There is no need for an additional silicone wet seal after the installation.

Bent edge plates are bolted to the profiles along the ring joints to the inner and outer sides of the glass skin. These hold the glass in place against wind suction loads, prevent broken panels from falling and ensure sufficient residual load-bearing capacity in case the stabilisation system based on the applied prestress should fail. The fittings butt-jointed at the intersections form a continuous ring.

The horizontal fabric bands are connected by a keder track to the inside of the spherical surface. The prestressing forces are transferred through the joint profile by edge compression to the glass ____ Fig. 37.

Two silicone U-channel gaskets wrap around the glass edge and seal the joint. To accommodate tolerances, aramide-reinforced hard rubber strips serve as setting blocks between the channels and the glass edges ____ Fig. 35. At the intersection of ring and meridian joint, the gap in the silicone U-channel is covered with a double-T dry gasket seal.

The fabric – *2000 TL*, a silicon-coated glass fibre fabric by *Interglas* – has excellent mechanical and optical properties. The fabric with basket weave (90° angle between warp and weft) has a breaking strength of 2000 N / 5 cm (see also GlassTex arch, p. 214).

Given the maximum fabrication width of 4.5 m, the fabric bands cannot be manufactured in one piece. To reduce joints and thus differing stiffnesses along the seams to a minimum, the fabric rings are composed of only two semicircular segments. The different expansion ratios that occur in the fabric due to the different angles of the fibre to the direction of force must be taken into consideration in the cutting of the fabric rings in order to ensure even transfer of force to the glass and a wrinkle-free geometry. The seams are connected to one another by keder rails. To achieve rings that are stretched without folds or wrin-

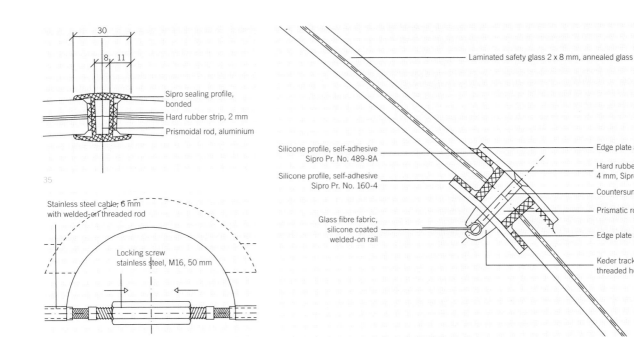

30
8 | 11

Sipro sealing profile, bonded
Hard rubber strip, 2 mm
Prismoidal rod, aluminium

35

Stainless steel cable, 6 mm with welded-on threaded rod

Locking screw stainless steel, M16, 50 mm

36

Laminated safety glass 2 x 8 mm, annealed glass

Silicone profile, self-adhesive Sipro Pr. No. 489-8A
Silicone profile, self-adhesive Sipro Pr. No. 160-4

Glass fibre fabric, silicone coated welded-on rail

Edge plate aluminium, 4 mm
Hard rubber aramide-reinforced, 4 mm, Sipro Pr. No. 377-1
Countersunk screws d = 6 mm
Prismatic rod, aluminium
Edge plate aluminium, 4 mm
Keder track aluminium, threaded hole d = 6 mm

37

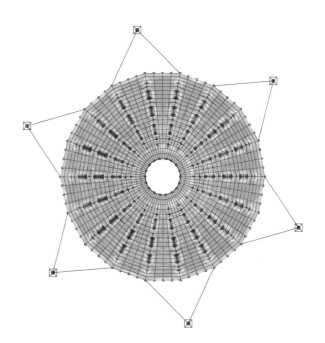

35 Connection detail of meridian joint

36 Detail prestressing element at edge cable

37 Keder connection detail track in ring joint

38 Even distribution of compression forces in dome surface
    in the FEM model under uniformly distributed load

38

kles, the membrane is pulled to the glass skin and into the tracks. A steel cable runs within a pocket along the inner edge of the fabric ring for minor adjustments to the prestressing ____ Fig. 36.

____FUNCTION AND FORM

Due to their louvred arranged in the cross-section, the textile rings serve as sun and glare protection in the interior of the dome. The depth of the fabric louvres has been selected to ensure that the interior is almost fully shaded at midday from the beginning of May until the end of August.

The fabric rings diminish in depth from bottom to top, thus reacting to the differing louvre distances. The fabric has a light reflectance of 46 percent and a light transmittance of 42 percent and supplies the interior with glare-free daylight. Since the solar shading is located in the interior of the dome, heat protection can only be achieved in conjunction with sufficient ventilation.

In addition to the open sides, a continuous opening between the acryl glass covering and the glass dome supports natural convection and ensures that accumulated warm air is extracted.

At night, the fabrics are illuminated from below with uplighting integrated in the floor construction: the rings appear to "float" ____ Figs 41, 42.

The fabrics reduce sound reflection and reverberation times, which can often lead to uncomfortable acoustic conditions for occupants in glass skin structures.

____SUMMARY

The glass forms both the exterior skin and the load-bearing structure and the connections serve simultaneously as load transfer elements and gasket seals. The prestressing fabric bands stabilise the structure. In addition, they also fulfil the building physical requirements of sun protection and acoustics, thus improving the quality of the environment beneath the glass dome for occupants. The appearance is dom-

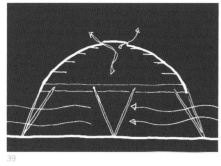

39

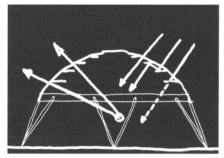

40

41

43

39 In combination with the ventilation openings at
    the joint, the open sides prevent overheating.

40 The fabric bands allow views of the sky.

41–43 At night, the fabric bands are illuminated
    from below and seem to "float".

42

inated by the visually attractive interaction between transparent glass
surfaces and translucent textiles. [7.4/2]

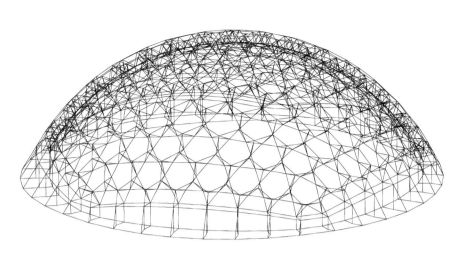

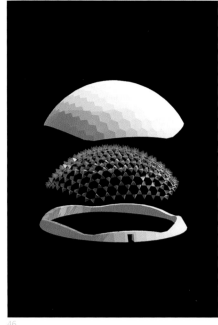

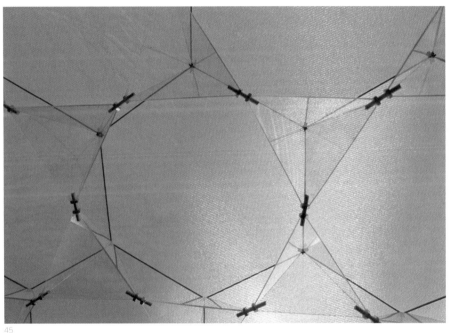

44 Computer model of space frame structure

45 Roof construction in structural model seen from below, scale of 1:50

46 Load-bearing structure: the membrane of the roof covering is stretched across a hexagonal netting system composed of rods; glass tetrahedra are connected to the nodes and stabilise the structure. A massive support ring is aligned with the edge geometry and support the shell structure.

BIOM "TETRASPHERE"

LOAD-BEARING SYSTEM AND CONSTRUCTION, 2002

___ DESIGN: STEFAN DAHLMANNS, NADINE
FISCHER, ALEXANDER KRUSE, NICOLE STOFF
___ PROJECT DIRECTOR: JAN WURM

The glass tetrahedron is an extraordinarily rigid, three-dimensional load-bearing module, as demonstrated in the "Tetra glass arch" and the "Tetra grid". The "Tetrasphere" studies the use of the module in double-curved, spherical structures. The point of departure for the project is the design for a biom with a span of 40 metres. A biom is a spherically curved climate skin, the compact volume and rise of which make it suitable for cultivating tropical plants.

A spherical triangle of the biom was realised on a scale of 1:50 as a detail model constructed of perspex and steel wire.

The construction is a spherically curved, double-layer space frame structure. The basic geometrical structure corresponds to the load-bearing structure of the Eden project in Cornwall.

The upper layer – top chord of the system – is formed by a hexagonal mesh system (hex-mesh). The bottom layer evolves from the upper layer in that the linear member centres are linked and shifted radially to the centre of the sphere with the result that the bottom layer represents a triangle-hexagonal mesh system (tri-hex-mesh). The nodes of the top and bottom chord layer are linked by diagonals, the geometry of which traces the edges of distorted tetrahedra.

The number of different linear and planar elements can be reduced by optimising the geodesic division of the sphere (see Section 6.2). In the "Tetrasphere" the edge length of the icosahedron was divided 16-fold by parallel displacement of the sides, resulting in 64 triangle surfaces with 15 different areas in plan. These triangles represent the area for the tetrahedron bodies, between the peaks of which

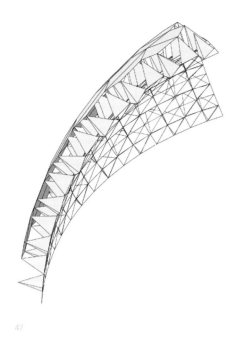

47 Sectional view of truss model

48 View of double-layered roof structure (model):
six tetrahedra arranged in a ring form a subsystem.
In the bottom chord plane, the vertices of the
tetrahedra are connected to one another and
form a triangle-hexagonal net (tri-hex-net).

49 View of complete structural model without
membrane

the hex-mesh is stretched. The asymmetrical bodies have an edge length ranging from 1.64 metres to 1.98 metres.

In the build-up of the "Tetrasphere", the edges of the triangular plate of the tetrahedron facing down form the bottom chord mesh; the edges of the lateral faces form the diagonals. The pyramid corners are connected by a steel rod system. As the hexagons can be displaced, the node connections in the top chord must provide bending stiffness. To reduce tensile forces in the glass elements, the skin of the "Tetrasphere" is utilised in the prestressing of the entire shell structure.

___FORM AND CONCLUSION

The interplay between the translucent weather skin and glass faces of the tetrahedra dissolves the materiality of the envelope through a play of light characterised by alternating transparency and reflection.
The project demonstrates structural ideas on linking stiff and flexible planar load-bearing elements. However, due to the complexity of the geometry and the number of differing glass components, the project also illustrates the limitations of structural glass skins.

8

OUTLOOK

1–2 Examples of texturing the surface of glass by means of sintering the flat glass pane or deep etching

4–6 Examples of forming glass by means of casting or hot bending of the flat glass pane

7–9 Examples of integrating layers and interlayers in insulating glass and laminated safety glass

The future developments of glass architecture will be based on the conceptual desire for reduction and abstraction in the appearance of the building skin. References to the constructional mastery of glass as an engineering material, such as point fixings, fittings and cable bracing – considered testimony of the engineer's and the architect's technical genius in the early days of structural glass architecture – continue to lose their appeal. The "legibility" of the construction and its components is relegated to lesser importance in comparison to the overall visual impression of the building skin, in which the versatile optical characteristics of the material are in the foreground.

As the interest in glass skin structures increases, exposed point fixings lose their structural significance in favour of discrete edge connections or shell-like modules, which obviate the need for connectors.

The architectural desire to minimise the construction and the number of components is not synonymous with a dematerialised appearance. Rather, the focus is on the many optical phenomena of glass, and mirror effects and colour impact are as much a part of the visual concept as translucency and transparency. The progressive use of semi-transparent or opaque glass in the building skin does not aim to "maximise" the amount of light that penetrates into the interior – contemporary glass construction has grown emancipated from this postulate. One can anticipate that the integration of active systems such as collectors, displays, logos and script, variable shading and lighting elements will come to define the image of high performance glass facades.

BUILDING MATERIAL

It is reasonable to assume that these design options will lead to larger panel sizes becoming available also for highly processed glass products and specialised architectonic applications. Heat treated, bent, laminated and printed glass is already manufactured by specialist firms in a large size of 3.21 m x 6 m. In the future, the discrepancy between

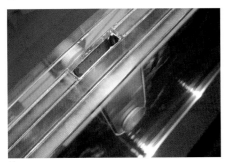

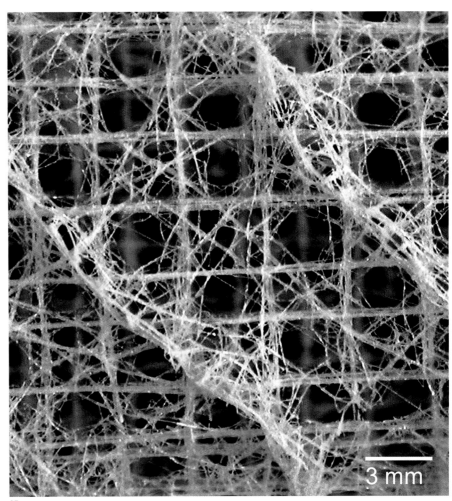

3 mm

10–12   Examples of new joining technologies through
lamination of steel elements into the composite glass
10, 11   Prototypes by *Glasbau Seele*, Gersthofen
12   Structurally bonded hybrid edge connection, prototype
Institut für Tragkonstruktionen, Stuttgart University

13   Inspiration for glass construction taken from nature:
Detail of the building principle of the glass skeleton of
the Euplectella marine sponge. The glass rods are
arranged vertically, horizontally and diagonally and woven
into the framework-like, highly load-resistant mesh.

sizes for "mainstream" and "high-profile" applications will continue to increase, until processing techniques will gradually become applicable even for the oversized jumbo size of 3.21 m x 12 m. Tremendous advances in factory design are anticipated in the area of heat forming and bending, with the result that more complex forms will be manufactured with better optical quality. It is our belief that the chemical strengthening of glass will also attain greater importance for building glazing, since it enables a more even force distribution – even in the case of complex forms – and a better optical quality than the thermal process.

In the future, colour and texture in the building skin will continue to gain in importance. In conjunction with the growing use of low-iron "white glass", the demand for multicoloured ceramic silkscreen prints and interlayers printed with photorealistic patterns or images will continue to increase. The customised surface texturing of the cast and rolled glass enhances the sensual and plastic appearance of the material

The performance of glazing with respect to building physics will likely continue to improve with the integration of innovative components that control the light and energy transmissivity in the cavity of insulating glazing and further advances in the development of thin film technology for photovoltaic modules.

___CONSTRUCTION

In terms of construction, composite construction will continue to gain in importance, whether it be planar as laminated safety glass, or in the area of linear or point fittings that enable "ghost" connections between building components.

Transparent and semi-transparent composite materials, similar to those already employed in automobile and airplane construction, will come into use and replace monolithic single glass panes. Glass with specialised composite film, the rigidity of which is optimised for each relevant application, can help reduce glass thicknesses and the dead load of glass constructions. With the development of more rigid "struc-

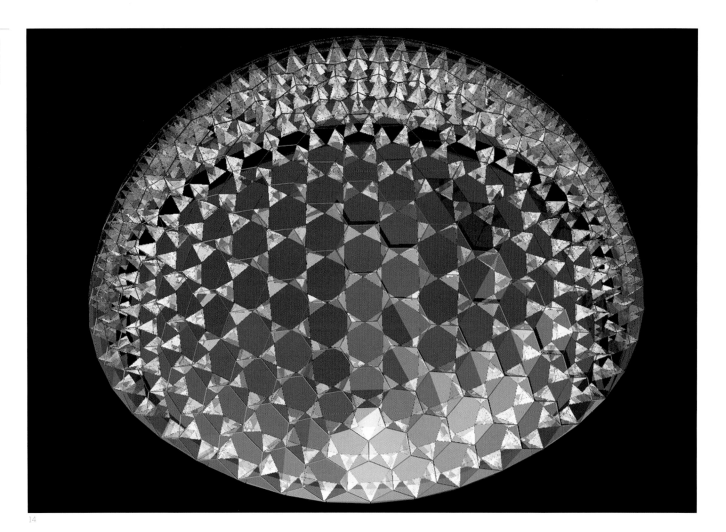

14

14 Computer model of a spherical space frame
    structure composed of glass tetrahedra Design:
    S. Dahlmanns, N. Fischer, A. Kruse, N. Stoff

tural" interlayers point fixings to the glass surface can be designed in a more advanced manner by incorporating thin sheets of a tough material in the laminate or by interlocking metal parts and glass notches. In composite constructions with titanium or specialised steel alloys, the thermal expansion rates of the structural components can be adjusted to allow for hybrid and rigid high-load connections.

Adhesive technology will improve with regard to transparent edge connections. In this area, there is a great demand to create options for controlling the quality of structurally bonded connections during production and the entire design life of the building. A desirable option would be structural adhesives that discolour as their strength decreases, thus providing a visual signal of a failure potential.

Another driving force in the development of glass construction is the desire to limit the production tolerances of the glass components by using float or chemically strengthened glass in order to obviate the need to compensate for tolerances caused by any heat treatment.

Semi-finished curved or double curved products with low manufacturing tolerances can be pre-assembled at the factory into standardised, cellular load-bearing modules with the help of thermal joining methods such as soldering or welding.

In comparison to lightweight constructions that are resistant to tensile forces and light-permeable film and membrane materials, the appeal of glass structures will increase greatly if the breakage behaviour caused by the brittleness of the material can be modified. Combinations of mineral glass with plastics, polymer layers and fibre and mesh inlays demonstrate greatly improved mechanical properties. Advances in micro- and nanotechnology open the door to the possibility of generating "self-healing" or restorative effects in the glass surface through special coatings, thereby reducing the compromising influence of scratches and cracks.

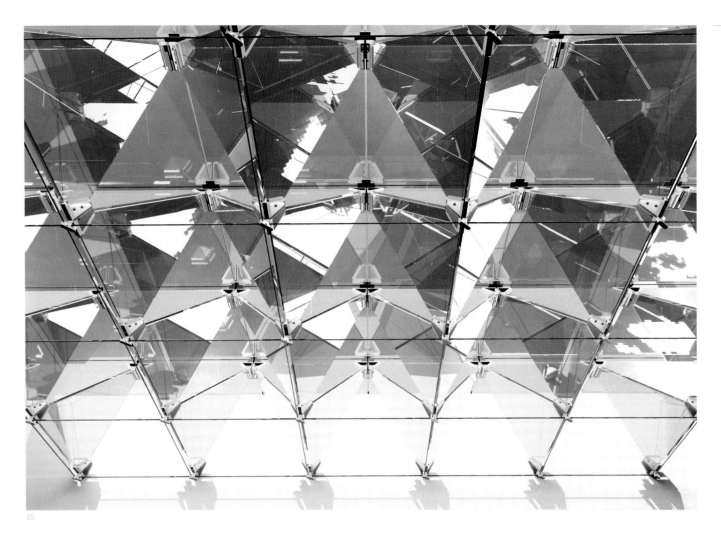

15

15 Computer model of a load-bearing structural space
frame composed of glass tetrahedra, Design:
J. Hlavka, S. Rullkötter, D. Seiberts, S. Spengler

____STRUCTURAL SKINS

The principles of structural skins will gain in popularity over skeleton construction. Continued research in the area of the load-bearing behaviour of redundant sandwich, folded-plate and truss structures, and also in the field of adhesive technology, could in the near future lead to load-bearing building "kits" approved by the building authorities. Construction modules for medium and large spans could be introduced to the building market in accordance with the design parameters outlined in this work.

Especially space frames, which are based on the prefabrication of cellular or prismatic load-bearing modules, will benefit from advances in 3D-forming and in the technology with transparent adhesives.

The synthesis of structural plates and enclosing panes in structural glass skins will create an obligation to furnish proof of the building physical requirements through integrated measures such as adaptive colouring or coatings of the glass or the interlayers. With continued progress in glass processing, irregular and quasi-periodic geometries will no doubt be realised in addition to the systems that are presented in this work.

The use of glass as a planar, multifunctional and visually variable load-bearing element creates the prospect for a new architectural language for glass enclosures:

"Multiple reflections on reflective glass: fluid transitions between colourful, geometrical patterns, crystals floating in the air. [...] We look up past our heads onto a wide-span, prismatic glass structure, a continually changing building skin. The eye only takes in surfaces on which images pass by, clouds, and people below. The surfaces seem to float, to move, they protect against wind and rain, heat or cold, separating inside and outside. [...] The image changes with the environmental conditions – the sun peaks out from behind the clouds and the surfaces or filling gases in the glass components change colour, reflect and direct the light or absorb energy." [8/1]

16

17

16, 17 Model of a quasi-periodic space frame composed of
        coloured glass plates, The Battersea Crystal, London,
        Arch. + Eng.: Arup for Parkview International

APPENDIX

BIBLIOGRAPHICAL REFERENCES

[P 1] Rice, P.; Dutton, H.: *Le Verre structurel*, Paris 1990

[P 2] Button, D.; Pye, B.: *Glass in Building*, Oxford 1993

[P 3] Wigginton, M.: *Glass in Architecture*, London 1996

[P 4] Gigon, A.; Guyer, M.: "Die Grammatik der Werkstoffe", in: *DAIDALOS 08/1995*, Magie der Werkstoffe II, pp. 48–55

[P 5] Siegel, C.: *Strukturformen der modernen Architektur*, Munich 1961

[1/1] Laugier, M.-A.; Bock, H. (eds): *Das Manifest des Klassizismus; based on the original: Essai sur l'architecture (1753)*, Zurich 1989

[1/2] Hix, J.: *The Glasshouse*, London 1996

[1/3] Knaack, U.: *Konstruktiver Glasbau*, Cologne 1998

[1/4] Schlaich, J.; Schober, H.: "Design Principles of Glass Roofs", conference report *Lightweight Structures in Civil Engineering*, 2002, pp. 815

[1/5] Tschumi, B.; Widder, L.: "Haus ohne Eigenschaften"; in: *DAIDALOS, 08/1995 Magie der Werkstoffe II*, p. 108

[1/6] Carpenter, J, Lowings, L.: "The material and the ephemeral", in: Behling, S.; Behling, St. (eds): *Glas(s) – Konstruktion und Technologie in der Architektur*, Munich 1999, pp. 86 et seqq.

[1/7] Siegel, C.: *Strukturformen der modernen Architektur*, Munich 1961

[1/8] cf.: Torroja, E.: *Logik der Form, based on the original: Razon y ser de los tipos estructurales*, Munich 1961, p. 12

[1/9] Fensterbusch, C. (ed.): *Vitruv: Zehn Bücher über Architektur; based on the original: De Architectura Libri Decem*, Darmstadt 1996

[1/10] Führer, W.: "Gedanken zur integralen Planung", catalogue for the exhibition *showreiff* at the DAM (German Museum of Architecture), Frankfurt am Main, Berlin 2001, pp. 108 et seq.

[2.1/1] Kohlmaier, G.; von Sartory, B.: *Houses of glass: a nineteenth-century building type*, Cambridge, Mass. 1996, pp. 33, 34

[2.1/2] Teubner, H.: *Vergessene Bauwerke – "Laubhütten" in Hessen*, brochures published by the Department of Conservation in Hessen, issue 01/1989; http://www.denkmalpflege-hessen.de

[2.1/3] Gräfe, R. (ed.): *Zur Geschichte des Konstruierens*, Stuttgart 1989

[2.1/4] Roemer, W.: *Kirchenarchitektur als Abbild des Himmels*, Kevelaer 1997, p. 14

[2.1/5] Geist, J. F.: *Arcades, the history of a building type*, Cambridge, Mass. 1983, p. 21

[2.1/6] Heinle, E.; Schlaich, J.: *Kuppeln*, Stuttgart 1996, p. 223

[2.1/7] Mark, R. (ed.): *Vom Fundament zum Deckengewölbe*, Basel 1995, pp. 62–66

[2.1/8] Hubala, E., quoted in Lindenmann, B. W.: *Bilder vom Himmel – Studien zur Deckenmalerei des 17. und 18. Jh.*, Worms am Rhein 1994, p. 49

[2.1/9] Kohlmaier, G.; von Sartory, B.: op. cit., p. 8

[2.1/10] Hix, J.: *The Glasshouse*, London 1996, pp. 56–72

[2.1/11] "Knight's Cyclopaedia of London", 1851; quoted in Hix, J.: op. cit., p. 141

[2.1/12] Taut, B.: *Haus des Himmels*, Frühlicht 1920, reprint as Bauwelt Fundamente 8, Berlin 1963, pp. 33–36

[2.1/13] Scheerbart, P.: *Glasarchitektur, XVIII – Die Schönheit der Erde*, Berlin 1914; http://www.gutenberg2000.de

[2.1/14] Fourier, Ch.: *The Theory of four Movements*, Cambridge, New York 1996; quoted in Schaper, R. M.: *Der gläserne Himmel*, Frankfurt am Main 1988, p. 24

[2.1/15] Loudon, J. C.: *An Encyclopaedia of Gardening*, 1822; quoted in: Hix, J.: op. cit., p. 44

[2.1/16] Liddell, I.: "Large Environmental Enclosures", in: *Widespan Roof Structures* (Barnes, M.; Dickson M., eds), London 2000, pp. 149–158

[2.1/17] quoted in Hix, J.: op. cit., p. 223

[2.1/18] N.N.: "Himmel, Erde und Wasser – Kurtherme in Bad Colberg", in: *DBZ 02/2001*, pp. 64–67

[2.1/19] N.N.: "Bunter Baldachin", in: *AIT 11/1999*, pp. 100 et seq.

[2.2/1] Torroja, E.: *Logik der Form, based on the original: Razon y ser de los tipos estructurales*, Munich 1961

[2.2/2] Geist, J. F.: *Arcades, the history of a building type*, Cambridge, Mass. 1983, pp. 55 et seq.

[2.2/3] Führer, W.; Ingendaaji, S.; Stein, F.: *Der Entwurf von Tragwerken*, Aachen 1995, pp. 37 et seq.

[2.2/4] Engel, H.: *Tragsysteme*, Ostfildern-Ruit 1997

[2.2/5] Führer, W.; Gerhardt, R.: *Tragkonstruktionen in Natur und Technik*, Lehrstuhl für Tragkonstruktionen, RWTH Aachen 2000

[3.1/1] Klindt, L. B.; Klein, W.: *Glas als Baustoff*, Cologne 1977, pp. 10 et seqq.

[3.1/2] Petzold, A.; Marusch, H.; Schramm, B.: *Der Baustoff Glas*, Berlin 1990, p. 13

[3.1/3] *DIN EN 572, Glass in Building*, Basiserzeugnisse aus Kalk-Natronglas, Berlin 2004

[3.1/4] Wörner, J.-D.; Schneider, J.; Fink, A.: *Glasbau – Grundlagen, Berechnung, Konstruktion*, Berlin 2001, pp. 61–76

[3.1/5] Sedlacek, G.: *Glas im Konstruktiven Ingenieurbau*, Berlin 1999, pp. 23 et seq.

[3.1/6] Button, D.; Pye, B.: *Glass in Building*, Oxford 1993, p. 215

[3.1/7] Heiringhoff, R: *Reflexion und andere optische Phänomene von Glas*, Studienarbeit am Lehrstuhl Tragkonstruktionen, RWTH Aachen 2001, pp. 16, 20, 25

[3.1/8] Schittich, Chr.; Staib, G.; Balkow, D.; Schuler, M.; Sobek, W.: *Glass Construction Manual*, Basel, Boston, Berlin 1999, p. 115

[3.1/9] The calculation of the g-value is in accordance with European standards EN 410 and ISO 9050.

[3.1/10] Wurm, J. P.: Archiooptix, *Kleine Einführung in die Optik für Architekten*, Heidelberg 2003

[3.1/11] *DIN EN 673*, January 2001; Glass in Building – Determination of Thermal Transmittance (U value) – Calculation Method (German version)

[3.2/1] Winter, M.: "Farbiges Glas", in: *ARCH+, vol. 134/135*, December 1996, pp. 110 et seqq.

[3.2/2] *DIN EN 572-4*, November 1994; Basic soda lime silicate glass products – Drawn sheet glass (German version)

[3.2/3] Technical information OPALIKA, Schott AG, 2004

[3.2/4] Technical information IMERA and ARTISTA, Schott AG, 2004

[3.2/5] Hager, W.: Saint-Gobain Glass, "Werk Mannheim setzt auf die Solartechnik", in: *GFF vol. 10/2002*, p. 100

[3.3/1] Hübinger, A.: Glasbearbeitung – über das Trennen, Schleifen, Bohren und Biegen von Glas, Studienarbeit am Lehrstuhl für Tragkonstruktionen, RWTH Aachen 2002

[3.3/2] Veer, F. A.; Zuidema, J.: The strength of glass, effect of edge quality, Glass Processing Days 2003

[3.3/3] Bucak, O.: Gutachterliche Stellungnahme zur gebogenen Überkopfverglasung beim Bauvorhaben Neubau Loggia Wasseralfingen, FH Munich, 2002

[3.3/4] Kasper, P.: "Die Polygenese elementarer Bauformen", in: *GFF-Zeitschrift für Glas Fenster Fassade, 10/2002*, pp. 28 et seq.

[3.3/5] Scholze, Th.: Reversibel gekrümmte Verbundglaselemente, Diplomarbeit am Institut für leichte Flächentragwerke, University of Stuttgart 2000, p. 132

[3.4/1] DIN 1259-1, Glass – Part 1: Terminology for glass types and groups, Issue 2001-09 (German version)

[3.4/2] DIN EN 12150-1, Glass in building – Thermally toughened soda-lime silicate safety glass, Part 1: Definition and description, Issue 2000-11 (German version)

[3.4/3] DIN EN 1863-1, Glass in building – Heat-strengthened soda-lime silicate glass, Part 1: Definition and description, Issue 2000-03 (German version)

[3.4/4] Kasper, A.: Spontanbruch von Einscheibensicherheitsgläsern am Bau – ein lösbares Problem, Tagungsband *Glas im Konstruktiven Ingenieurbau 2*, FH Munich, November 2001

[3.4/5] Wörner, J.-D.; Schneider, J.; Fink, A.: *Glasbau – Grundlagen, Berechnung, Konstruktion*, Berlin 2001, pp. 13 et seq.

[3.4/6] Richtlinie zur Beurteilung der visuellen Qualität von Glas im Bauwesen, Bundesinnungsverband des Glaserhandwerks und Bundesverband Flachglas, Version June 2004

[3.4/7] Technical information *berlinglas*, http://www.berlinglas.de

[3.4/8] Technical information *BI-Color, BI-ThermColor*, BGT Bischoff Glastechnik, 2004

[3.4/9] *Glashandbuch* von Flachglas Markenkreis, Issue 2004, pp. 146 et seq.

[3.4/10] Scholze, Th.: "Thermische Veredelung von Flachglas", in: *GLASS II*, Pub.: Verband Deutscher Maschinen- und Anlagenbau e.V. (VDMA) und Messe Düsseldorf GmbH, 2002, pp. 128–141

[3.4/11] Technical information Tambest, 2004

[3.4/12] Scheideler, J.: "Die Statik gebogenen Glases", in: *Glaswelt 08/2000*

[3.5/1] DIN EN ISO 12543-1 to -6, Glass in building – Laminated glass and laminated safety glass, Parts 1 to 6, Issue 1998-08 (German version)

[3.5/2] Brockmann, W.: "Flachglas-Veredelung durch Fügen", in: *GLASS II*, Pub.: Verband Deutscher Maschinen- und Anlagenbau e.V. (VDMA) und Messe Düsseldorf GmbH, 2002, pp. 160 et seq.

[3.5/3] Handbuch der Trosifol AG, http://www.trosifol.com/ger/handbuch

[3.5/4] Bucak, Ö.: "Glas im konstruktiven Ingenieurbau", in: *Stahlbaukalender 1999*, Berlin 1999, pp. 534 et seq.

[3.5/5] Bucak, Ö.; Heger, F.: "Fassaden", in: *Stahlbaukalender 2003*, Berlin 2003, pp. 632 et seq.

[3.5/6] Schuler, Chr.; Gräf, H.: "Verbundtragverhalten von VSG", paper at seminar *Glas im Konstruktiven Ingenieurbau* at FH Munich on 8 November 2001

[3.5/7] Bohmann, D.: *Ein numerisches Verfahren zur Berechnung von Verbundglasscheiben*, Dissertation at Lehrstuhl für Stahlbau, RWTH Aachen, 1999

[3.5/8] Product information Vanceva Design-Folien, Solutia, 2002

[3.5/9] Product information Sentry Glass Expressions, DuPont, 2002

[3.5/10] Technical information Gesellschaft für Licht und Bautechnik mbH, Cologne 2000

[3.5/11] Technical information PRIVA-LITE von SGG Germany, 2002

[3.5/12] Haase, W.: Smart Materials – "Intelligente" Werkstoffe, Anwendungsmöglichkeiten in Hüllsystemen, Proc. *GlasKon* Munich 2003, pp. 12–23

[3.5/13] Erban, Chr.: Photovoltaik zur Gebäudeintegration, Proc. *GlasKon* Munich 2001, pp. 23–27

[3.6/1] Scheideler, J.: "Verfahren zur Veränderung der Flachglasoberfläche", in: *GLASS II*, Pub.: Verband Deutscher Maschinen- und Anlagenbau e.V. (VDMA) and Messe Düsseldorf GmbH, 2002, pp. 144 –157

[3.6/2] Product information "Sunenergy" and "Sungate" from PPG and "Sunguard" from Guardian, 2002

[3.6/3] Technical information Amiran, SCHOTT AG, 2004

[3.6/4] Reuters, N.: James Carpenter – "Glas und Licht", student research project at the Lehrstuhl für Tragkonstruktionen, RWTH Aachen 2000, pp. 111–114

[3.6/5] Technical information Prinz Optics GmbH, 2000

[3.6/6] Technical information Spacia, Nippon Sheet Glass http://www.nsg-spacia.co.jp

[3.6/7] Product information GEWE-therm TPS, Scholl Glas, 2004

[3.6/8] Siebert, G.: *Entwurf und Bemessung von tragenden Bauteilen aus Glas,* Berlin 2001, pp. 98–110

[3.6/9] Product information Thermur HM, Glasfischer, 2004

[3.6/10] Product information Kapilux, Okatech and Okalux, Okalux GmbH, 2004

[3.6/11] Product information Micro solar control louvre, Siteco Beleuchtungstechnik GmbH, 2004

[3.6/12] Haase, W.: "Smart Materials", in: Proc. *GlasKon* 2003, pp. 18 et seq.

[3.6/13] The weighted sound reduction index RW is determined in accordance with DIN EN 20140-3, *Issue 1995-05 and DIN EN ISO 717-1, Issue 1997-01.*

[4.1/1] Techen, H.: *Fügetechnik für den konstruktiven Glasbau,* Dissertation at the Institut für Statik, TU Darmstadt, 1997

[4.1/2] Schadow, Th.: "Beanspruchungsgerechtes Konstruieren mit Glas", in: Proc. *glasbau2004*, Institut für Baukonstruktion, TU Dresden, pp. 63–74

[4.1/3] Burchhardt, B.; Diggelmann, K.; Kock, S.; Lanzendörfer, B.: *Elastisches Kleben – Technologische Grundlagen und Leitfaden für die wirtschaftliche Anwendung,* Landsberg/Lech 1998, pp. 25 et seqq.

[4.1/4] Weller, N.; Pottgiesser, U.; Tasche, S.: "Kleben im Bauwesen – Glasbau, Teil 2: Grundlagen", in: *DETAIL 12/2004,* pp. 1488–1494

[4.1/5] Schneider, H.: "Stand der Normung im Glasbau", in: Proc. *glasbau2004*, Institut für Baukonstruktion, TU Dresden, pp. 41–50

[4.1/6] Reidt, A.: "Allgemeine bauaufsichtliche Zulassungen für Glaserzeugnisse", in: Proc. *glasbau2004*, Institut für Baukonstruktion, TU Dresden

[4.1/7] Technische Regeln für die Verwendung von linienförmig gelagerten Verglasungen (TRLV), Issue 1998-09, published in *DIBt Mitteilungen 6/1998*

[4.1/8] Technische Regeln für die Verwendung von absturzsichernden Verglasungen (TRAV), Issue 2003-01, published in *DIBt Mitteilungen 2/2003*

[4.1/9] Entwurfsfassung Technische Regeln für die Bemessung und Ausführung punktförmig gelagerter Verglasungen August 2005, DIBt

[4.1/10] ETAG No. 002: Leitlinie für die europäische Zulassung für geklebte Glaskonstruktionen (Structural Sealant Glazing Systems – SSGS), Teil 1: Gestützte und ungestützte Systeme; Issue: 1998-07

[4.1/11] Regierungspräsidium Tübingen / Landesstelle für Bautechnik Baden-Württemberg: Allgemeines Merkblatt zur Erlangung einer Zulassung im Einzelfall, Issue 23.01.2005

[4.1/12] Bucak, Ö.: "Glas im konstruktiven Ingenieurbau", in: *Stahlbau-Kalender,* Berlin 1999, pp. 621 et seq.

[4.1/13] Wörner, J.-D.; Schneider, J.; Fink, A.: *Glasbau – Grundlagen, Berechnung, Konstruktion,* Berlin 2001, pp. 121–128

[4.1/14] Siebert, G.: "Möglichkeiten der Bemessung von Bauteilen aus Glas", *Stahlbau 73/2004*, Vol. 5, pp. 348–355

[4.1/15] Blank, K.: *Dickenbemessung von vierseitig gelagerten rechteckigen Glasscheiben unter gleichförmiger Flächenlast,* Forschungsbericht, Vol. 3 der Veröffentlichungsreihe des Instituts für konstruktiven Glasbau IKG, Gelsenkirchen 1993

[4.1/16] Shen, X.: *Entwicklung eines Bemessungs- und Sicherheitskonzeptes für den Glasbau,* VDI Report, Series 4, No. 138, 1997

[4.1/17] Güsgen, J.: *Bemessung tragender Bauteile aus Glas,* Dissertation at the Lehrstuhl Stahlbau, RWTH Aachen 1998

[4.1/18] prDIN EN 13474-1: Glass in building – Design of glass panes – Part 1: General basis of design, analysis and design, Issue 1999 (German version)

[4.1/19] Laufs, W.: *Ein Bemessungskonzept zur Festigkeit thermisch vorgespannter Gläser,* Dissertation at the Lehrstuhl Stahlbau, RWTH Aachen 2000

[4.1/20] Wörner, J.-D.; Schneider, J.; Fink, A.: *Glasbau – Grundlagen, Berechnung, Konstruktion,* Berlin 2001, pp. 172–180

[4.1/21] Four-point test in accordance with DIN 52303: Determination of bending strength (DIN EN 1288-1, Issue 2000-09)

[4.2/1] Schittich, Chr.; Staib, G.; Balkow, D.; Schuler, M.; Sobek, W.: *Glass Construction Manual,* 2nd, revised and expanded edition, Basel, Munich 2006

[4.2/2] Charlier, H.; Feldmeier, F.; Reidt, A.: Erläuterungen zu den "Technischen Regeln für die Verwendung von linienförmig gelagerten Verglasungen", *Mitteilungen des DIBt 3/1999*

[4.2/3] Regierungspräsidium Tübingen / Landesstelle für Bautechnik Baden-Württemberg: Merkblatt G2, Zusammenfassung der wesentlichen Anforderungen an zustimmungspflichtige Vertikalverglasungen, Issue 10.05.2004

[4.2/4] Fachverband Konstruktiver Glasbau: Merkblatt "Betretbare Verglasungen", Cologne, Issue 13.05.2002

[4.2/5] Hauptverband der gewerblichen Berufsgenossenschaften (Pub.): Prüfgrundsätze GS-BAU-18 – Grundsätze für die Prüfung und Zertifizierung der bedingten Betretbarkeit oder Durchsturzsicherheit von Bauteilen bei Bau- und Instandsetzungsarbeiten, Karlsruhe, Issue 02/2001

[4.2/6] Zulassungsbescheid Z 70.6-90: Begehbare Verglasung SGG LITE-FLOOR, DIBt Berlin, 11.02.2004

[4.2/7] Anforderungen an begehbare Verglasungen; Empfehlungen für das Zustimmungs-verfahren, *Mitteilungen des DIBt 02/2001*, pp. 60 et seqq.

[4.2/8] Regierungspräsidium Tübingen / Landesstelle für Bautechnik Baden-Württemberg: Merkblatt G4, Zusammenfassung der wesentlichen Anforderungen an begehbare Verglasungen im Rahmen einer Zustimmung im Einzelfall, Issue 10.05.2004

[4.2/9] Haas, Ch.; Haldimann, M.: Entwurf und Bemessung von Tragelementen aus Glas – Wissensstandbericht, Rapport ICOM 493, Ecole Polytechnique Fédérale de Lausanne (EPFL), Lausanne, 2004, pp. 85–89

[4.2/10] Bucak, Ö.: Glas im konstruktiven Ingenieurbau, *Stahlbau-Kalender*, Berlin 1999

[4.2/11] Lehmann, R.: Auslegung punktgehaltener Gläser, *Stahlbau 67* (1998) Vol. 4, pp. 270–274

[4.2/12] Fachverband Konstruktiver Glasbau e. V.: Merkblatt Punktförmig gelagerte Verglasungen, 2000

[4.2/13] Brodin, S.: *Experimentelle und numerische Untersuchungen zu einem neuartigen Hinterschnitt-Dübelsystem für punktgehaltene Stahl-Glas-Konstruktionen*, diploma thesis at the Lehrstuhl Stahlbau, RWTH Aachen 2001

[4.2/14] Technical information SGG POINT XS – Punktgehaltenes Verglasungssystem von Saint-Gobain Glass 08/2003

[4.2/15] ETAG No. 002, Leitlinie für die europäische Zulassung für geklebte Glaskonstruktionen (Structural Sealant Glazing-SSGS), Teil 1: Gestützte und ungestützte Systeme; Issue 1998-07

[4.2/16] DC 993 and DC 895: Tragende Klebstoffe zur Verwendung in geklebten Glaskonstruktionen, ETZ No. 01/0005 dated 07.03.2001

[4.2/17] Elastosil SG 500 – Klebstoff zur Verwendung in geklebten Glaskonstruktionen, ETZ No. 03/0038, dated 02.02.2004

[4.2/18] Havemann, K.: *Untersuchung geklebter Verbindungen aus Glas*, diploma thesis at the Institut für Baukonstruktion, TU Dresden 2003

[4.2/19] Fleckenstein, M.: *Tragfähigkeit geklebter Punkthalter*, diploma thesis at the Lehrstuhl für Stahlbau, RWTH Aachen 2000

[4.2/20] Nägele, T.: "Modifizierte Acrylat-Klebstoffe für hochtransparente Glasverklebungen", Proc. *GlasKon* Munich 2005, pp. 30 et seq.

[4.3/1] Hübinger, A.: *Stabilität von Tragelementen aus Glas*, Dissertation EPFL 3014, Ecole Polytechnique Fédérale de Lausanne (EPFL), Lausanne, 2004, pp. 93–106

[4.3/2] Liess, J.: *Bemessung druckbelasteter Bauteile aus Glas*, Dissertation am Fachgebiet Tragwerksplanung, Kassel University 2001

[4.3/3] Geist, J. F.: *Arcades, the history of a building type*, Cambridge, Mass. 1983, p. 12

[4.3/4] Wellershoff, F.: *Schubaussteifung bei Stahl-Glas-Konstruktionen*, AIF-Research project, Chair of Steel Construction, RWTH Aachen 1999/2000

[4.3/5] Schmid, J.; Spengler, R.; Niedermaier, P.; Gräf, H.; Hoeckel, C.: *Ansätze zur Berücksichtigung und Entwicklung von Bemessungsvorschlägen zur aussteifenden Wirkung der Verglasung bei Wintergärten aus Holz*, Final report on a research project at the Institut für Fenstertechnik Rosenheim (ift) und Fachgebiet Holzbau TU Munich, 1999

[4.3/6] Mohren, R.: *Konzeption und Bemessung einer schubaussteifenden Glasscheibe für Stabtragwerke aus Glas und Stahl*, diploma thesis at the Lehrstuhl für Stahlbau, RWTH Aachen 2000

[4.3/7] Luible, A.: *Stabilität von Tragelementen aus Glas*, Dissertation EPFL 3014, Ecole Polytechnique Fédérale de Lausanne (EPFL), Lausanne, 2004, pp. 166 et seqq.

[4.3/8] N.N.: "Aussteifungssystem mit Glas", in: *glasforum 03/2003*, pp. 7–10

[4.3/9] Nijsse, R.: *Glass in Structures*, Basel 2003, pp. 16 et seqq.

[4.3/10] Güsgen, J.: *Bemessung tragender Bauteile aus Glas*, series published by the Lehrstuhl Stahlbau, RWTH Aachen 1998

[4.3/11] Kasper, T.: *Analytische und experimentelle Untersuchungen zum Biegedrillknicken thermisch vorgespannter Glasschwerter*, diploma thesis at the Lehrstuhl für Stahlbau, RWTH Aachen 2000

[4.3/12] Luible, A.: *Stabilität von Tragelementen aus Glas*, Dissertation EPFL 3014, Ecole Polytechnique Fédérale de Lausanne (EPFL), Lausanne 2004, pp. 145–155

[4.3/13] Proc. "glasbau2005", Institut für Baukonstruktion, TU Dresden, pp. 52 et seqq., pp. 104–114

[4.3/14] Haas, Ch.; Haldimann, M.: "Entwurf und Bemessung von Tragelementen aus Glas – Wissensstandbericht", *Rapport ICOM 493*, Ecole Polytechnique Fédérale de Lausanne (EPFL), Lausanne, 2004, p. 30

[4.3/15] Bucak, Ö.: "Glas im konstruktiven Ingenieurbau", *Stahlbau-Kalender*, Berlin 1999, p. 595

[4.3/16] Technical Datasheet HIT-HY 50 for glass construction, 2003

[4.3/17] Hagl, A.: "Aktuelles aus der Arbeitsgruppe Verkleben des Fachverbands Konstruktiver Glasbau (FKG)", conference minutes *Glas im konstruktiven Ingenieurbau 4*, FH Munich 2004

[5.1/1] Alberti, L. B: *The Ten Books of Architecture*, Florence 1485

[5.1/2] Miloni, R. P.: "Die emanzipierte Jalousie", in: *FASSADE / FACADE 03/2002*, pp. 11–15

[5.1/3] Bauernschmidt, Chr.; Hodulak, M.: "Umhüllte öffentliche Räume – Behaglichkeit und technischer Ausbau", in: *DETAIL 02/1995*, pp. 168–172

[5.1/4] Siebert, G.: *Bauklimatischer Entwurf für moderne Glasarchitektur*, Berlin 2002

[5.1/5] von Gerkan, M.: Der gläserne Himmel – Glas als Raumhülle und Informationsmedium, yearbook *VDI-Bau, 2000*, p. 222

[5.1/6] Gibiec, Chr.: "Tageslicht ist wertvoller als jedes Kunstlicht", *VDI-Nachrichten 1/2 2002*, pp. 36 et seq.

[5.1/7] Brandi, U.: "Daylight Control", in: *DETAIL 04/2004*, pp. 368 et seqq.

[5.1/8] Humm, O.: *Niedrig-Energie-Häuser*, Staufen bei Freiburg, 1990, pp. 103 et seqq.

[5.1/9] Pültz, G.: *Bauklimatischer Entwurf für moderne Glasarchitektur,* Berlin 2002, p. 45

[5.1/10] Grimm, F.: *Energieeffizientes Bauen mit Glas*, Munich 2004, pp. 78 et seq.

[5.1/11] Lang, W.: "Is it all 'just' façade? The functional, energetic and structural aspects of the building skin", in: Schittich, Chr. (ed.): *Building Skins*, Basel 2001, pp. 29 et seqq.

[5.1/12] Informationen Fachverband Lichtkuppel, Lichtband und RWA e.V. (FVLR): Projektierung RWA, http://www.fvlr.de

[5.1/13] Flachglas Markenkreis: Merkblatt "Reinigung von Glas", from: *Glas Handbuch 2004*, pp. 214 et seqq.

[5.1/14] Fischer, K.: *Reinigen und Warten von Glaskonstruktionen*, Proc. GlasKon, Munich 1998

[5.1/15] Steinbicker, O.: *Überdachte Einkaufsstraßen*, diploma thesis at the Fakultät Raumplanung, Dortmund University 2000

[5.1/16] Schittich, Chr.; Staib, G.; Balkow, D.; Schuler, M.; Sobek, W.: *Glass Construction Manual*, Munich 1999, p. 142

[5.1/17] Jauer, M.: Bora Bora im Spreewald, *Süddeutsche Zeitung* dated 17.12.2004

[5.1/18] Davies, D.: "Mezotecture", contributing article in: Barnes, M.; Dickson M. (pub.): *Widespan Roof Structures*, London 2000, pp. 133 et seqq.

[5.2/1] Compagno, A.: "Sonnenschutzmaßnahmen an Fassaden", in: *GLAS 02/2003*, pp. 42–50

[5.2/2] Fuchs, H. V.; Drotleff, H.; Wenski, H.: "Mikroperforierte Folien als Schallabsorber für große Räume", in: *Technik am Bau 10/2002*, pp. 67–71

[5.2/3] Technical information Microsorber, Kaefer-Gruppe, http://www.kaefer.com

[5.2/4] Erban, Chr.: "Gestaltungsmöglichkeiten von gebäudeintegrierten Photovoltaik-Elementen", Proc. *Glas im Konstruktiven Ingenieurbau 2*, Munich 2001

[5.2/5] Daniels, K.: *The Technology of Ecological Building*, Basel 1997, p. 166

[5.2/6] Sobek, W; Kutterer, M.: "Flache Dächer aus Glas – konstruktive Aspekte bei Horizontalverglasungen", in: *DETAIL 05/1997*, pp. 773-776

[5.2/7] Hix, J.: *The Glasshouse*, London 1996, pp. 32 et seqq.

[5.2/8] Krewinkel, H.: "Glaskuppel im Weltbild Verlag in Augsburg", *GLAS 03/99*, pp. 39–41

[5.2/9] Wack, R.; Fuchs, H. V.: "Mikroperforierte Akustik-Segel in Versammlungsräumen", *Mitteilungen des Fraunhofer Institut für Bauphysik (IBP)*, No. 31/2004

[5.2/10] Hillmanns, N.: Der Kuppelputzer, "Blickpunkt Bundestag", from: *Deutscher Bundestag*, Berlin 12/99

[6.1/1] Makowski, Z. S.: *Räumliche Tragwerke aus Stahl*, Düsseldorf 1963, p. 8

[6.2/1] Emde, H.: *Geometrie der Knoten-Stab-Tragwerke*, Würzburg 1978

[6.2/2] Mengeringhausen, M.: *Komposition im Raum*, Gütersloh 1983, p. 24

[6.2/3] Heyden, J.-W.: *Räumliche Knotenstabtragwerke*, dissertation at the Lehrstuhl für Tragkonstruktionen, RWTH Aachen 2001, pp. 101 et seqq.

[6.2/4] Emde, H.: *Geometrie der Knoten-Stab-Tragwerke*, Würzburg 1978, p. 52

[6.2/5] Museum für Gestaltung Zurich (ed.): "Design als Kunst einer Wissenschaft", from: *Buckminster Fuller – Your Private Sky*, Baden 1999

[6.2/6] Schober, H.: "Geometrieprinzipien für wirtschaftliche und effiziente Schalentragwerke", in: *Bautechnik 79 (2002)*, Vol. 1, pp. 16 et seqq.

[6.2/7] Schober, H.: "Die Masche mit der Glas-Kuppel", *deutsche bauzeitung, 10/94*, pp. 152 et seqq.

[6.2/8] ENV 1991 – Part 1 (EC 1): Basis of design and actions on structures – Basis of design, 1994 (German version)

[6.2/9] Knaack, U.; Führer, W.; Wurm, J.: *Konstruktiver Glasbau II*, Cologne 2000, p. 90

[6.2/10] Ackermann, K.: *Tragwerke in der konstruktiven Architektur*, Stuttgart 1988, p. 30

[6.3/1] Emde, H.: *Geometrie der Knoten-Stab-Tragwerke*, Würzburg 1978, p. 39

[6.3/2] Hess, R.: *Glasträger*, research report, ETH Zurich 1999

[6.3/3] Knaack, U.: *Konstruktiver Glasbau*, Cologne 1998

[6.3/4] Nijsse, R.: *Glass in Structures*, Basel 2003

[6.3/5] Wurm, J.: *Das Glasschwert*, Seminar report Lehrstuhl für Tragkonstruktionen, RWTH Aachen 2004

[6.3/6] Schittich, Chr.; Staib, G.; Balkow, D.; Schuler, M.; Sobek, W.: *Glass Construction Manual*, Munich 1999, p. 102

[6.3/7] Koschade, R.: *Die Sandwichbauweise*, Berlin 2000, pp. 28 et seqq.

[6.3/8] Leitner, K.: *Tragkonstruktionen aus plattenförmigen Holzwerkstoffen mit der Textilen Fuge*, Dissertation at Lehrstuhl für Tragkonstruktionen, RWTH Aachen 2004

[6.3/9] Engel, H.: *Tragsysteme*, Ostfildern-Ruit 1997

[6.3/10] Führer, W.: Seminar presentation Glasbau, Lehrstuhl für Tragkonstruktionen, RWTH Aachen 08/01/03

[6.3/11] Borrego, J.: *Space Grid Structures*, Cambridge MA, 1968

[6.3/12] Makowski, Z. S.: *Räumliche Tragwerke aus Stahl*, Düsseldorf 1963

[6.3/13] Schulz, Chr.: "Konstruieren mit Glas", *Proc. Vol. 3*, Congress "Innovatives Bauen mit Glas", Munich 1995

[6.3/14] Eekhout, M.: *Product Development in Glass Structures*, Rotterdam 1990, p. 70

[6.3/15] Knaack, U.: "Fachwerke aus Glas", in: *Bauwelt Vol. 05/2001*, pp. 20 et seq.

[6.3/16] Führer, W.; Ingendaaij, S.; Stein, F.: *Der Entwurf von Tragwerken*, Aachen 1995, pp. 249 et seqq.

[6.3/17] Borrego, J.: *Space Grid Structures*, Cambridge MA 1968, p. 116, pp. 111 et seq.

[6.3/18] Knaack, U.: *Konstruktiver Glasbau*, Cologne 1998, p. 129

[7.1/1] Kuff, P.: *Tragwerke als Elemente der Gebäude- und Innenraumgestaltung*, Cologne 2001, pp. 37 et seqq.

[7.2/1] Courtesy of Graham Dodd, Arup, London

[7.2/2] Courtesy of Chris Jofeh, Arup, London

[7.2/3] N.N.: "Glasdach auf Glasträgern", in: *Glas 01/2003*, pp. 35 et seqq.

[7.2/4] Project documentation Glas- und Metallbau Andreas Oswald GmbH

[7.2/5] Project documentation Glas Trösch

[7.2/6] Maedebach, Mario, "Alte Mensa und Rektorat der TU-Dresden", In: *glasbau 2005*, ed. By Prof. Dr. Ing. Bernhard Weller, Institut für Baukonstruktion TU Dresden, 2005

[7.2/7] Maedebach, Mario, "Konstruktiver Glasbau - Ein Glasdach ganz aus Glas", from: *Berichte und Informationen, wissenschaftliche Zeitschrift der HTW-Dresden*, 1/2006

[7.2/8] Knaack, U.: *Konstruktiver Glasbau*, Cologne 1998, pp. 112 et seq., pp. 194 et seqq.

[7.2/9] Knaack, U.: *Konstruktiver Glasbau*, Cologne 1998, pp. 176 et seqq.

[7.2/10] Först, S.; Hübinger, A.: *Dachelemente aus Trapezblech und Glas – Projektmappe*, Lehrstuhl für Tragkonstruktionen, RWTH Aachen 2001

[7.2/11] Wellershoff, F.; Sedlacek, G.: *Structural Use of Glass in Hybrid Element*, seminar proceedings Glass Processing Days 2003, pp. 268–270

[7.2/12] Exhibition catalogue for "showreiff" at the German Museum of Architecture (DAM) in Frankfurt, Aachen 2001

[7.2/13] Student competition 4. ArchiCAD prize for innovative glass applications, protocol of jury proceedings on 07.12.04

[7.2/14] Eggert, I.; Weber, A.: *Glasbrücke – Dokumentation und statische Analysen des gebauten Prototyps*, seminar report, Lehrstuhl für Tragkonstruktionen, RWTH Aachen 2003

[7.2/15] Flake, F.; Langer, L.; Pirwitz, M.: *Fachwerkbrücke*, seminar report, Lehrstuhl für Tragkonstruktionen, RWTH Aachen 2003

[7.2/16] Türk, I.: *Untersuchungen zum Tragverhalten des Glass-Screen*, Lehrstuhl für Tragkonstruktionen, RWTH Aachen 2002

[7.2/17] Bandekow, K.; Knoke, J.; Meder, P.; Menken, P.-R.: *Der Glass Screen*, seminar report, RWTH Aachen 2002

[7.2/18] Catalogue for exhibition "glass-technology live" at the glasstec fair in Düsseldorf, 2002

[7.3/1] Knaack, U.: *Konstruktiver Glasbau*, Cologne 1998, pp. 242–245

[7.3/2] The tests and expert reports required for approval were carried out at the FH-Munich by Prof. Dr.-Ing. Ö. Bucak and Chr. Schuler and at the TU Darmstadt by J.-D. Wörner, X. Shen and M. Fahlbusch.

[7.3/3] Product information Maier-Bogenglas, 2003, http://www.magla.de/bogenglas-produktinfo.html

[7.3/4] Breuninger, U.; Stumpf, M.; Fahlbusch, M.: "Tragstruktur der Loggia in Wasseralfingen", in: *Bautechnik 80, 06/2003*, pp. 355–361

[7.3/5] N.N.: "Maximilianmuseum in Augsburg", in: *DETAIL 05/2001*, pp. 873 et seqq.

[7.3/6] N.N.: "Glasdach im Maximilianmuseum in Augsburg", in: *GLAS 02/2000*, pp. 20–25

[7.3/7] Ludwig, J.; Weiler, H.-U.: "Tragstrukturen aus Glas am Beispiel einer Ganzglastonne", in: *Bautechnik 04/2000*, pp. 246–249

[7.3/8] Schadow, Th.; Vellguth, F.: *Entwurf, Berechnung und Bemessung eines Fachwerkbogens aus Glas und Stahl*, study carried out at the Lehrstuhl Stahlbau, TU Hamburg, Harburg 1999

[7.3/9] Bosbach, H; Einhäuser, S.; König, M.; Sobotta, A.: *Der GlasTex-Bogen*, project documentation at the Lehrstuhl für Tragkonstruktionen, RWTH Aachen 2001

[7.3/10] Führer, W.; Wurm, J.: Der GlasTex-Bogen, *FASSADE/FACADE* 03/2002, pp. 5–8

[7.3/11] Ackermann, K.: *Tragwerke in der konstruktiven Architektur*, Stuttgart 1988, pp. 123 et seqq.

[7.3/12] Führer, W.; Wurm, J.: *Der Glasbogen auf der glasstec 2000*, seminar report, Lehrstuhl für Tragkonstruktionen, RWTH Aachen 2001

[7.3/13] Führer, W.; Weimar, Th.: *Statische Analyse des Glasbogens für die glasstec 2000*, Lehrstuhl für Tragkonstruktionen, Aachen 2000

[7.3/14] Wurm, J.: Glasbogen auf der glasstec 2000, *GLAS 02/2001*, pp. 5–10

[7.4/1] Wurm, J: "Innovationen in Glas", in: Architektur & Bau Forum, 04 / Februar 2003, pp. 9 et seq.

[7.4/2] Herkrath, R.: *Die GlasTex-Kuppel*, student research project carried out at the Lehrstuhl für Tragkonstruktionen, RWTH Aachen 2003

[8/1] Wurm, J.: "Glasvisionen", in: *DBZ Vol. 11/2004*

PICTURE CREDITS

[1, Fig. 4] from: Hix, J.: *The Glasshouse*, London 1996, p. 41

[1, Fig. 5] from: Mc Grath, A. C.: *Glass in Architecture and Decoration*, London 1961

[1, Fig. 9] James Carpenter Design Associates, New York

[1, Fig. 10] Ulrich Knaack, Lehrstuhl für Tragkonstruktionen, RWTH Aachen

[2.1, Fig. 2] The Chapter of Gloucester Cathedral

[2.1, Fig. 5] from: Rykwert, J.: On Adam's House in Paradise, Cambridge 1989, p. 39

[2.1, Fig. 6] Kaefer Isoliertechnik GmbH & Co KG, Bremen

[2.1, Fig. 13] Rolf Gerhardt, Aachen

[2.1, Fig. 15] from: Hix, J.: *The Glasshouse*, London 1996

[2.1, Fig. 16] Picture archives Marburg, from: Hix, J.: *The Glasshouse*, London 1996, p. 53

[2.1, Fig. 17] Courtesy: The Estate of R. Buckminster Fuller

[2.1, Fig. 18] from: Heinle, E.; Schlaich, J.: *Kuppeln*, Stuttgart 1996, p. 191, © Fritz Dressler, Worpswede

[2.1, Fig. 19] Courtesy: The Estate of R. Buckminster Fuller

[2.1, Fig. 20] © Heide Wessely

[2.1, Fig. 22] © Ulrike Grothe, CLMAP GmbH, Munich

[2.1, Fig. 23] Kitka-river, 2004, 1820 mm x 3000 mm, cromogenic digital print on aluminium, of Ilkka Halso, Orimattila

[2.2, Fig. 12] Clemens Dost, Aachen

[2.2, Figs 13, 16] Ulrich Knaack, Lehrstuhl für Tragkonstruktionen, RWTH Aachen

[2.2, Fig. 18] Schlaich, Bergermann und Partner sbp GmbH, Stuttgart

[2.2, Fig. 24] James Carpenter Design Associates, New York

[2.2, Fig. 28] © Wolfgang Dürr, Würzburg

[3.1, Fig. 15] James Carpenter Design Associates, Inc.; © Balthazar Korab, New York

[3.1, Fig. 16] Schott AG, Grünenplan

[3.1, Figs 17, 19–21, 23, 24, 26, 28–33, 35, 36, 38, 39] Ron Heiringhoff, Aachen

[3.2, Figs 1, 5] Saint-Gobain Glass, Chantereine, Frank Dunouau

[3.2, Figs 2, 4] Saint-Gobain Glass, archives

[3.2, Fig. 6] © Reiner Meier, Wittmar, Schott AG, Grünenplan

[3.3, Fig. 3] Saint-Gobain Glass, Chantereine, Frank Dunouau

[3.3, Fig. 18] Maier Glas, Heidenheim

[3.4, Fig. 9] Saint Gobain Glass, Aachen

[3.4, Fig. 18] Lucio Blandini, ILEK, Universität Stuttgart

[3.4, Fig. 20] Glasid AG, Essen

[3.4, Figs 23, 24] © Thomas Kramer, WSP GmbH, Aachen

[3.4, Fig. 28] KSE GmbH / Division TROSIFOL, Rainer Hardtke, Dow Corning

[3.4, Fig. 38] Seele GmbH & Co. KG, Gersthofen

[3.4, Figs 41, 42] The Greenhouse Effect Ltd., UK

[3.4, Figs 43, 44] Fusion Glass Design Ltd, London

[3.5, Figs 3, 6] Saint-Gobain Glass, archives

[3.5, Figs 7, 8] KSE GmbH / Division TROSIFOL

[3.5, Fig. 9] Pilkington Architectural, UK

[3.5, Fig. 10] Weischede, Herrmann und Partner GmbH, Stuttgart

[3.5, Figs 14, 16] Saint-Gobain Glass, Aachen

[3.5, Fig. 20] KSE GmbH / Division TROSIFOL, Flughafen Köln/Bonn GmbH

[3.5, Figs 28, 29] KSE GmbH / Division TROSIFOL, Rainer Hardtke, Dow Corning

[3.6, Figs 4, 10] Saint-Gobain Glass, archives

[3.6, Figs 8, 9] KSE GmbH / Division TROSIFOL, Engelhardt/Sellin

[3.6, Fig. 28] Ulrich Knaack, Düsseldorf

[4.1, Fig. 12] Maren Krämer, Aachen

[4.1, Figs 17–19] By courtesy of Sika Technology AG, Zurich, from: Koch, S.: *Elastisches Kleben im Fahrzeugbau – Beanspruchungen und Eigenschaften*, thesis, Munich Technical University

[4.1, Fig. 38] Lehrstuhl Stahlbau, RWTH Aachen

[4.1, Fig. 41] Saint-Gobain Glass UK, Eggborough

[4.2, Figs 3, 25, 26, 28] Dorma-Glas GmbH, Bad Salzuflen

[4.2, Fig. 10] Verlinden

[4.2, Figs 11, 12] Saint Gobain Glass, Aachen

[4.2, Fig. 42, 43, 45] Hunsrücker Glasveredelung Wagener

[4.2, Fig. 46] Silke Tasche, Institut für Baukonstruktion, Technische Universität Dresden

[4.3, Fig. 1] © Adam Mork

[4.3, Figs 2, 3, 46] Arup

[4.3, Fig. 4] © Picture archives, Institut für Leichtbau Entwerfen und Konstruieren (ILEK), Universität Stuttgart

[4.3, Fig.Figs 5, 6, 52] Dorma-Glas GmbH, Bad Salzuflen

[4.3, Figs 7, 9, 10, 24, 34, 36] from: Luible, A.: *Stabilität von Tragelementen aus Glas*, thesis EPFL 3014, Ecole Polytechnique Fédérale de Lausanne (EPFL), Lausanne 2004

[4.3, Figs 22, 28, 42] Ulrich Knaack, Lehrstuhl für Tragkonstruktionen, RWTH Aachen

[4.3, Figs 26, 27] Frank Wellershoff, Lehrstuhl für Stahlbau, Aachen

[4.3, Figs 31, 32] Fred Veer, Delft University of Technology

[4.3, Fig. 35] Rubert App GmbH, Leutkirch

[4.3, Fig. 53] Marquardt und Hieber Architekten, Stuttgart

[4.3, Fig. 57] Thomas Schadow, Lehrstuhl für Baukonstruktion, Universität Dresden

[5.1, Fig. 16] Garigliano Tomaso, Maria Elena Motisi, RWTH Aachen

[5.1, Fig. 24] © Christian Kandzia, Esslingen

[5.2, Figs 23, 25, 33, 34] Ulrich Knaack, RWTH Aachen

[5.2, Fig. 28] Clemens Dost, Aachen

[5.2, Fig. 30] Silke Först, RWTH Aachen

[5.2, Fig. 31] © Fraunhofer Institut für Fabrikbetrieb und -automatisierung, Magdeburg

[5.2, Fig. 41] © Nigel Young, Foster + Partners

[5.2, Fig. 46] Kaefer Isoliertechnik GmbH & Co. KG, Bremen

[5.2, Fig. 44] KSE GmbH / Division TROSIFOL

[6.2, Figs 10, 19, 26] Ulrich Knaack, Lehrstuhl für Tragkonstruktionen, RWTH Aachen

[6.2, Fig. 13] from: Emde, H.: *Geometrie der Knoten-Stab-Tragwerke*, Würzburg 1978, p. 45

[6.2, Figs 16, 17] © Hans Schober, Schlaich Bergermann und Partner, Stuttgart / New York

[6.2, Figs 39–42] Tobias Unterberg, RWTH Aachen

[6.2, Fig. 37] Henrike Bosbach, Michael König, RWTH Aachen

[6.3, Fig.1] Fred Veer, Delft University of Technology

[6.3, Figs 7, 21, 31, 33, 35–37, 58] Ulrich Knaack, Lehrstuhl für Tragkonstruktionen, RWTH Aachen

[6.3, Fig. 11] Dewhurst Macfarlane and Partners, London

[6.3, Fig. 17] Daniel Seiberts, Sebastian Spengler, RWTH Aachen

[6.3, Fig. 18] Zamil Glass Industries, Riyadh

[6.3, Fig. 29] Chr. Helmus, M. Mevissen, Aachen

[6.3, Fig. 43] Nicole Leiendecker, Pamela Schmitz, RWTH Aachen

[6.3, Fig. 46] Reyhan Ada, Mina Ayoughi, RWTH Aachen

[6.3, Figs 50, 51] Henriette Kosel, Uwe Ernst, RWTH Aachen

[6.3, Fig. 57] Proposals for the atrium roof of ABN AMRO Bank in Den Haag, design: Mick Eekhout

[7.2, Figs 1–6] Arup, London

[7.2, Figs 7, 9, 10] © Lance McNulty

[7.2, Figs 8, 11, 12] © ssGreat Britain Trust

[7.2, Fig.13] Dewhurst Macfarlane and Partners, London

[7.2, Figs 14–18, 20] Andreas Oswald GmbH, Munich

[7.2, Figs 21–23] Glas Trösch, Butzberg

[7.2, Figs 24, 25, 27, 29–34, 38] Maedebach, Redeleit & Partner, Dresden

[7.2, Figs 26, 28] © Werner Huthmacher, Berlin

[7.2, Figs 35–37] Institut für Baukonstruktion TU Dresden

[7.2, Figs 39–43] Ulrich Knaack, Lehrstuhl für Tragkonstruktionen, RWTH Aachen

[7.2, Figs 44–46] Ulrich Knaack, Lehrstuhl für Tragkonstruktionen, RWTH Aachen

[7.2, Figs 52, 56, 57] Andrea Hübinger, Silke Först, RWTH Aachen

[7.2, Figs 73, 74] Frank Wellershoff, Lehrstuhl Stahlbau, RWTH Aachen

[7.2, Fig. 78] Christof Helmus, Marc Mevissen, RWTH Aachen

[7.2, Figs 80–82, 84, 86] Rüdiger Schmidt, RWTH Aachen

[7.2, Figs 96–103, 106, 108] Iljana Eggert, Anna Weber, RWTH Aachen

[7.2, Figs 114, 115] Frank Flake, Lutz Langer, Mario Pirwitz, RWTH Aachen

[7.2, Fig. 118] Rainer Baumann, RWTH Aachen

[7.2, Figs 117, 128, 130, 132] Kerstin Bandekow, Jona Knoke,
    Malgorzata Meder, Peter-René Menken, RWTH Aachen

[7.2, Figs 137, 138, 142, 145, 147, 148] Jan Cyrany, Ron Heiringhoff,
    Dalibor Hlavacek, Florian Nitzsche, RWTH Aachen

[7.2, Fig. 149] Christof Erban, Saint-Gobain Glas Solar, Aachen

[7.2, Figs 155, 160, 162–164] Jiri Hlavka, Sascha Rullkötter, Daniel
    Seiberts, Sebastian Spengler, RWTH Aachen

[7.3, Figs 1, 2] Ulrich Knaack, Lehrstuhl für Tragkonstruktionen, RWTH Aachen

[7.3, Figs 3, 5] © Dietmar Strauß, Besigheim

[7.3, Fig. 4] Maier Glas, Heidenheim

[7.3, Figs 9–12] Thomas Schadow, Frithjof Vellguth, Arbeitsbereich
    Baustatik und Stahlbau, TU Hamburg-Harburg

[7.3, Figs 15, 17, 18, 23] Henrike Bosbach, Sabine Einhäuser,
    Michael König, Agi Sobotta, RWTH Aachen

[7.3, Figs 33–37] Arup archives

[7.3, Fig. 40] Andre Bauer, Tobias Unterberg, RWTH Aachen

[7.3, Fig. 41] Christian Leffin, Daniel Stuttmann, RWTH Aachen

[7.4, Figs 1–3] © Jens Willebrand, Cologne

[7.4, Figs 5, 6] Lucio Blandini, ILEK, Stuttgart University

[7.4, Figs 18, 20, 21, 23–25] Ewout Brogt, Marjon Doeser, Gerard Engel,
    Roy Hendriks, Xander Windsant, Delft University of Technology

[7.4, Figs 33, 34] Ralf Herkrath, RWTH Aachen

[7.4, Figs 38] Thorsten Weimar, Dresden

[7.4, Figs 44, 46, 47] Stefan Dahlmanns, Nadine Fischer,
    Alexander Kruse, Nicole Stoff, RWTH Aachen

[8, Fig. 13] Max-Planck-Institut für Kolloid- und Grenzflächenforschung, Potsdam

[8, Fig. 14] Stefan Dahlmanns, Nadine Fischer, Alexander Kruse, Nicole Stoff, RWTH Aachen

[8, Fig. 15] Jiri Hlavka, Sascha Rullkötter, Daniel Seiberts, Sebastian Spengler, RWTH Aachen

[8, Figs 16, 17] Francis Archer, Arup Advanced Geometry Unit, London

All other figures are supplied by the author.

Every effort was made to acknowledge and obtain permission for all pictures.
We deeply regret any mistakes or oversights that might have occurred.

PARTNERS

The author gratefully acknowledges the firms, whose extensive sponsorships made the realisation of the research projects documented in chapter 7 possible:

[7.2]
Self-supporting, semi-transparent roof module
Prototype for a modular roof system
    Saint-Gobain Glass Deutschland GmbH, Aachen;
    Thyssen Bausysteme GmbH, Dinslaken

Multifunctional Glazing
Prototype for composite insulating glass unit with integrated solar shading
    Sika Deutschland GmbH, Bad Urach
    August Krempel GmbH, Vaihingen;
    Röchling Haren KG, Haren;
    Glas Engels GmbH, Essen;

Exhibition Architecture "Gläserner Himmel" (Glass Sky)
    Brugg Drahtseil AG, Birr (CH);
    Saint-Gobain Glass Deutschland GmbH, Aachen;
    Kerschgens Stahlhandel GmbH, Stolberg

Projection wall "Glass-Screen"
    TC-Kleben GmbH, Übach-Palenberg;
    Glas Engels GmbH, Essen;
    Carl Stahl GmbH, Süssen

Glass roof "Solar Bridge"
prototype for a roof element with integrated photovoltaic modules
    Saint-Gobain Glass Solar Deutschland, Aachen

"Tetra-Grid"
Prototype for a glass roof as luminous ceiling
    Wilhelms Industriebedarf GmbH, Würselen;
    Röhm GmbH, Darmstadt

[7.3]
"GlassTex Arch"
Prototype of a Glass roof with integrated solar shading
    Flachglas Wernberg GmbH, Wernberg-Köblitz;
    Aeronatec GmbH, Seeon;
    Carl Stahl GmbH, Süssen

"Tetra Glass Arch"
Construction system for arched roofs
    Saint-Gobain Glass Deutschland GmbH, Aachen;
    Dorma Glas GmbH, Bad Salzuflen;
    HILTI Deutschland GmbH, Leinfelden-Echterdingen;
    DELO Industrieklebstoffe, Landsberg

[7.4]
"Delft Glass Dome"
Prototype for a garden pavilion
    Octatube Space Structures B.V., Delft (NL);
    Van Noordenne Groep B.V., Hardinxfeld (NL)

My special thanks are due to the following companies which generously contributed to making the publication of this book possible:

Sponsoring firms:

ARUP
13 Fitzroy Street
London W1T 4BQ
UK
www.arup.com

Kuraray Europe GmbH
Division TROSIFOL
Mülheimer Straße 26
53840 Troisdorf
www.trosifol.com

DORMA-Glas
Max-Planck-Straße 33-45
32107 Bad Salzuflen
www.dorma-glas.de

Supporting firms:

Saint-Gobain Glass Deutschland
Viktoriaallee 3–5
52066 Aachen
www.saint-gobain.de

SCHOTT AG
Hüttenstraße 1
31073 Grünenplan
www.schott.com

DELO Industrie Klebstoffe
Ohmstrasse 3
86899 Landsberg am Lech
www.delo.de

Hilti Deutschland GmbH
Hiltistr. 2
86916 Kaufering
www.hilti.de